Missouri Railroads

Railroads Past and Present

Thomas Hoback and Carlos Arnaldo Schwantes, *editors*
H. Roger Grant, *founding editor*

Missouri Railroads

A Modern Crossroads, 1921–2023

**Don L. Hofsommer
and Carlos Arnaldo Schwantes**

INDIANA UNIVERSITY PRESS

This book is a publication of

Indiana University Press
Office of Scholarly Publishing
Herman B Wells Library 350
1320 East 10th Street
Bloomington, Indiana 47405 USA

iupress.org

© 2025 by Don L. Hofsommer and Carlos Arnaldo Schwantes

All rights reserved
No part of this book may be reproduced or utilized in
any form or by any means, electronic or mechanical,
including photocopying and recording, or by any
information storage and retrieval system, without
permission in writing from the publisher.

First Printing 2025

Manufactured in China

Cataloging information is available
from the Library of Congress.

ISBN 978-0-253-07285-6 (hdbk.)
ISBN 978-0-253-07287-0 (ebook)
ISBN 978-0-253-07286-3 (web PDF)

**Dedicated to the Memory of
Peter A. Hansen**

FIG 0.1. Soaring: Missouri Pacific issued a special brochure to promote its attractive post–World War II streamliners, the "Eagles," that linked St. Louis with destinations in Colorado and Texas. Schwantes-Greever-Nolan Collection.

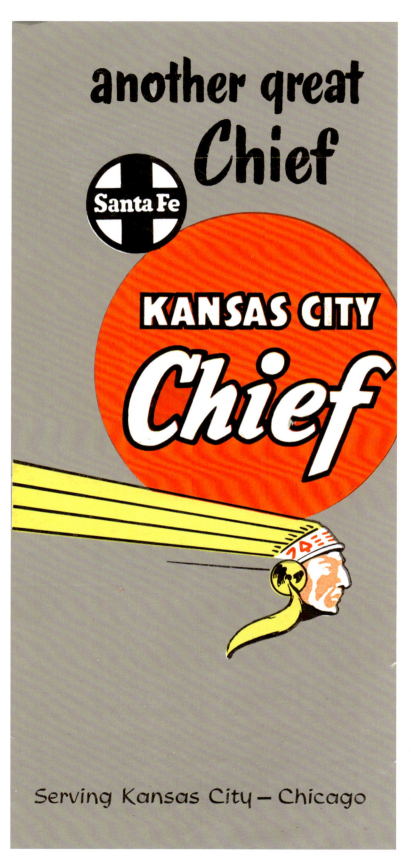

FIGURE 0.2. Atchison, Topeka & Santa Fe issued a colorful brochure in 1950 to salute one of its many fine trains as well as the one hundredth birthday of the western Missouri metropolis. Schwantes-Greever-Nolan Collection.

FIGURE 0.3. A brawny steam locomotive powers a St. Louis Southwestern freight through Dupo, Illinois, located on the Cotton Belt line that linked Missouri with Arkansas and Texas. Don L. Hofsommer Collection.

The Missouri Pacific is pleased to have you as a guest on its *Texas Eagle*, so named because it links St. Louis and Memphis with the major cities of the Lone Star State. . . . The route of the Eagles connects the staid Mississippi at St. Louis and Memphis with the blue waters of the Gulf of Mexico at Galveston; to the shrine of all Texans at San Antonio— the Alamo—and to the turgid waters of the Rio Grande at El Paso.

—*Along the Way . . . Texas Eagle*, circa-1950s route
guide issued by the Missouri Pacific Lines

Enroute between St. Louis and San Antonio . . . on the TEXAS SPECIAL

—"New *Texas Special* Streamliners," an undated post–World War II brochure issued jointly by the St. Louis–San Francisco and Missouri–Kansas–Texas railroads

Contents

xii	Overview and Acknowledgments
2	**Introduction**
16	**1. Spirit of St. Louis: New Competitors**
46	**2. The Dark Decade**
86	**3. Of War and Peace**
126	**4. A Fluid State**
170	**5. Debilitated and Downsized**
198	**6. Winds of Change**
236	**7. Rail Industry Survivors Face an Uncertain Future**
265	Notes
277	Selected Bibliography and Further Reading
281	Index

FIGURE 0.4. At the close of the grim decade of the 1930s, the situation for Missouri's railroads was not rosy, but neither was it desperate. Implying optimism for the present and the future alike was Burlington's impressive new *General Pershing Zephyr*. Schwantes-Greever-Nolan Collection.

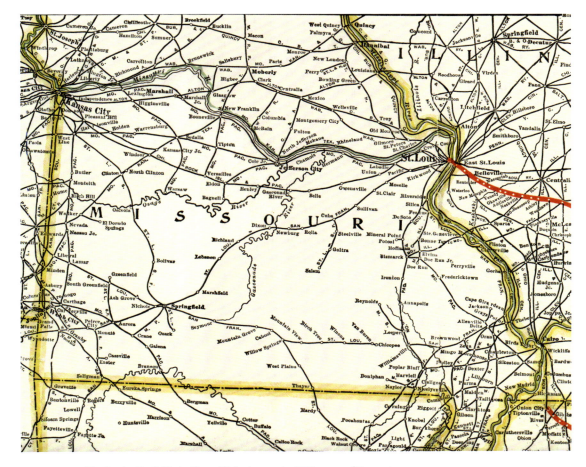

FIGURE 0.5. The Louisville & Nashville published an early-1950s map of its service territory, which at the time included St. Louis. Schwantes-Greever-Nolan Collection.

Overview and Acknowledgments

The *North Star Limited*—a New Train Between St. Paul-Minneapolis and St. Louis. Electric Lighted Sleepers and Chair Cars. Dining Service.

—Minneapolis & St. Louis advertisement, 1902

Born of compromise, Missouri entered the Union as the twenty-fourth state in 1821. As the nation eventually developed, Missouri would find itself nearly in the geographic center, and, served as it was by marvelous natural highways—the Mississippi and Missouri Rivers—Missouri quickly came to control much of the nation's internal transportation needs. But full flower for Missouri's transportation prominence would come only with the age of railways coupled with the dramatic evolution of St. Louis on the east and Kansas City on the west—twin and fiercely competitive entrepots to and from which radiated a complex and comprehensive rail network that blanketed the state and linked Missouri to all quarters of the nation—the state in that way truly becoming the crossroads of a continent.

Volume 1, titled *Crossroads of a Continent*,[1] was a survey of Missouri's early railroad experience—a time of feverish construction, laissez-faire economics, heroic entrepreneurship, absence of regulation (initially), the conquering of space, and ending the tyranny of distance. It was the time of Fred Harvey and Arthur Stilwell, intense rivalry between Chicago and St. Louis, the rise of Kansas City as an important new metropolitan center, erection of the elegant St. Louis Union Station, and the exciting World's Fair of 1904. It was a time of streetcars, electric interurban railways, and, yes, the time of "Limiteds, Locals, and Slow Trains to Everywhere." And, as it developed, the early twentieth century became a time of fully pollinated regulation that threatened to stifle enterprise. In sum, it was a time in which Missouri and its railroads grew up together.

FIGURE 0.6. Still powered by steam, New York Central's *Gateway* has just completed its lengthy journey from New York's Grand Central Station to St. Louis Union Station. Don L. Hofsommer Photo.

All of that was in the one-hundred-year span of 1820–1920. Missouri's railroads during the following ten decades found themselves in a remarkably changed and ever-changing environment. Increasingly they were faced with stultifying regulation at the state and federal levels that choked innovation, onerous and unproductive work rules, a smothering "this is the way we have always done it" mentality among union leaders and managers alike, and especially aggressive and creative modal competition very often subsidized by tax dollars from the public purse. The age of railways was imperiled.

Of course, that was not the end of the story, and the question was, how would railroads of Missouri respond to this new circumstance? Marvelously appointed "Limited" passenger trains still strutted boldly across Missouri in the 1920s, and elegant new streamliners appeared during the next decade even as the pall of the Great Depression ravaged railroads large and small alike. But then came World War II, when carriers turned in their finest hour (furnishing 97 percent of domestic troop movements and expediting nearly 90 percent of military goods and equipment). The 1950s witnessed several important adjustments, much stiffer modal competition—water, air, and particularly roadway—and

Retrospective: When Missouri's First Successful Railroad Served as the Crossroads for the Continent

In our first volume, titled *Crossroads of a Continent*, we provided an illustrated overview of Missouri railroads from the 1850s until 1921. A primary theme was the growth of the state's track network. The 1850s witnessed the emergence of the earliest predecessors to the great systems that by 1900 came to dominate transportation. During those early years, progress was halting for the pioneer lines that would later form key portions of the Missouri Pacific, St. Louis–San Francisco, and Wabash, three St. Louis–based railroads. One other railroad of note crossed the northern part of the state: the Hannibal & St. Joseph, which by the end of the 1850s had clearly emerged as the state's most successful railroad. It enjoyed the financial blessing conferred by a generous grant of land across the fertile northern part of the state, though it soon gravitated to the Chicago, Burlington & Quincy, which used it to complete a line of tracks between Chicago and Kansas City that

FIGURE 0.1.1. At the end of the 1850s, the Hannibal and St. Joseph was the first railroad to cross the state to link the Mississippi and Missouri Rivers. Schwantes-Greever-Nolan Collection.

the end of most local and branch-line passenger operations. The 1960s brought increased mergers, depot closings, line abandonments, and the near end of passenger service by investor-owned railroads. Amtrak, with a highly abbreviated passenger network (skeletal in Missouri) was bypassed St. Louis, much to the consternation of Missouri's largest (and perhaps proudest) city.

The Hannibal & St. Joseph also made history in 1862 as the first railroad in America to operate an RPO mail car. Two years earlier, on April 3, 1860, the railroad is supposed to have forwarded the first mail west to California via the fabled Pony Express that linked St. Joseph with Sacramento. Here is one early example of how Missouri served as the crossroads of a continent.

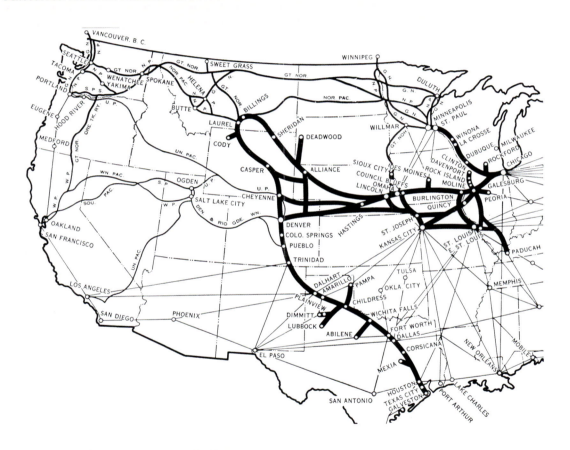

FIGURE 0.1.2. One hundred years later, the Hannibal & St. Joseph formed one small segment of the sprawling Chicago, Burlington & Quincy in 1961. Schwantes-Greever-Nolan Collection.

born in the early 1970s. Acute malaise enveloped the industry, and earnest and sober prognosticators forecast that the railroad industry was headed for the dustbin of history. They got it wrong. Important if partial deregulation coupled with a cadre of imaginative and innovative

Missouri's "Big Seven" Railroads in 2023: A Summary History

On January 1, 2023, just seven Class I railroads accounted for most of the track network that crisscrossed North America. That changed in less than four months with the April 14 merger of the Canadian Pacific Railway with Kansas City Southern to form a twenty-thousand-mile network that currently conducts business as CPKC.

Incidentally, the definition of a Class I railroad as set in 1992 was one that earned revenue greater than $250 million annually. Of course, that figure has increased with inflation. Ranking somewhat lower in the economic pecking order were regional, local, and switching and terminal railroads, all of which formed important components of Missouri's ever-evolving transportation landscape.

Below we offer a list of the state's current Class I railroads and a few words on how they came to be. More in-depth information is included in later chapters of *Missouri Railroads*.

BNSF Railway (headquartered in Fort Worth, Texas)

Today's BNSF Railway forms one of two sprawling rail systems that dominate the American West. It includes two railroads with a significant historical presence in Missouri. The St. Louis–San Francisco, or "Frisco," maintained its headquarters in St. Louis for more than a century until the Burlington Northern takeover. The other railroad was the Atchison, Topeka & Santa Fe, which for decades served the Kansas City area, with that Missouri metropolis forming a vital link in a network of tracks that stretched west from Chicago to Los Angeles and San Francisco and southwest to Oklahoma and Texas.

The original Burlington Northern was formed from the Great Northern and Northern Pacific lines that connected St. Paul across the Northern Tier to Seattle and Tacoma, two gateway cities to the Pacific. Track of the Chicago, Burlington & Quincy, meanwhile, blanketed the Midwest and served St. Louis, Kansas City, and many other Missouri communities. The Burlington Northern Railroad increased its presence in Missouri with its acquisition of the Frisco in 1980, followed by its 1996 merger with Santa Fe to create the Burlington Northern Santa Fe Railway. The carrier took the name BNSF Railway Company in 2005.

Components Related to the History of Missouri Railroads since 1921

- Atchison, Topeka & Santa Fe (Santa Fe)
- Chicago, Burlington & Quincy (Burlington)
- St. Louis–San Francisco (Frisco)

Canadian National Railway (headquartered in Montreal, Quebec)

One of the most venerable railroads to link the Midwest with the Gulf Coast was the Illinois Central, which dates from the 1850s. Though its track stopped just short of Missouri, it used local connections to run passenger trains north between St. Louis and Chicago and south from St. Louis to Memphis, New Orleans, and other cities of the Deep South. Canadian National was for years a sleepy ward of the Canadian government, a vast and in many places redundant system cobbled together shortly after World War I (1919) from several of the Dominion's ailing railroads. After privatization in 1995, it exhibited unexpected nimbleness. It shed unprofitable track and added Illinois Central in 1998 to give it a major presence in mid-America.

Components Related to the History of Missouri Railroads since 1921

- Illinois Central

Canadian Pacific Railway (headquartered in Calgary, Alberta)

Canadian Pacific was a venerable railroad, one that literally stitched the new Dominion of Canada together when track opened between Montreal and Vancouver during the mid-1880s. For years it was the majority shareholder of the Minneapolis, St. Paul & Sault Ste. Marie (Soo Line), a Minnesota-based carrier with tracks that stretched across Wisconsin to Chicago, east through Michigan's natural-resource-rich Upper Peninsula, and west to the High Plains of North Dakota. Comparatively recent is its footprint in Missouri, which dates from the 1985 acquisition of the former Chicago, Milwaukee, St. Paul & Pacific line to Kansas City.

Components Related to the History of Missouri Railroads since 1921

- Soo Line (including parts of the former Milwaukee Road)

CSX Transportation (headquartered in Jacksonville, Florida)

CSX Transportation, one of the two big railroads that today dominate the eastern half of the United States, takes its corporate moniker from its Wall Street stock symbol. Among its historic components are the Baltimore & Ohio, Missouri's first rail connection to the East, and the Louisville & Nashville, a major southern line that linked St. Louis with Kentucky and the southern United States. Other building blocks essential to the CSX rail edifice were the Chesapeake & Ohio, Atlantic Coast Line, and Seaboard Air Line. With dismemberment of Conrail in 1999, it gained the former Pennsylvania main line that linked St. Louis and Indianapolis with cities of the East Coast. Earlier, during the 1980s, Conrail removed rails from the New York Central's former main line that had extended across central Illinois to connect St. Louis with Indianapolis, Cleveland, Buffalo, Boston, and New York City.

Components Related to the History of Missouri Railroads since 1921

- Baltimore & Ohio
- Chicago & Eastern Illinois (divided with the Missouri Pacific)
- Louisville & Nashville
- New York Central
- Pennsylvania

Kansas City Southern (headquartered in Kansas City, Missouri)

Kansas City Southern was a prominent newsmaker in early 2023 because the Kansas City–based railroad, a fixture in Missouri's ever-changing rail landscape for more than 120 years, was acquired by Canadian Pacific. At the time of its 2023 merger, it was the only big railroad still headquartered in Missouri.

Components Related to the History of Missouri Railroads since 1921

- Gulf, Mobile & Ohio (former Chicago & Alton line across Missouri)

Norfolk Southern Railway (headquartered in Atlanta, Georgia)

The Norfolk & Western was a major coal carrier across West Virginia when it boldly reinvented itself and greatly extended its reach in 1964 by acquiring several Midwestern railroads, including the Nickel Plate and Wabash. The latter was a fixture in Missouri. With its headquarters in St. Louis, its tracks fanned out to Kansas City, Omaha, Des Moines, Chicago, Toledo, Detroit, and Buffalo. After Norfolk & Western acquired the Southern Railway in 1982, it acquired its present name. Along the way, the acquisitive Norfolk Southern in 1981 also gained Illinois Terminal, the electric interurban that joined St. Louis with Peoria and several other major cities within Illinois.

Components Related to the History of Missouri Railroads since 1921

- Illinois Terminal (Illinois Traction until 1937)
- New York, Chicago & St. Louis (Nickel Plate)
- Southern Railway
- Wabash

Union Pacific Railroad (headquartered in Omaha, Nebraska)

Union Pacific was one of the partners that completed the original transcontinental railroad across the American West in 1869. In recent years it acquired several St. Louis–based railroads—namely, the Missouri Pacific, Missouri–Kansas–Texas, and St. Louis Southwestern. The Missouri Pacific was the state's rail pioneer, the Pacific Railroad of Missouri, which in 1851 struck out for the West Coast from St. Louis but never advanced any farther than the base of the Rocky Mountains at Pueblo, Colorado, where it had access to Denver. The Missouri–Kansas–Texas, or "Katy," was always focused on the Southwest.

Components Related to the History of Missouri Railroads since 1921

- Chicago & Eastern Illinois (divided between Missouri Pacific and Louisville & Nashville)
- Chicago & North Western (including the former Chicago Great Western)
- Denver & Rio Grande Western
- Gulf, Mobile & Ohio (former Chicago & Alton line between St. Louis and Chicago)
- Missouri Pacific (including the former St. Louis, Iron Mountain & Southern)

FIGURE 0.2.1. Headquartered in St. Louis, the Wabash operated an extensive network of tracks across the Midwest. The railroad offered "new all-steel equipment" on its passenger runs serving St. Louis and Kansas City markets. "No Better Trains Anywhere," claimed Wabash. This promotion dates from 1925. Schwantes-Greever-Nolan Collection.

- Missouri–Kansas–Texas (Katy)
- St. Louis Southwestern (Cotton Belt)
- Southern Pacific
- Union Pacific

What Is Missing?

Harder to classify are the former Chicago, Rock Island & Pacific and the Chicago, Milwaukee, St. Paul & Pacific, two Chicago-based carriers that played historically significant roles in Missouri's complex railroad history. However, the Rock Island collapsed before it could be merged into a stronger railroad, and its former competitors were eager to acquire the viable segments, most notably its north-south "Spine Line" between Minneapolis and Kansas City, which Chicago & North Western gained before it was itself acquired by Union Pacific.

As for the Chicago, Milwaukee, St. Paul & Pacific, its trains had for years linked Kansas City and the northwest quadrant of Missouri with Chicago and a sprawling network of tracks that extended north and west to Seattle, Tacoma, and Puget Sound. By the 1970s it was no longer a viable network, and despite several attempts to save it, the Milwaukee Road, too, was broken up and viable portions sold to other railroads. The line that served Missouri went to the Soo Line, a Canadian Pacific satellite. Ironically, the segment serving Missouri and Kansas City, which had been of secondary importance in Milwaukee Road days, served as a crucial component of Canadian Pacific Kansas City (CPKC) to stitch the two merged systems together.

managers in the next decades combined to bring about what might be called the "rebirth" of the industry if in much smaller form. Railroads serving Missouri reflected all of these national trends—change, yes, dramatic changes, but in all cases with a local flavor.

This, then, is a survey of Missouri's railroad experience during the years 1920–2023. It moves from mountaintop to mountaintop, so to speak, offering a snapshot of a fascinating and critically important element in the state's rich history—with emphasis on the tight symbiotic relationship between the state and its steel highways.

* * *

This book is dedicated to the late Peter A. Hansen (1957–2020), our valued collaborator on volume 1 of *Crossroads of a Continent*. It may have been Pete who suggested our expansive title. He was an unfailing source of good cheer as well as a gifted writer. We miss him.

No project of this magnitude could succeed without the earnest, diligent, and generous assistance of several persons who contributed in numerous ways. Norbert Shacklette, Jeff Schmid, Steve Patterson, John Friedmann, Lawrence Thomas, Conrad Cheatham, Pat Hiatte, James Rueber, Chris Burger, William Siegel, Jennifer McDaid, Dale Hearn, and James House provided or helped round up illustrations. Insights, suggestions, and hard data came from William Hoenig, Bob Huff, Kent Hannah, Pete Rickershauser, Jim Johnson, and Dennis Opferman. Rollin Bredenberg, Michael Haverty, Michael McCarthy, Tom Hoback, and Gregory P. Ames read all or parts of the manuscript and offered excellent advice as to content and presentation. To all the above and to others whom we might regrettably have overlooked, we are grateful. For errors of fact or infelicities of style, we alone are responsible.

* * *

Finally, for the record, here is an enumeration of who was primarily responsible for individual chapters: Carlos A. Schwantes for the introduction, chapter 1, and text boxes devoted to the Hannibal & St. Joseph, the Rock Island line across central Missouri, Leonor Loree, the demise of passenger trains, railroad publishing, and the index; and Don L. Hofsommer for the overview and acknowledgments, chapters 2 through 7, and all text boxes not mentioned above. Each individual chapter can be read as a stand-alone essay. Hence, some repetition is inevitable, and perhaps even desirable, to provide the necessary historical context and sustain the chapter narratives.

FIGURE 0.7. Many turn-of-the-century carriers combined to form Missouri's largest railroads today. Schwantes-Greever-Nolan Collection.

Missouri Railroads

The period of development of the new sections of this country has very largely passed. From now on it must be an intensive development. Where we have single track railroads now, we shall require double tracks. Where we have double tracks now, we shall require a third or even a fourth track. We require now greatly enlarged terminals, more automatic signal devices, more sidings, a reduction of grades, straightening out of curves—all to make our transportation more efficient for the service of the public.

—*Proceedings of the St. Louis Railway Club*, April 8, 1921[1]

Introduction

A handful of landmark events defined the course of Missouri railroad history prior to 1921. The first of these took place in 1851 with the July 4 launch in downtown St. Louis of the state's first railroad, the grandly titled Pacific Railroad of Missouri. Other key events were the long-awaited completion of a railroad west from St. Louis to Kansas City (1865), construction of the Eads Bridge across the Mississippi (1874), completion of monumental union stations in both St. Louis (1894) and Kansas City (1914), and federal takeover of the nation's railroads during the waning hours of 1917 as a wartime measure.

From 1851 to 1917, the prevailing motif of Missouri railroad history was optimism. Just consider, for example, the incredible optimism represented by the "Pacific" portion of the name of Missouri's pioneer railroad. No railroad anywhere else in the United States prior to 1851 had dared to dream of extending a line of tracks over the Rocky Mountains and west to the Pacific Ocean. The challenge, given the still rudimentary state of railroad technology and the many formidable geographical hurdles that railroad builders needed to surmount as they peered across the continent from St. Louis to the Pacific Coast, could have resulted in doubt and a paralyzing form of defeatism, and yet Missouri's first generation of railroad builders looked to the far horizon with optimism as they talked of forging an iron pathway to California and beyond. Their grand dream was to create nothing less than a passage all the way to India using a multimodal combination of rails and ships that would link Missouri with one of the richest nations on the planet.

Likewise, these railroad optimists envisioned Missouri as forming nothing less than the buckle that knitted together a network of tracks that ultimately spanned the continent. The monumental bridge that James Buchanan Eads extended across the Mississippi River at St. Louis

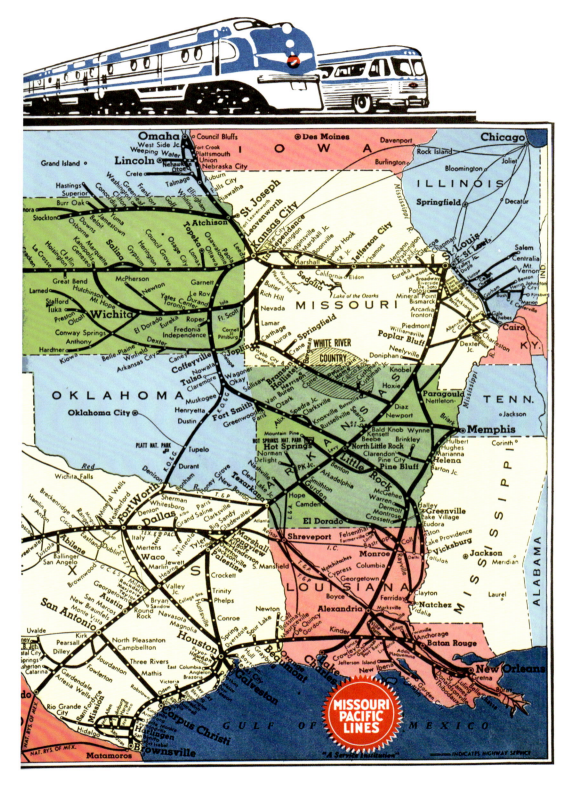

FIGURE INTRO.1. In its post–World War II timetables, Missouri Pacific included a multicolor map of its sprawling St. Louis–based system. Schwantes-Greever-Nolan Collection.

FIGURE INTRO.2. "Railroad fever!" swept Missouri during the late nineteenth century. Don L. Hofsommer Collection.

in the early 1870s to defy the many naysayers who claimed it could not be done represented yet another statement of optimism, as did the St. Louis Union Station that opened in 1894. At one time, the passenger trains of more than twenty different railroads began or ended their journeys in the imposing structure, one of the largest rail terminals in the United States. These trains not only connected St. Louis horizontally with the great cities of the East and West Coasts but also ran vertically from North Star to Lone Star—that is, from Minnesota (and Canada) deep into the heart of Texas (in fact, all the way to Mexico City in the early twentieth century).

Although the Pacific Coast was the stated ambition of two of Missouri's earliest railroads, the Pacific Railroad of Missouri and the St. Louis–San Francisco, neither of them got there. The Missouri Pacific (MoPac), successor to the state's original Pacific Railroad, stalled at

Introduction 5

FIGURE INTRO.3.
"The steamcar civilization" was a term commonly used to describe the rail industry's onetime dominance of American life. Don L. Hofsommer Collection.

the foot of the Rocky Mountains, and the St. Louis–San Francisco (Frisco) extended no farther west than the high plains of Oklahoma. Both railroads remained ambitious and soon discovered a lucrative consolation prize in Texas and the Southwest. The MoPac and Frisco changed course as they now headed south instead of continuing west. Joining them in extending the commercial reach of St. Louis all the way to Texas were St. Louis, Iron Mountain & Southern (soon to become a Missouri Pacific subsidiary), Missouri–Kansas–Texas ("Katy"), and St. Louis Southwestern ("Cotton Belt"). On the opposite side of the state, Kansas City Southern created a Gulf Coast outlet for Midwestern grain and other commodities. In all, no fewer than five Missouri-based railroads forged a long-term relationship with the Lone Star State. After the landmark discovery of oil at Beaumont in 1901, the prelude to many more black-gold gushers, many Texans spent their newfound wealth in St. Louis, which for a time served as the de facto economic and cultural capital of the suddenly rich Lone Star State. For fast-talking peddlers of oil securities, rail connections made the Missouri metropolis an easily accessible source of suckers willing to invest in the latest Lone Star oil bonanzas, many of which were frauds that left investors with little more than their handsomely engraved stock certificates.

* * *

More was obviously better, and that was true also for the numerous railroad lines built within Missouri in the nineteenth and early twentieth

FIGURE INTRO.4. St. Louis–San Francisco promoted oil and other valuable natural resources located along its sprawling network of tracks. For years St. Louis served as the de facto economic capital of Louisiana, Oklahoma, and Texas oil ventures, and in the early twentieth century the city's small-time investors offered tempting targets for promoters, their dubious dealings made possible by Missouri's direct rail connections to the Southwest and Gulf Coast. Schwantes-Greever-Nolan Collection.

centuries. Tracks crisscrossed the state by 1900, and the building boom was by no means over at the dawn of the new century. At the same time that St. Louis hosted the 1904 World's Fair, the Chicago, Rock Island & Pacific completed one more rail link across Missouri between St. Louis and Kansas City. The 1904 fair itself offered yet another statement of optimism, not just in its several "palaces" intended to call public attention to the technological wonders of the age but also in the enormous size of the fairgrounds. Never before or since has any world's fair covered more acreage than Missouri's Louisiana Purchase Exposition.

The exposition's Palace of Transportation showcased Missouri's prevailing optimism and the pride the state derived from its railroads, both steam and electric. Although it never had a network of interurban electric railways equal in size those in neighboring Illinois, Indiana, or Ohio, several manufacturers based in St. Louis were recognized worldwide for the quality of their trolley and interurban cars. One of them, St. Louis Car Company, claimed to operate the world's largest plant devoted to the construction of electric railway cars. The latest rail cars made in Missouri were proudly displayed at the 1904 fair.

In the early twentieth century, a number of major American railroads were based in Missouri. These included Kansas City Southern, which

Introduction 7

FIGURE INTRO.5. Missouri–Kansas–Texas used the "Miss Katy" image to advertise trains to the Southwest and to the St. Louis World's Fair of 1904. Schwantes-Greever-Nolan Collection.

formed as a vital conduit all the way south to Port Arthur, an outlet on the Gulf of Mexico named for the railroad's founder, Arthur Stilwell. Five more major railroads were headquartered in St. Louis: Missouri Pacific, St. Louis Southwestern, St. Louis–San Francisco, Missouri–Kansas–Texas, and Wabash. In addition, railroads based in Chicago extended lengthy lines of track across the agriculturally rich northern half of Missouri. Some, like Atchison, Topeka & Santa Fe and Chicago Rock Island & Pacific, ran tracks through the state on their way to destinations farther west, while four additional Illinois-based railroads—Chicago Great Western; Chicago, Milwaukee & St. Paul; Chicago, Burlington & Quincy; and Chicago & Alton—ran tracks into Missouri as far west as Kansas City. Finally, scattered across the state were numerous short lines that served a variety of local transportation needs. One of these, Terminal Railroad of St. Louis, facilitated the movement of passenger and freight trains through the bi-state metropolitan area that extended along both sides of the Mississippi River.

In 1916, the nation's railroad network attained its peak mileage. Construction of new lines had slowed noticeably by that date; nonetheless, plans for additional rail links across the Southwest and elsewhere (including a proposed Santa Fe connection to St. Louis) remained viable and could well have been spiked into place during the subsequent years to increase the 254,000 miles already in use had not World War I intruded.

In April 1917, the United States joined the conflict that had already been raging across Europe for three years. It was hard to remain optimistic in the face of the awful carnage that took place in the frontline trenches or when confronted with terrible new weapons of war like poison gas. Federal takeover of America's railroads eight months after the

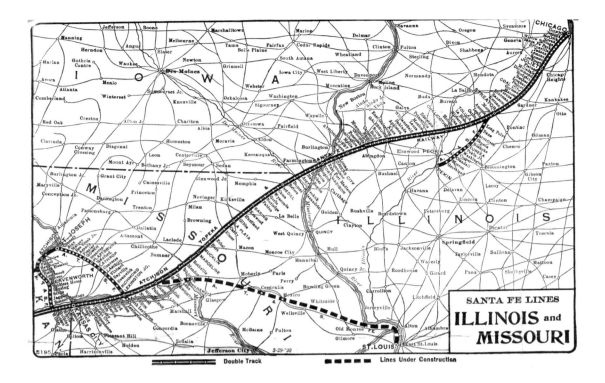

FIGURE INTRO.6. Atchison, Topeka & Santa Fe completed a line between Kansas City and Chicago in 1888 to provide it a through route between the Great Lakes and the Pacific Ocean, but as this 1920s map illustrates, the railroad still desired to extend tracks of its own to St. Louis. Schwantes-Greever-Nolan Collection.

United States entered the Great War effectively eliminated any remaining rail-industry optimism. There were plenty of reasons now for railroad executives to view the future with pessimism. In fact, the big question was whether the wartime takeover was but a prelude to permanent government ownership of the nation's largest and most important industry.

Creation of the United States Railroad Administration in December 1917 represented the culmination of nearly two decades of regulatory mission creep, and accompanying the increasingly heavy burden of federal and state regulations imposed since 1900 came competition such as the rail industry had never known before. During the first seventeen years of the twentieth century, the time widely acclaimed as the "Progressive Era," the multiplication of regulations was anything but progressive because they discouraged investment and retarded railroad modernization. By 1916, the year of the mileage apogee of the American rail, highway competitors attracted increased attention. The number of private automobiles (and additionally during the 1920s, the number of intercity bus and truck lines) multiplied annually, and these rail competitors operated at first largely unregulated and often untaxed.

Investors took notice of how the compass of opportunity pointed in a new direction, and while some venture capitalists almost threw their dollars at anything connected with the rising automotive industry, they shunned the railroads. It grew increasingly difficult for railroads to raise

FIGURE INTRO.7. Missouri railroads were called to perform a monumental duty as part of America's World War I participation. Don L. Hofsommer Collection.

FIGURE INTRO.8. The federal government took control of the nation's railroads during World War I and also extended forceful dominion over the population at large. Don L. Hofsommer Collection.

UNITED STATES RAILROAD ADMINISTRATION
OFFICE OF THE DIRECTOR GENERAL

WASHINGTON, AUGUST 12, 1918.

GENERAL ORDER NO. 39.

The sale of liquors and intoxicants of every character in dining cars, restaurants and railroad stations under Federal control shall be discontinued immediately.

W. G. McAdoo,
Director General of Railroads.

76172—18

St. Louis, Kansas City & Colorado:
Missouri Railroad History in Microcosm

The cross-state line that the Rock Island completed to St. Louis in 1904 never amounted to much more than a marginal addition to the map of Missouri railroads. Nonetheless, its hundred-year saga mirrored many of the prominent twists and turns that shaped the rail network across the state between the 1880s and 1980s, and we explore the specifics in later chapters.

When the Chicago, Rock Island & Pacific commenced running trains across Missouri between Kansas City and St. Louis on its newly completed line in early June 1904, it expected to benefit from passenger and freight traffic likely to swell that year because of the Louisiana Purchase Exposition, the world's fair extravaganza hosted by St. Louis. Officially sanctioned world's fairs had previously been held in the United States only twice: in Philadelphia in 1876 and Chicago in 1893. It was thus quite an honor for the nation's fourth-largest city to host America's first official world's fair of the twentieth century.*

Magazines of all varieties devoted extensive coverage to the St. Louis exposition, and railroads blanketed North America with travel brochures and other publications intended to urge people see for themselves the greatest wonders of the age

FIGURE INTRO.1.1. Railroads across the United States issued special brochures to promote the St. Louis World's Fair of 1904, all of them expecting to reap a revenue bonanza from the crowds journeying to see the latest wonders on display. Schwantes-Greever-Nolan Collection.

11

displayed in a gleaming array of "palaces." Two of the largest buildings were devoted to transportation and electricity, technologies that generated considerable excitement among inventors, investors, and users. In one out-of-the-way corner of the Palace of Transportation was a small display of automobiles, still regarded mainly as curiosities, at best playthings of the idle rich. Their full potential as a competitor to America's almighty railroads was not yet recognized, and so Rock Island and other carriers continued to lay additional miles of track and acquire other railroads to expand their systems. They expected to dominate Missouri transportation for years to come because rural and small-town residents had no viable alternatives. They endured the plodding pace of branch-line locals because that was their only option—until reliable automobiles and all-weather roads upended all presumptions during the 1920s.†

The Rock Island line to St. Louis no doubt benefited temporarily from world's fair traffic, but it would be a mistake to view it as a significant addition to Missouri's rail landscape. It had originated two decades earlier as the Saint Louis, Kansas City, and Colorado, and the fact that it took twenty years to complete a 296-mile line across Missouri (and not a very good one at that) suggests that its dismal history illustrates in microcosm the ups and downs typical of many other rail lines opened across the state.‡ The Pacific Railroad of Missouri, the state's first, required from 1851 until 1865 to spike tracks into place between St. Louis and Kansas City. But over time it became the main line of the Missouri Pacific (and later Union Pacific) between the state's two largest cities. The line the Rock Island opened in 1904 was beset by a continuous series of up-and-down grades, the bane of rail operators, and its trains plodded through a rural landscape with few population centers of consequence. In addition, it was the longest of the several rail routes—Missouri Pacific, Wabash, Burlington, and Chicago & Alton—that linked St. Louis and Kansas City.§

With the financial and physical collapse of the Rock Island, St. Louis Southwestern in 1980 picked up this remnant in hopes of creating a transcontinental

the dollars they needed to modernize their support structures or their rolling stock, and thus when faced with the unprecedented demands that the war economy placed on their passenger and freight equipment, the railroads were unprepared. Traffic soon clogged rail networks serving the East Coast ports from which soldiers and war cargoes departed for battlefields in Europe. When coupled with years of investment starvation, the ensuing struggle to deliver goods provided a pretext for Uncle Sam to take over the railroads.

Seventy years of optimism were over. No longer could eccentric but highly capable railroad builders like Arthur Stilwell or Jay Gould implement their dreams across a landscape that offered boundless possibilities. Regulators made certain of that, and the many restrictions they imposed speedway that used the "Golden State Route" across Kansas, Oklahoma, Texas, New Mexico, and Arizona to link St. Louis with Los Angeles. It was not to be. The former Rock Island route across Missouri cost too much to rehabilitate and handled too little online traffic to be viable. As was true for numerous other marginal miles of Missouri rail line, the addition of other options—private automobiles most importantly, but also intercity trucks and buses—first grew worrisome to rail managers in the 1920s. During subsequent decades, the competition only increased. The best financial option was to abandon service and pull up poorly utilized tracks. Most of the Rock Island line reverted to nature, though a portion in western Missouri provided the right-of-way for a cross-state hiking and biking trail. An easternmost segment continued to see an occasional train hauling coal from St. Louis to an electric generating plant at Labadie, a distance of fifty miles.¶

---

* *Railway Journal*, January 1904, 5.

† Perhaps it is quibbling to list only these officially sanctioned world's fairs because Buffalo, New York, hosted a major fair, the Pan-American Exposition, in 1901. Alas, history recalls the event mainly because of the assassination of President William McKinley. For a more detailed account of railroads and the St. Louis world's fair of 1904, see Peter A. Hansen, Don L. Hofsommer, and Carlos Arnaldo Schwantes, *Crossroads of a Continent: Missouri Railroads, 1851–1921* (Bloomington: Indiana University Press, 2022), chap. 14. Providing a case study of the excitement that all things electrical inspired during the 1890s and into the early years of the twentieth century is Carlos A. Schwantes, *Electric Indiana: The Rise and Fall of the World's Greatest Interurban Railway Center, 1893–1941* (Bloomington: Indiana University Press, 2023).

‡ The railroad was incorporated in late 1884 in Kansas, and it proposed to locate general offices at both ends of the line in Fort Scott, Kansas, and St. Louis, Missouri. During the 1880s when the St. Louis, Kansas City & Colorado still existed mainly on paper, the Atchison, Topeka & Santa Fe considered purchasing the rail line to gain entrance to St. Louis. That was only one of Santa Fe's several attempts to access Missouri's largest city, a goal it still sought to achieve during the 1920s, but never with success. *Topeka Daily Capital*, December 21, 1884; *Kansas City Times*, January 19, 1887; *Saint Louis Globe-Democrat*, May 18, 1887; *Daily Commonwealth* (Topeka, KS), August 26 and 27, 1887.

§ Chicago, Rock Island & Pacific, public timetable (October 1929), 24–25; H. Roger Grant, *A Mighty Fine Road: A History of the Chicago, Rock Island & Pacific Railroad Company* (Bloomington: Indiana University Press, 2020).

¶ Gregory L. Schneider, *The Rock Island Requiem: The Collapse of a Mighty Fine Line* (Lawrence: University Press of Kansas, 2013).

---

on the railroads after 1900 forever changed the world in which they operated. As a result, Missouri's network of railroad lines had grown as large as it would ever be. The same was true for the United States. In fact, during the Great War the national rail network began to shrink for the first time with the abandonment, most notably, of the Colorado Midland. The immediate future for Missouri railroads also required that they cope with the rising tide of competition and its impact on both freight and passenger revenue.

Thus, the milestone events of 1917 to 1921, when the federal government acquired and then almost reluctantly returned the railroads to their investor owners, offer a logical place for us to break our history of Missouri railroads into two distinct volumes. The decades after 1921

FIGURE INTRO.9. Missouri–Kansas–Texas throughout its long history was a tireless and innovative promoter of its trains, both passenger and freight, and the southwestern region they served. Schwantes-Greever-Nolan Collection.

formed a new era very different from the boundlessness, in terms of both opportunity and optimism, that had propelled the growth of Missouri railroads during the nineteenth and early twentieth centuries. That is not to claim that optimism had completely disappeared, but increasingly it was tempered by periodic bouts of industry pessimism about what the future held. A whole new set of challenges and opportunities confronted rail leaders during the century after 1921, and the industry evolved as it responded to circumstances wholly unimaginable to earlier generations of Missourians. This dynamic gave rise to many events recalled in *Missouri Railroads: A Modern Crossroads, 1921–2023*, the second of our two Crossroads of a Continent volumes.[2]

Besides, a good road is often really better for a town
than a poor railroad, especially when most of the
products are disposed of in neighboring towns.

—*Good Roads Magazine*, 1903

1

Spirit of St. Louis

New Competitors

Missourians in the opening years of the twentieth century were not building railroads as they had in former years. The pace of construction had slowed noticeably since the late 1880s when the Atchison, Topeka & Santa Fe completed its main line diagonally across Missouri between

FIGURE 1.1. Pennsylvania Railroad publicists issued a colorful brochure during the late 1940s to salute the *Spirit of St. Louis*, the carrier's premier train between New York City, Philadelphia, Washington, and St. Louis since the late 1920s. The name saluted the most famous aircraft of the day, the Spirit of St. Louis, which Charles A. Lindbergh flew solo from New York to Paris in 1927. His St. Louis backers, most notably Albert Bond Lambert, provided money to make the epochal flight possible. Schwantes-Greever-Nolan Collection.

FIGURE 1.2. By the time this advertisement for St. Louis–manufactured Moon cars appeared in 1916, the automobile had become a potent competitor of urban streetcar systems and would soon challenge steam railroad passenger service. Schwantes-Greever-Nolan Collection.

Kansas City and Chicago. Until the eve of World War I in 1917, Santa Fe's system maps continued to suggest that the transcontinental railway intended to extend its reach into St. Louis, the state's largest city at the time, but it never did. Missouri's last new rail link of any substantial length was the one Rock Island opened between St. Louis and Kansas City on June 5, 1904, the summer of the St. Louis World's Fair. The new line gained Rock Island backdoor access into the St. Louis market (which was already well served by more than two dozen other railroads), but it was never a particularly prosperous venture in terms of either freight or passenger traffic. Rock Island's St. Louis–Kansas City corridor plus a substantial new bridge that opened across the Mississippi River at Thebes the following year, 1905, essentially completed Missouri's rail network.

Initially, two daily passenger trains steamed along Rock Island tracks each way between Missouri's largest cities. By the onset of the Great Depression in 1930, one had evolved into a make-all-stops motor train ("doodlebug"), though the better of the pair, the *St. Louis and Colorado Express*, carried through Pullman sleeping cars for Denver and Los Angeles. During the decade of hard times, it became obvious that the line's primary function was to serve local communities, a source of income that proved especially vulnerable to highway competition. Indeed, the same was true across Missouri for lightly patronized passenger trains that served mainly rural communities.[1]

During the opening decade of the twentieth century, railroads across North America had anticipated and planned for continued growth. The era of competition first noticeable during the century's second decade was both unexpected and unsettling, and the intensified competition prompted railroads to respond in a variety of ways during the 1920s, not all of them successful.

The single greatest threat to railroad hegemony was the automobile and the sense of personal freedom it gave motorists. Since 1894, the year the nation's two earliest horseless carriages sputtered along the streets of Massachusetts and Indiana, technological improvements to automobiles that resulted in their ever-greater reliability together with the thousands of miles of government-funded highways unspooling each year across America in every direction conferred on the growing legions of motorists the illusion that they now had the freedom to go anywhere at any hour and at any almost speed. It was a combination railroads found hard to beat, but one, ironically, that railroads themselves had initially helped foster by their promotion of speed as an important feature of modern rail travel.

⋆　⋆　⋆

Since the early days of the Republic, Americans had been thrilled by speed—the faster the better. No doubt the enormous physical size of the United States contributed to popular interest in any form of transportation that ran fast and offered a better way to conquer time and space. A powerful and sleek racehorse had long epitomized the national fascination with speed, but during the late nineteenth century, bicycle races enjoyed enormous popularity, too, and in the early twentieth century, when the motor car was still less than a decade old, an automobile race was guaranteed to attract big crowds. In Indianapolis in 1911, the city's

FIGURE 1.3. New York Central, the Pennsylvania's main competitor, used a 1925 timetable to advertise its *Southwestern Limited*, one of the railroad's several daily trains that linked New York City and St. Louis by way of Buffalo, Cleveland, and Indianapolis. Schwantes-Greever-Nolan Collection.

famous five-hundred-mile race was born—five hundred miles being an unimaginable distance at the time for an automobile race, or even for an ordinary automobile to travel without one or more breakdowns.

Railroads recognized the popular fascination with speed and had done their best to capitalize on it. Americans in 1893 were captivated by the record-breaking run of New York Central and Hudson River Railroad's Engine 999. The railroad's publicist George H. Daniels proclaimed it the first locomotive in the world to attain a speed of more than a hundred miles per hour. So famous did Engine 999 become that it was a featured exhibit at the Chicago World's Fair that same year, and it also appeared on a United States postage stamp. The fast-running locomotive engineer likewise became a popular hero—a tragic hero in the person of Casey Jones, who died in 1900 trying to make up lost time on the Illinois Central. He became the subject of a popular ballad, and like Engine 999 he was immortalized on a United States postage stamp.

Of course, the national fascination with speed had its tragic results. Eddie Rickenbacker, a speed-addicted daredevil who competed four different times in the Indianapolis 500 before becoming America's most successful military aviator during World War I and later the president of Eastern Airlines, once quipped, "If it can move, it can crash." That tragic reality was affirmed once again on the afternoon of August 5, 1922, when a Missouri Pacific passenger train racing north from Texas to St. Louis smashed at full speed into the rear car of a local train stopped on the main line at Sulphur Springs to take water. The crash killed 34 people and injured 150, making it an even more grisly smashup than the Warrensburg wreck of a Missouri Pacific special train headed to the St. Louis World's Fair of 1904. The Sulphur Springs crash was, in fact, the worst train wreck in Missouri history.[2]

*   *   *

In terms of the "conquest of time and space," a cliché always popular in the United States, aviation held the winning hand even though few Americans in the early twentieth century understood its competitive potential. The Louisiana Purchase Exposition had treated aviation with almost grudging condescension in 1904 by relegating airships to a far corner of the grounds instead of showcasing at least some aspects of aviation in the Palace of Transportation. Seven years later, however, Missourians could follow in their daily newspapers the saga of a daring young man in a flying machine who in 1911 did for aviation what Doctor Horatio Nelson did in his Winton automobile back in 1903 to win a fifty-dollar bet by becoming the first person to cross the United States by automobile. Calbraith Perry Rodgers became the first person to cross the United States by air.

This time, considerably more money than fifty dollars was at stake. The publisher William Randolph Hearst had offered a prize of $50,000 to the first person who could fly from one coast to the other in less than thirty days. Rodgers, a young man with a big ambition but little flying experience, was determined to claim Hearst's money. Backed by Armour & Company of Chicago and flying a spindly Wright-built craft named Vin Fiz for Armour's popular grape soft drink, the determined aviator did finally make it across the United States to Pasadena, California, despite repeated malfunctions, time-consuming repairs, and several hospital visits necessitated by his numerous crashes.

The historic feat took him forty-nine days, nineteen days too long to claim Hearst's $50,000. A few months later in April 1912, as Rodgers gave an exhibition flight over Long Beach (ostensibly to demonstrate how safe aviation had become), he ran into a flock of gulls, crashed into the surf, and died of a broken neck. He was thirty-three years young. Like his great-great-uncle, Commodore Matthew Perry, who boldly opened Japan to the world in 1854, the late aviator had relished the role of pioneer, though several years would pass before the full significance of his journey became clear. As amazing as the first transcontinental

FIGURE 1.4. Railways clearly stood at the center of American life. Their clocks set the tempo for every community, large or small. Don L. Hofsommer Collection.

air journey was, Rodgers's travail probably confirmed for railroad executives that commercial aviation posed no threat whatsoever to the long-established supremacy of the passenger train.

Warning signs of the rail industry's coming competition were perhaps visible as early as 1909, but they were clearly distinguishable to executives only from hindsight. That October, several thousand St. Louisans attended the city's first air show. The star of the event was a young American motorcycle racer turned aviator, Glenn Curtiss, who

22   Missouri Railroads

was legitimately billed as the fastest man in the air because three months earlier he had won a French contest by achieving the blazing speed of forty-eight miles per hour. That was fast enough to impress an American among the half-million spectators, Missouri industrialist Albert Bond Lambert, who offered Curtiss a guarantee of $5,000 if he would repeat his feat before a crowd of spectators in St. Louis. Curtiss so wowed his "Show Me State" audience that he and other aviators enthusiastically agreed to hold an even bigger spectacle a few months later in balmy Southern California.[3]

This, then, was the Missouri background to the first-ever airshow held in the United States: the Los Angeles International Air Meet in January 1910. Some 250,000 spectators attended the eleven-day event. The name itself was a bit of a joke, as were some of the planes that never lifted off the ground. It could claim to be "international" only because among the aviators was a French tightrope walker who had taught himself how to fly. Curtiss was once again the star of the event, and one observer, a furniture maker from Seattle named Boeing, was so overcome by enthusiasm that he offered to pay the dashing young aviator to teach him how to fly. Curtiss refused, but history would record that the Curtiss name would later be forever linked with that of the Wright brothers in the Curtiss-Wright engines that powered the aircraft built by William E. Boeing, the furniture maker turned aviation industrialist.

Back in Missouri, the Lambert name also attained a measure of immortality when the local flying field was officially named the St. Louis Lambert International Airport. That was a fitting honor for the Missouri visionary who used the fortune he had earned from a mouthwash named Listerine to help finance a young St. Louis aviator named Charles A. Lindbergh, who made history in 1927 by successfully completing the first solo trans-Atlantic flight in his Spirit of St. Louis. So compelling was his feat that Lindbergh became an instant hero, and the Pennsylvania Railroad christened its premier New York–St. Louis train the *Spirit of St. Louis*.[4]

Although nearly a quarter of a century had passed since the Wright brothers' first manned flight in North Carolina in 1904, it required Lindbergh's epochal flight across the Atlantic to awaken Wall Street to the money-making possibilities commercial aviation offered. In their frenzied enthusiasm, investors in the late 1920s rushed to buy stock in any newly founded airline, and that even included stock in the Seaboard Air Line Railroad, a nonaviation carrier whose name dated to 1900, three years before the Wrights' first flight, and simply connoted a straight line of track.

*　*　*

Spirit of St. Louis

A Railroad Dog's Life

FIGURE 1.1.1. Many railroad companies provided for their passenger waiting rooms long, wooden benches with firm armrests spaced to facilitate seating for individual people but really designed to discourage vagrants or other nonrevenue elements from choosing depot facilities for occasional slumber. Itinerant hounds foiled such plans. Don L. Hofsommer Collection.

Dogs were frequent tenants around the railroad—especially at rural depots, switch shanties, round houses, and interlocking plants where they found admiring and sheltering friends among employees. No doubt the most famous of these dogs was Owney, a Scotch-Irish terrier, who became a beloved mascot of clerks on Railroad Post Office cars and traveled with them across much of the United States and Canada—rolling up an estimated 143,000 miles of travel before his untimely death in 1907. In Missouri, a mutt named Jack hung around Hannibal Union Station, where railroaders shared their lunches with the appreciative dog. Dick, a small yellow mongrel, was the loyal companion of St. Louis, Iron Mountain & Southern engineer Jerry Phalen, who fashioned a bed in the cab of locomotives assigned to him on his various runs. Another dog, part chow, answering to the name of Blackie, earned his keep at the Gulf, Mobile & Ohio station at East St. Louis by joining the company's special agent on nighttime patrols. A fixture at St. Louis Union Station for years was Mack, he of white body, black spots, gray eyes, and questionable parentage, who was friend to all hands and who "jumped trains" for various destinations and then quickly returned. Old Jim, a yellow bulldog, was the favorite at the Bremen Avenue switch shanty in St. Louis, where he trotted at the heels of switchmen and often boarded switch engines over to Madison and back.*

* Freeman Hubbard, *Railroad Avenue: Great Stories and Legends of American Railroading* (New York: McGraw-Hill, 1945), 270–87; *St. Louis Post-Dispatch*, March 13 and 24, 1906, May 23 and 24, 1912.

If there was a milestone year that clearly marked the emergence of the competitive threat that during the 1920s became so visible and annoying to the railroads of Missouri and elsewhere, it was probably 1914. Even if a prophet had accurately predicted the rail industry's coming decade of gloom and doom, what executive would have had the courage to act at a time when the future of rail transportation still seemed so bright? True, the railroads of the United States found themselves having to adapt to reforms foisted on them by numerous political reformers who flattered themselves as "progressives," and an economic slump in 1914 drove some of the weaker rail lines into receivership, but the industry as a whole seemed healthy and likely to continue to grow—physically by expanding and modernizing their already huge fleet of cars, spatially in terms of adding miles to their already impressive national network (something they had done every year since 1830), and financially in terms of passenger and freight traffic and revenue. In short, the railroad industry in 1914 remained the undisputed king of American transportation.

A decade earlier, the automobile was considered a plaything of the rich, and driving one on a country jaunt of any distance was viewed as a refined sport not unlike polo. Automobile enthusiasts in conjunction with the St. Louis Exposition decided to enjoy a five-day tour across Missouri to Kansas City. It was considered highly newsworthy that one participant drove his Stevens-Duryea automobile the entire 293 miles "without even inflating a tire or cleaning a spark plug." In 1904 the best road across Missouri included a five-mile stretch of sand that took these intrepid motorists fully five hours to inch across.[5]

The newest warning sign of trouble ahead for the railroads was Henry Ford's commitment to assembly-line production of his Model T automobile, a technological innovation that allowed him to produce more cars in 1914 than all other American makers combined. The subsequent price drop placed the Model T within easy reach of the average American, and if a person could not afford a new car, an increasing number of used ones were available. Second, the Panama Canal opened in 1914, and ocean ships used it to transport nonperishable commodities like lumber and oil from West Coast ports to East Coast markets, all of it transcontinental traffic that the railroads had formerly dominated.[6]

Finally, on the streets of St. Louis, Kansas City, and other major urban centers across the United States in late 1914, the first automobile "jitneys" appeared seemingly out of nowhere. This spontaneous and enormously popular fad with its profoundly negative implications for future streetcar and local passenger train patronage spread to large cities across the United States. Streetcars ran nearly empty, while the ubiquitous jitneys typically carried more passengers than they could safely accommodate. The sensation of riding in an automobile on rubber tires filled with a cushion of air was new to most Americans in 1914, and they eagerly climbed aboard any unlicensed jitney just to experience the novelty of "automobility."[7]

So many people became jitney operators or joined them as passengers that streetcar companies howled in protest that the fad was ruining their long-established public monopoly. Some city governments actively sought to put the growing legions of jitney operators out of business, while others merely administered a slap on the wrist and looked the other way. Trolley revenue across the United States slumped noticeably in 1915, and even after the industry bounced back, the ubiquitous jitney continued to bedevil some local streetcar operators for years to come.[8]

FIGURE 1.5. Offering an early hint of the coming highway competition was the sudden appearance of the jitney during 1914–15, unregulated private vehicles that captured public fancy. This image appeared on the cover of sheet music titled "Mr. Whitney's Jitney." Schwantes-Greever-Nolan Collection.

In short, the jitney phenomenon and its negative financial impact on the American street railway industry foreshadowed what steam railroads might expect as an ever-enlarging circle of automobile owners demanded that governments provide them more and more miles of good roads. Theirs was a crusade that had won new converts ever since 1893 and the great Chicago Exposition that did so much to showcase the bicycle. At the time, hundreds of manufacturers made bicycles, and bicycling became the great American craze.

Little noticed by the railroad industry was that the nation's growing legions of bicycle riders functioned as a pressure group to demand better public roads for their vehicles. The typical rural road at the time ranged from a nearly nonexistent trace to a primitive dirt path usable as long as the weather was dry. Urban bicycle owners in the 1890s wanted to enjoy pleasure rides into the nearby countryside, and through the League of American Wheelmen and various good-roads associations, they pressured state legislatures and Congress to take action to improve abominable rural roads. One of the largest of their periodic conferences—probably more accurately described as pep rallies—was held in St. Louis in 1903.

Most members of Congress in the early twentieth century were unenthusiastic about good roads. Not since the 1830s had Uncle Sam willingly shouldered the burden of constructing good public roads for Americans, and many legal authorities in the 1890s thought such federal intrusion into the domain of state and local governments was unconstitutional. Three decades of lobbying bore fruit in 1916 when revolutionary violence along the Mexican border convinced a majority on Capitol Hill that good roads were necessary for national security. That year and again in 1921, Congress allocated the federal dollars needed to launch a national system of all-weather public highways.[9]

Therein lay an irony. Early in the twentieth century, some of the nation's largest railroads, most notably the Illinois Central, St. Louis–San Francisco (Frisco), and Southern, had eagerly embraced the cause of good roads in the belief that they would benefit farmers who could use them to haul their crops more efficiently from fields to the nearest rail line. The rail industry, in other words, anticipated that farm-to-market roads would function as feeders to extend the reach of railroads into agricultural hinterlands. Executives never imagined that the anticipated farm-to-market roads would coalesce into a national network of highways for which Henry Ford and hundreds of lesser-known automobile manufacturers eagerly supplied the vehicles that created a devastating new form of competition. In the end, rail advocates of better roads learned a lesson about unintended consequences.[10]

Missouri, perhaps surprisingly, functioned as a national center for the increasingly popular movement demanding that state and federal governments fund better roads and highways. St. Louis was home to the National Good Roads Association. In late April 1903, in conjunction with the official dedication ceremonies of the upcoming Louisiana Purchase Exposition, the city hosted the largest Good Roads gathering to date in American history.[11]

That event attracted a glittering array of prominent persons, including President Theodore Roosevelt; the Democratic Party's frequent presidential nominee, William Jennings Bryan; and the commanding general of the United States Army, Nelson A. Miles, who predictably spoke on the military necessity of good roads. Another speaker, a farmer from the town of Macon, Missouri, asserted that the state's agrarians "lose thousands of dollars every year because they cannot reach the markets with their produce when they wish to: that while they should be governed in selling by the market price, they must now be governed by the condition of the roads."[12]

President Roosevelt closed the conference with one of his typical rousing speeches, in which he noted the historical importance of the imperial roadways of Rome. Closer to home, he observed that "trolley lines, the telephone, rural free delivery are doing a great deal to render it possible to live in the country and yet not lose the advantages of the town, but no one thing can do as much to offset the unhealthy trend from the country into the city as the making and keeping of good roads." The United States in 1903 was still predominantly rural, but its population balance was rapidly tipping toward the city, a disturbing trend that rural isolation accelerated and that Roosevelt and most other speakers thought good roads could slow or reverse.[13]

Perhaps in response to the two good-roads conferences of 1903 and 1904 held in St. Louis in conjunction with the Louisiana Purchase Exposition, one hometown railroad, Frisco, put together a National Good Roads train and dispatched it on a three-month educational tour along its lines in Missouri and elsewhere during the fall of 1904. Frisco even offered special excursion rates to enable as many Missourians as possible to view road-building demonstrations held in Lebanon, Springfield, and Neosho. In addition, Frisco's passenger department published a magazine devoted to "development of the resources and the promotion of the mercantile, manufacturing, and agricultural interests" in the territory contiguous to the railroad.[14]

In his speech at the National Good Roads Conference in 1903, Missouri's governor Andrew M. Dockery boldly suggested that "the time has fully come when the great railroad systems of the United States should be supplemented by an improved system of public roads." The key word was *supplemented*. One wonders if any attendees of the St. Louis conference dared to think that good roads and automobiles could ever supplant, or even simply compete with, the mighty railroad industry's thousands of daily passenger and freight trains.[15]

*   *   *

Further accelerating the rail industry's rendezvous with a decade of unprecedented competitive challenges was the entry of the United States into World War I in April 1917. During and immediately after the conflict, the railroads of Missouri and their counterparts across North America discovered just how transformative the war years had been. Foremost was the federal takeover of the railroads in 1918. The pretext was that the railroad industry had failed to meet the demands suddenly placed on it by the wartime economy, a somewhat specious argument that ignored the many ways "progressive" legislation enacted by federal and state governments since 1900 had pleased voters who worried that America's largest industry had grown too powerful, reelected scores of antirailroad politicians, but crippled the railroad industry by making it unattractive to investors and thereby restricted the infusion of dollars needed to fully modernize its locomotives, cars, and infrastructure. In short, railroad profit margins steadily shrank from 1907 to 1914, though during those same years their traffic increased by 25 percent. Twice, in 1914 and again in 1915, the increasingly meddlesome Interstate

Big Business

Railroads constituted America's first big business. They were prodigious consumers of coal, forest products, iron and steel, and lubricants, among many other material goods. They also were huge consumers of capital and, not surprisingly, provided jobs to tens of thousands of Americans. In general offices such as the Missouri Pacific and Frisco based in St. Louis and Kansas City Southern in Kansas City could be found an army of clerks, stenographers, accountants, dispatchers, civil engineers, and draftsmen, along with middle managers and executives; at shops in Sedalia and elsewhere were boilermakers, machinists, carpenters, pipefitters, painters and assorted others; agents and telegraphers along with track laborers and water tenders proliferated at stations across the state; extra gangs and bridge and building crews were part of the mix, as were bridge tenders, carmen, linemen, and signal maintainers; and operating crafts included engineers, firemen, brakemen, conductors, and flagmen. This said nothing of significant employment by railroad equipment suppliers (rail cars, trucks, underframes, etc.). Rail employment that had nationally tallied 163,000 in 1870 (1.3 percent of the national labor force) mushroomed to 1,700,000 in 1916 (4.2 percent of the national labor force).*

---

* John F. Stover, *American Railroads* (Chicago: University of Chicago Press, 1961), 177; John H. Armstrong, "Working on the Railroad," in *Rails across America: A History of Railroads in North America*, ed. William L. Withuhn (New York: Smithmark, 1993), 12–89. See also Richard Reinhardt, *Workin' on the Railroad: Reminiscences from the Age of Steam* (Palo Alto, CA: American West, 1970).

FIGURE 1.2.1. Railways constituted America's first big business. They offered employment to a huge number of Missourians. Among the array of specialized workers were those in train service and maintenance of way as well as train dispatching.

FIGURE 1.2.2. The train dispatcher's job was to direct the movement of all trains in an orderly and safe manner along a section of rail line so as to prevent delays. Don L. Hofsommer Collection.

Commerce Commission refused to grant them the rate increases they desperately needed. Because the rail industry lacked the money required to update and enlarge its fleet of cars and locomotives and modernize its physical plant, the government-enforced frugality negatively impacted car builders and suppliers in St. Louis as well as long-established locomotive builders like Baldwin in Philadelphia.[16]

The pioneer airlines that took to the air in 1928 and 1929 posed no significant competitive threat to railroads—at first. That was not true for the growing competition railroads faced on the ground, where their rivals operated largely unburdened by regulations but benefited from every new mile of all-weather highway that federal, state, and local governments financed with money derived in part from the taxes they had placed on the railroads.[17]

*   *   *

Initially, it must have been difficult for rail executives to imagine that the balky personal mobility vehicles called horseless carriages, motor cars, and automobiles—even "devil wagons" by some farmers who resented the intrusion of city folks and their noisy machines into the quiet countryside—might amount to a serious competitive threat. Nonetheless, Union Pacific executives as early as 1916 voiced concern about the growing number of automobiles nibbling away at patronage on some of the railroad's branch-line passenger trains. Farmers in Nebraska, Missouri, and elsewhere had in recent years quietly dropped their opposition to motor vehicles and become automobile owners themselves. Henry Ford had made this transition much easier with the mass production of his Model T, an inexpensive car well designed for rutted rural roads and mechanically simple enough to appeal to the many farmers who were natural-born tinkerers.[18]

At the time of the St. Louis exposition in 1904, a drive of any distance was such a novelty that a motorist could travel from Chicago to St. Louis, for example, and likely get the story of the epic automobile adventure published in any number of popular magazines. Just completing the trek was a feat not unlike exploring the Amazon jungles of Brazil, and magazine and newspaper readers would likely have found the story fascinating. A decade or so later, professional writers and novelists launched what might be described as pioneering road-trip literature. Theodore Dreiser produced a fat and rambling book called *A Hoosier Holiday* in 1916; three years later, young Sinclair Lewis, destined to win a Nobel Prize in 1930 for his later novels, penned a road-trip novel called *Free Air*; and F. Scott Fitzgerald published a short story in which he and his wife Zelda drive south from their home in the Northeast to Alabama to surprise her parents, only to find that her parents had at the same time driven north to surprise the Fitzgeralds. Because of the sprawling landscape of the United States and its numerous interesting features, the road trip remained a popular personal adventure for decades to come—even after cars were air-conditioned and the four-lane interstate highways made it possible, in the words of novelist John Steinbeck, to drive from coast to coast and not see a thing.

As thousands of miles of new or improved highways were extended across the countryside after 1916, automobile ownership more than kept pace. Uncle Sam did not number the main routes for at least another decade, but various private associations emerged to create a series of marked trails for intrepid motorists to follow. One early trail was called the Lincoln Highway, its construction funded mainly through private contributions; when completed in 1914, it formed America's first cross-continent motor route. It was literally cobbled together, with occasional short portions of brick pavement interspersed with lengthy stretches of gravel or even graded dirt.

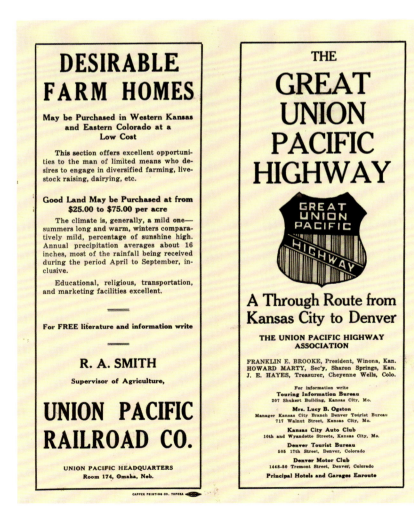

FIGURE 1.6. Before federal highways were numbered during the late 1920s, a variety of named "auto trails" crisscrossed the United States. One of these was the Great Union Pacific Trail between Kansas City and Denver, a route that later became part of US 40, the transcontinental highway that linked St. Louis and Kansas City. The original road across Kansas closely paralleled Union Pacific tracks. A road map, including those given away free by service stations until the gasoline shortage of the early 1970s, was in many ways a motorist's counterpart to the railroad timetable. Schwantes-Greever-Nolan Collection.

Spirit of St. Louis 31

FIGURE 1.7.
Those in charge of Missouri's investor-owned railroads complained with good reason that their competitors received generous taxpayer support, a disparity highlighted by this newspaper cartoon. Don L. Hofsommer Collection.

The Lincoln Highway bypassed Missouri in favor of Iowa, but soon linking St. Louis with Kansas City as well as extending overland more than three thousand miles to the distant coasts was the National Old Trails Road, also known as the Ocean-to-Ocean Highway. The idea for this route originated in Missouri with public pressure for a highway originally intended to link St. Louis with Kansas City. The state chapter of the Daughters of the American Revolution amplified the idea by proposing a motor route that roughly followed the route of the historic Santa Fe Trail from Missouri to the Southwest and east along the route of the old National Road to Baltimore.

Like the Lincoln Highway, the National Old Trails Highway was one of several dozen named but as-yet-unnumbered routes that crisscrossed the United States by the mid-1920s. Each was typically identified by a distinctive set of colored stripes painted around telephone poles to guide motorists. Color coding was not a success. It caused problems for colorblind motorists, and where several highway trails converged, a confusing array of colors might encircle a telephone pole from top to bottom. In the late 1920s when many original highway trails were numbered to form a national grid, the National Old Trails route across Missouri became US 40 (the letters being an abbreviation for "uniform system," not United States).[19]

The rail industry remained optimistic about the future of its long-distance passenger business, and during the 1920s it spent millions of dollars to upgrade its best trains, increase their speeds, and improve service. Pullman cars continued to offer a luxurious and popular way to travel—aboard parlor cars on the several day trains that connected St. Louis, Chicago, and Kansas City and by sleepers at night. The network of Pullman sleepers that nightly journeyed out from St. Louis and Kansas City effectively traced each city's spatial outreach and highlighted its major commercial and social connections. In 1929, the last prosperous year of the decade, the bible of rail passenger travel in North America, the monthly *Official Guide*, attained its greatest thickness with more than 1,700 pages, and that was despite rail mergers, the abandonment of many lightly used lines, and the steady pruning of local and branch-line trains since the end of federal control in March 1920.

FIGURE 1.8. Rock Island vigorously promoted Excelsior Springs as "America's Haven of Health," and several of its finest trains connected the Missouri resort with nearby Kansas City and also Chicago, Minneapolis, and St. Paul. Schwantes-Greever-Nolan Collection.

Spirit of St. Louis   33

Regulated Railroads versus Their Unregulated Competitors

Federal control did not end with the World War I armistice in November 1918. The United States Railroad Administration maintained a heavy hand on the throttle for another year and a half. Not until March 1920 did Uncle Sam finally relinquish control of the nation's railroads to their investor-owners, and that took place almost reluctantly and only after lengthy public debate about whether American railroads should remain a state enterprise, as was typical of rail systems in Europe.

Even after the ownership issue was settled, the railroads of the United States discovered that their familiar prewar environment had vanished forever. No longer did it make any economic sense for them to build new lines or even to operate some of their existing track and trains. The rail network of the United States peaked at 254,000 miles in 1916, and shortly thereafter the war's appetite for scrap steel claimed the Colorado Midland along with other miles of lightly used track considered superfluous in 1918. Across the Mississippi River from Missouri, the fate of the Chicago, Peoria & St. Louis Railroad provided a case study in just how much the railroad world had changed. Back in December 1890, Santa Fe, which had long desired to enter the St. Louis market if only to break the Gould family's control of many railroads headquartered there, had partnered with the Illinois railroad to run an overnight passenger train called the *Red Express* between Chicago and St. Louis. Although the *Red Express* featured the most luxurious appointments of its day, it faced an uphill struggle to compete successfully with long-established routes already running passenger trains between the two cities. Realizing it could never win a rate war and buffeted by the nation's latest economic downturn, Santa Fe abruptly discontinued the *Red Express* during the summer of 1893. A short time later both the mighty Santa Fe and its short-line gateway into St. Louis went bankrupt. Chicago, Peoria & St. Louis bumbled along until foreclosure in 1924 resulted in miles of its line being abandoned and the viable remnants parceled out to four separate railroads.

Chicago, Peoria & St. Louis Railroad was a small carrier of limited impact on Missouri or anywhere else, but during the postwar recession year of 1921 even the largest American railroads complained that they suffered the worst downturn in their industry's history, and they naturally blamed their woes on overregulation. During the next several years, the economy improved, but no single pattern prevailed among the American railroads: some companies enjoyed record prosperity, while others stumbled from one crisis to another. The biggest shock came in 1925 when one of the largest railroads in the United States, and one that had been for

FIGURE 1.3.1.
Steam ruled Missouri rails until the late 1930s. Some locomotives were as modest as the one puffing up and down the St. Louis & Hannibal in Perry, Missouri, in May 1923. Conrad Cheatham Collection.

decades synonymous with prosperity, fat dividends, and the almighty Rockefeller family, went bankrupt. It was, in fact, the largest corporate bankruptcy in American history to date, and the fate of the Chicago, Milwaukee & St. Paul was no doubt sobering to Missourians because one of its several western lines crossed the northeast corner of the state to link Kansas City and Chicago.*

Although railroads during the 1920s complained a great deal in print about the unfairness of overregulation, they were not powerless to fight back. In innovative ways they sought to adapt to the harsh new reality. Missouri Pacific, for example, improved its operating efficiency and enhanced its profits by becoming a national pioneer in extending the distance that steam locomotives ran at the head of its freight and passenger trains. Along some stretches of track, such as the 485 miles between Wichita and St. Louis, it more than doubled the length of their runs between 1926 and 1928. That saved money by using fewer locomotives, less fuel, and less labor.†

---

* The unexpected bankruptcy distressed many people who looked for a villain to blame. Actually, the causes were many, but a primary culprit was the expense associated with the new transcontinental line the Milwaukee Road completed from the Missouri River in South Dakota to Seattle and Tacoma on Puget Sound in 1909. To compound its misjudgment, the company soon thereafter electrified two sections of the line, but the light traffic the Pacific Extension generated never justified the cost of its construction or its electrification.

† *Railway Age*, October 6, 1928, 650–52.

Interurban Fever

At the height of the national interurban craze in the first decade of the twentieth century, dreamers and schemers put forth a blizzard of possibilities—most of them modest and local, but a few grandiose and strategic. In the latter camp was a plan to put down a double-track electric railroad in straight-line fashion linking New York City with Chicago. Another bold interaction had an interurban route strung out from East St. Cloud in Minnesota all the way to New York City. Perhaps the most expansive of all appeared in 1909 from visionaries and advocates of the Minneapolis, Kansas City & Gulf Electric Railway, which proposed a double-track thoroughfare from Minneapolis to Galveston—a route that would clip northwest Missouri to serve Bethany, Weatherby, Plattsburg, and Kansas City (with branches to Gallatin and St. Joseph) before jutting southward through Kansas, Oklahoma, and Texas. "No well-informed person doubts its completion," asserted a company

FIGURE 1.4.1.
A typical single-car interurban car cuts across the landscape. Electric railways provided clean, frequent, and economical service until automobiles and taxpayer-funded highways wiped them out. Don L. Hofsommer Collection.

spokesman, referring to the Panama Canal. "When completed, vessels from the Orient, with their millions of tons of freight, will seek a Southern port. This means Galveston." Moreover, said the company, "electricity is the coming motive power. Few are so obtuse as to doubt it." Demand would be immediate and would be met with satisfaction: "We will provide fast, through passenger and freight trains . . . to properly care for all local demands, and when this is supplied, no one will question but what we will receive the support of the entire population." Northwestern Securities Company, with offices in the Equitable Building in St. Louis, promised an "Easy Payment Plan of Buying Stock," par value $25 per share, "$50 buys 5 shares, $5 down and $5 per month for 9 months." The route was ostentatious in its design, and ostentatious would it be in its failure to birth.*

* *Fort Dodge Messenger*, May 11, 1906; *Minneapolis Journal*, June 23, 1909; *Railway Age*, September 13, 1907, 341.

FIGURE 1.4.2. At the dawn of the twentieth century, the St. Louis Car Company claimed that its Missouri trolley manufactory was the largest in the world. Schwantes-Greever-Nolan Collection.

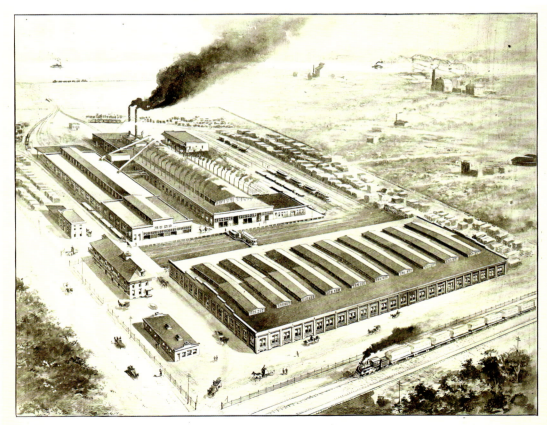

WORKS OF THE ST. LOUIS CAR CO., ST. LOUIS, MO.

Main-line passenger service continued and in many cases even grew better during the 1920s. At that time, it was possible for Missourians to travel in comfort and style aboard Pullman cars through to nearly every big city in the United States and even far south of the border all the way to Mexico City. A vacation in balmy Texas became a popular way to escape the chill of a Missouri winter, while a summer's idyll beside one of the many lakes of Michigan or Wisconsin provided a bracing escape from the heat and humidity that blanketed St. Louis and Kansas City during the years before air-conditioning.

*   *   *

Since the beginning of modern railways in the late 1820s, steam had served as their primary means of propulsion. A handful of companies added electricity to the mix in the late 1890s when they used it to power clean-running locomotives along stretches of track where the smoke from steam locomotives created major problems—as it did in the Baltimore & Ohio's cramped tunnels beneath the streets of Baltimore or the Milwaukee Road's westward extension over the northern Rocky Mountains of Montana and Idaho and the Cascade Mountains of Washington. No steam railroad in Missouri electrified its tracks, and electric interurban companies never constructed many miles of line within the state either. Nonetheless, the industry was important to Missouri if only because miles of electric trolley line interlaced city streets, and the industry was also the bread and butter of the venerable St. Louis Car Company, which in the 1920s remained one of the world's largest manufacturers of streetcars.

The pages of the *Electric Railway Journal* remained surprisingly optimistic about the industry's status. Even more than the steam railroads, however, interurban lines faced an insurmountable problem in the growing network of all-weather highways and the increasing number of automobiles. Some weaker ones sought salvation through mergers, some added freight to their traffic mix, some substituted buses for trains until they had fully morphed into highway carriers, and some pulled up their tracks but found new life as electric utilities. One of the strongest interurban lines was the Illinois Terminal, which until the 1950s continued to run frequent passenger trains between its station in downtown St. Louis and over the Mississippi River to Illinois cities as distant as Springfield, Decatur, and Peoria.[20]

*   *   *

All through the 1920s, the railroads' new competitors remained largely unfettered by federal regulations even as the rail industry itself

Express by Rail

The movement of packages and parcels was the responsibility of privately owned express companies—of which there were several early on, but now reduced to just one: the Railway Express Agency. Express cars, or combination baggage-and-express cars, were in the consist of most passenger trains, and this service blanketed the country with a highly integrated system. In larger communities, the express companies had their own offices, but in small towns the "depot agent" was also the express agent, and customers transacted business at the railroad office.

Railroads not only provided transportation services but also served as the major arteries of communication. Passengers, crewmen, and even tramps moved quickly from one place to another taking news, views, and rumors with them. And newspapers from metropolitan centers reached the interior by means of the cars. But it was the trackside telegraph with its ability to transmit any message at lightning-like speeds that captured the fancy of the American public. Those who could read Morse code—the telegraph operators—were held in special awe not only

FIGURE 1.5.1. During its heyday, the Railway Express Agency was synonymous with package delivery, including the latest Christmas gifts ordered from merchandisers like Sears, Roebuck of Chicago and sped by train to cities and villages across the United States. Schwantes-Greever-Nolan Collection.

for their particular talent but also because they were the first in any community to know important news. As with the express business, initially there were many telegraph companies, but over time these fell by the wayside, leaving the field to Western Union. Again, like express companies, the telegraph companies maintained special offices in larger centers but relied on depot agents in smaller places to send and copy messages.

It was to such telegraph offices that traveling salesmen—"knights of the grip" or "drummers," mysterious but omnipresent fixtures—repaired to communicate with their employers. Most were hired by manufacturers or wholesale houses whose businesses had expanded with the railroad. Armour & Company, the meatpacker, alone employed four thousand, who were dispatched throughout the country to drum up business. Indeed, the evolution of railroads and the telegraph, metropolitan centers and outlying areas, and manufacturing, wholesale, and jobbing collectively provides a prominent case study of symbiosis. Typically, the salesman launched forth from his point of origin on a Monday morning and stopped off at some wayside

FIGURE 1.5.2.
Traveling salesmen—"knights of the grip" or "drummers"—were ubiquitous, and it was at the depot where the drummer arrived, where his trunks were unloaded, where he wired his orders to headquarters, where he purchased a ticket to his next destination, where his trunks were reloaded, and where goods he sold to local merchants would soon arrive. Don L. Hofsommer Collection.

location to unpack sample cases and trunks so that local merchants could inspect goods.*

The drummer was usually a "live wire" who, as Meredith Willson pointed out in the *Music Man*, had "to know the territory." He also seemed to know the latest slang, the latest song, and the newest dance, was attired in the latest style, was known as a ladies' man, knew the most recent gossip, and, of course, could tell the best jokes. He was a link to the great outside world—a man who knew of and trafficked in the finest hotels and eateries around his circuit.†

It was at the depot where the drummer arrived, where his trunks were unloaded, where he wired his orders back to headquarters, where he purchased a ticket to his next destination, where his trunks were reloaded, where the goods he sold to local merchants would one day soon arrive by express or by freight in less-than-carload lots or on "trap" or "package" cars attached to the local freight train.‡ The depot, of course, was the focal point of any community, large or small, throughout the era of the steam-car civilization, the funnel through which people, goods, and information passed—the prism through which country folk and small-town America looked to the outside and urbanites pondered the great beyond.§

FIGURE 1.5.3. Handling baggage of all shapes and sizes contributed to the depot hubbub at train arrival and departure times. Don L. Hofsommer Collection.

---

* Kendrick W. Brown, "Memories of a Commercial Traveler," *Palimpsest* 52 (May 1971): 225–88.

† Susan Strasser, "'The Smile That Pays': The Culture of the Traveling Salesman, 1880–1920," in *The Mythmaking Frame of Mind: Social Imagination and American Culture*, ed. James Gilbert et al. (Belmont: Wadsworth, 1993), 155–77.

‡ Don Marquis, "My Memories of the Old-Fashioned Drummer," *American Magazine*, February 1929, 20–21, 152–54; Truman E. Moore, *The Traveling Man: The Story of the Traveling Salesman* (Garden City: Random House, 1972), 21–39.

§ John R. Stilgoe, *Metropolitan Corridor: Railroads and the American Scene* (New Haven, CT: Yale University Press, 1983), 193–211; George H. Douglas, "Down by the Depot," *Locomotive & Railway Preservation*, November–December 1992, 11–27; H. Roger Grant and Charles W. Bohi, *The Country Railroad Station in America* (Boulder: Pruett, 1978), 3–10.

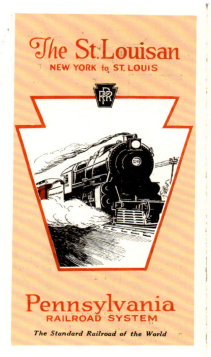
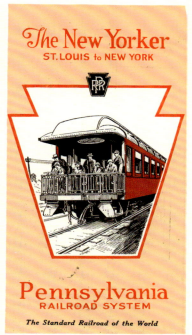

FIGURES 1.9, 1.10, AND 1.11. Railroads during the 1920s and 1930s eagerly promoted their premier passenger trains, such as the Pennsylvania's *St. Louisan*, the Missouri Pacific's *Sunshine Special* ("Out of St. Louis at Sunset—Into Texas at Sunrise"), and the Milwaukee Road's *Southwest Limited* between Chicago and Kansas City. These three represented only a sample of the splendid assortment of named trains that served Missouri patrons. The color images on the facing page come from the Schwantes-Greever-Nolan Collection, while the black-and-white image on this page comes from the Don L. Hofsommer Collection.

was forced to shoulder an increasingly odious burden of regulation. If ever there was a case of the past determining the future, this was it. Railroads during their golden years before 1900 had attained a level of financial power and public prominence never seen by any industry in American history, and Americans grew scared and resentful. Theodore Roosevelt enhanced his popularity in the early twentieth century by challenging unfettered railroad power as no previous president had done, the so-called Progressives in Congress joined the fight to constrain railroad power by piling one new regulation atop another, and the individual states did likewise. By the 1920s this was clearly an example of the biblical warning that the sins of the fathers would later vex their children for many generations. That is, the regulators and the public at large in the 1920s continued to treat the nation's railroad industry as if it still possessed the unfettered power it had enjoyed back in the 1880s, and thus they largely ignored the impact of the growing legion of unregulated competitors.[21]

Federal operation of the railroads during World War I followed by the unfettered competition during the 1920s extinguished the exuberance, sometimes irrational, that had formerly motivated the individuals who did the most to expand and shape the rail network of Missouri and the nation. No longer did promoters dare to dream and then implement great railroad-building projects, and no longer did many smaller railroads embrace passenger service with any degree of optimism or enthusiasm. They ran their trains simply as a public service and nothing more. Contributing to further changes within the railroad industry was the Great Depression that began with the stock market crash of late 1929.[22]

Between 1927 and 1937 the various governments in the
United States spent no less than $19 billion for new roadways
or improvements and another $12 billion for maintenance,
or a total of $31 billion—a sum greater than the total capital
investment in railroads of the United States in 1939.

—*Going Places: Transportation Redefines the
Twentieth Century West*, 2003[1]

2

The Dark Decade

All was not well with the American railroad industry. The age of railways had passed, but that reality had not adequately settled in on the public, its policymakers, or even railroaders. The industry's illness was reflected in annual reports to shareholders, which presented a dreary record of inadequate return on investment—an average of merely 4.48 percent in 1923 and about 5.25 percent in 1926. Railroad stocks in 1927 typically traded at levels lower than in 1906. The result was that investors favored the auto, steel, copper, and electrical industries.[2]

Then came the calamitous stock market crash of October 1929, a prelude to the Great Depression of the 1930s when industrial production slumped, unemployment skyrocketed, and consumer demand plummeted. Key statistics highlight the woes that resulted from the onset of hard times. Domestic manufacturing in 1932 slowed to just half of what it had been in 1929. Sales of motor vehicles in 1929 hit 4.6 million; the comparable figure for 1933 was a mere 1.3 million. American Locomotive Company erected an average of six hundred locomotives annually during the 1920s. During 1932 it sold just one locomotive! America's rail carriers in 1933 acquired only six passenger cars and 1,685 freight cars. Housing starts slid from 509,000 in 1929 to only 93,000 in 1933. Business failures as early as 1930 were epidemic; unemployment in the nonagricultural sector eventually reached 25 percent or maybe higher, and reductions in income were customary for those remaining on the payroll. Bank suspensions—9,765 around the country during the five-year period 1929–1933—deepened the national malaise. Missouri would not be spared.[3]

Hard times in industry and commerce were quickly manifest in agriculture, already smarting after a decade of trauma during the 1920s. Exports of grain and meat fell off due to shrunken demand abroad in conjunction with counterproductive tariffs; domestic consumption fell,

FIGURE 2.1.
The cover image used on a Missouri–Kansas–Texas timetable from 1935 emphasized the primacy of steam to power passenger trains. Schwantes-Greever-Nolan Collection.

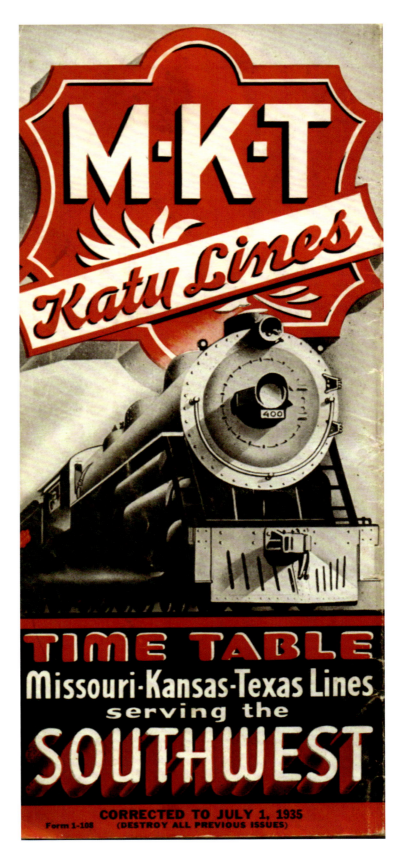

Railroad Customers across Missouri

Under normal circumstances, Missouri railroads could count on significant and regular freight billings from major manufacturers, wholesalers, meat packers, and even smaller firms located in the state's larger cities. They could also bank on carload, less-than-carload, and express business generated at hundreds of small stations sprinkled across Missouri. Listed here is a sample of the traffic mix that benefited rail carriers: R. M. Cuber, wallpaper, drugs, and furniture at Jacksonville (Wabash) and an axe-handle factory at Huntsville (Wabash); Marblehead Lime and Fullgraf Quarries at Hannibal (St. Louis & Hannibal); Chess & Wymand, oak barrels and food containers at Cuba (Frisco); Goodwin Company, poultry and eggs at Delta (Cotton Belt); Hi-Land Farms, hatchery at Hermann (Missouri Pacific) and Anchor Milling at Bagnoli (Missouri Pacific); Caldwell Brothers, caskets at Flat River (Missouri–Illinois); Yowell Saddlery, harness at Monroe City (Burlington); Gowgill Grain, feed, grain, and coal at Gowgill (Milwaukee Road); Regal Printing, publisher and printing at Plattsburg (Santa Fe); Wilson Bell Rock Crushing at Iron Mountain (Missouri Pacific); Superior Mineral Co. at Cabot (Missouri Pacific); Milne & LeGrand Quarry at Doe Run (Missouri Pacific); Missouri Reduction Co. at Flat River (Missouri Pacific); J. Rich Saw Mill at Mountain View (Frisco); Moran Silica Sand at Pacific (Missouri Pacific); Ben & Max Hirschowitz Horses & Mules at Oran (Missouri Pacific); Day Lumber Co. at Salem (Frisco); Crystal Carbonite at Louisiana (Burlington); and Imperial Broom Company, brooms and brushes at Pleasant Hill (Rock Island).*

* *Reference Book of Dun & Bradstreet* (New York: Dun & Bradstreet, 1937), 1436–536.

too, the result of inadequate buying power and changed dietary habits. Gross farm income nationwide in 1932 was but 40 percent of what it had been in 1929. Land values slid uncontrollably; the market value of an average acre of farmland in 1932 was about half of what it had been three years earlier. Foreclosures by lending agencies were predictable, but prices lenders realized because of severely diminished market value often threw them into bankruptcy; that, in turn, ruined others. As one observer recalled, because of the vicious cycle, it took faith, fortitude, and patience to remain in farming. That was no less true for businessmen in small towns who depended economically on the producing countryside as well as industries and workers connected in any way to agriculture. One element hinged on another; economic malaise of service territories impacted the health of railroad companies connected to those areas.[4]

Railroaders were as startled as others by the stock market crash and the Great Depression that followed only weeks later. Late in November

1929, *Railway Age* editorialized that "fundamental economic conditions of the country have changed but little," suggesting that "a mild recession in business" had been brewing since late summer. Illinois Central's L. A. Downs two months later admitted that "the recession of [late] 1929 had carried into 1930," but he believed that a "recovery seemed definitely under way." President Herbert Hoover argued that "any lack of confidence in the economic future or the basic strength of business in the United States" was foolish, and he extracted from railroad leaders a unanimous determination to "co-operate in the maintenance of employment and business progress." He also gained promises to "proceed with full programs of construction and betterments" undeterred by nervousness or uncertainty. They could not know, of course, just how serious matters would become or how long hard times would last.[5]

Economic dislocation of this magnitude and scope was immediately part of the political landscape. President Herbert Hoover and fellow Republicans hoped to aid the commercial and industrial areas with the Reconstruction Finance Corporation (RFC), a bank of last resort that essential but down-and-out companies might turn to. Hoover was fond of predicting that prosperity was "just around the corner," but the economic downturn in 1932 proved so devastating that many normally conservative citizens were radicalized. In November voters turned Hoover out of office and instead embraced Franklin D. Roosevelt and the promise of a "New Deal" by the president and his fellow Democrats.[6]

Nothing was of greater interest to railroaders than what the new Democratic administration in Washington had in mind as to overall transportation policy. In September 1932, Roosevelt as part of a nationally broadcast speech at Salt Lake City had declared that the preservation of railroads was essential to the well-being of the entire nation as well as to the protection of investors and employees. Railroaders took heart.[7]

What emerged during the first half of 1933 was bankruptcy legislation that benefited railroads in their struggle. A much more aggressive Reconstruction Finance Corporation soon became the nation's largest bank and also its largest single investor. To oversee implementation of key legislation beneficial to railroads, President Roosevelt appointed Joseph B. Eastman, a well-regarded Interstate Commerce Commissioner.[8]

American railroads needed all the help they could get. In 1932 they handled 646 million tons of freight and earned $2,451 million, statistics that compared unfavorably to those recorded for 1929 when rail carriers had hauled 1,339 million tons and had taken in $4,826 million. Passenger revenues were worse, dropping from $874 million in 1929 to $377 million in 1932. Carriers cut operating expenses by nearly half and reduced dividends by almost three-quarters, but taxes fell by less than a third, and bonded interest actually rose. Aggregate net income

FIGURE 2.2.
Freight paid the bills on most railroads, but promotion of passenger travel garnered the advertising dollars. Schwantes-Greever-Nolan Collection.

of $897 million in 1929 melted into a deficit of $130 million for 1932. Fifty-eight roads operating 43,681 miles of line were in receivership during the six-year period 1929–1934.[9]

Among those roads were several serving Missouri: Cape Girardeau Northern; Chicago & Eastern Illinois; Missouri & North Arkansas; Missouri–Illinois; Missouri Pacific; Mobile & Ohio; Chicago, Rock Island & Pacific; St. Louis–San Francisco; and Wabash. To these Chicago, Milwaukee, St. Paul & Pacific and St. Louis Southwestern soon would be joined. The Cape Girardeau Road simply expired, but most others underwent arduous and often lengthy reorganization proceedings and would emerge intact.[10]

Mobile & Ohio and Cotton Belt followed a jagged path to financial and corporate realignment, as did Chicago & Alton. As it eventually developed, Mobile & Ohio joined with Gulf, Mobile & Northern to form Gulf, Mobile & Ohio on September 13, 1940. Chicago & Alton, which had been in receivership since 1922, was sold at public auction to Baltimore & Ohio on December 11, 1930, but Alton remained in receivership,

The Dark Decade 51

FIGURE 2.3.
Depressed freight billings and reduced passenger boardings thrust Chicago, Rock Island & Pacific into receivership. All of it was reflected at Rock Island's St. Louis engine terminal, where 0-6-0 number 283 slumbered between fewer and fewer calls to make up and break up trains or perform switching duties for trackside customers. Don L. Hofsommer Collection.

and on May 31, 1947, it passed from Baltimore & Ohio control and was merged into the expansion-minded Gulf, Mobile & Ohio. Cotton Belt, meanwhile, had passed to control by the Chicago, Rock Island & Pacific in 1925, then to Kansas City Southern in a scheme floated by Leonor F. Loree to combine St. Louis Southwestern, Missouri–Kansas–Texas, and Kansas City Southern into a large new southwestern rail system. That project foundered, and on January 12, 1932, Cotton Belt found itself under the broad umbrella of the San Francisco–based Southern Pacific.[11]

Not all railroad companies serving Missouri were financially distressed—Pennsylvania prided itself as "The Standard Railroad of the World" with "Dividends Paid Every Year Since 1847"—but especially during the first half of the Dark Decade of the 1930s, none could boast of financial vibrancy. Freight billings spun downward, seemingly out of control. Passenger receipts followed a similarly dreary path. Railroad companies had little choice but to cut service. Freight train starts were trimmed and yard jobs eliminated. Other cuts were more difficult and subject to governmental review. All of Missouri's railroads hastened to reduce costs by eliminating open stations and by curtailing passenger service, but it was a tricky business. The age of railways had passed, but that did not mean that rails had been completely suspended by some other mode or modes. Much of Missouri remained "in the mud" in terms of all-weather highways, and many communities remained tightly bound to rail carriers. Beyond that there was the very legitimate fear of losing even more jobs during this awful depression—good jobs, relatively high-paying jobs. Even at the tiniest open station, there was

FIGURE 2.4.
Mobile & Ohio and Gulf, Mobile & Northern joined to form the Gulf, Mobile & Ohio on September 13, 1940. Schwantes-Greever-Nolan Collection.

the depot agent and likely the section foreman—these among the very few at such a location who received regular and reliable incomes. Any loss was immediate and significant. It was the same in every Missouri village. And reduction in freight starts and discontinuance of passenger trains had the instant result at larger division points of layoffs among operating personnel—enginemen and trainmen but also support staff such as coach cleaners, carmen, roundhouse laborers, and the like. The ripple effect was palpable. The state's great metropolitan centers—Kansas City, St. Joseph, St. Louis—were linked inextricably to the hinterland—to Trenton, Elmer, Marceline, Hermann, Eldon, and Boonville. The health of one was the health of the other. Small wonder politicians paid attention.[12]

Change was essential. Cuts had to come, no matter the pain. Missouri's rail mileage contracted from 7,897 during the 1930s to 7,042 a decade later. The pattern was bits and pieces—no substantial line segments were pulled up. Examples of mileage eliminated during those years included the following:

The Dark Decade   53

Santa Fe	Henrietta to North Lexington, 3.11 miles (1933)
Rock Island	Edgerton Junction to Wallace, 12.8 miles (1930)
Rock Island	Rockville to Wallace, 11.9 miles (1934)
Missouri Pacific	Crosmo to Belmont, 3.93 miles (1933)
Frisco	Wardwell to Frailey, 4.50 miles (1933)
Frisco	Yuko to Deering Junction, 4.00 miles (1933)
Frisco	Bangert to DeCamp, 12.8 miles (1933)
Frisco	Vanduser to Bloomfield, 17.3 miles (1933)
Salem, Winona & Southern	Herse to Winona Junction, 19.0 miles (1930)

These abandonments were part of a nationwide reduction in mileage—down from 249,052 in 1930 to 233,670 in 1940—and were explained by mines that played out, diminished agricultural production, failure of on-line sawmills, and simply inadequate customer bases in a changed and changing local economy.[13]

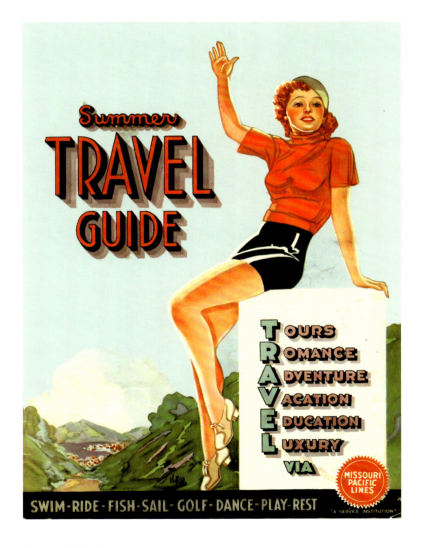

FIGURE 2.5. Passenger departments advertised attractive vacation destinations for patrons who had discretionary income. Missouri Pacific was especially aggressive in such matters. It used this image in the mid-1930s. Schwantes-Greever-Nolan Collection.

Leonor Loree's New Southwestern System

During the first three decades of the twentieth century, Leonor Fresnel Loree (1858–1940) was an oversized presence in Missouri's railroad landscape. He was without doubt one of the brightest and most capable Americans ever to run a railroad. Though Illinois-born and never a Missouri resident, at various times he guided the fortunes of the Kansas City Southern, St. Louis–San Francisco, and St. Louis Southwestern (Cotton Belt). From an office in Chicago, he briefly oversaw the Chicago, Rock Island & Pacific System, a major railroad presence in Missouri, but his tenure lasted only a few months in 1904. During that time Loree garnered probably unwelcome fame as the highest-paid railroad president in the United States. Perhaps because in the eyes of American journalists as well as some Rock Island investors, his big salary appeared outrageous, he soon ran headlong into the buzzsaw of corporate politics. After a stormy week of confrontation with majority shareholders, he was forced to resign, though his reputation as a railroad genius remained intact.*

The *Kansas City Star* opined that "Mr. Loree was a luxury" who cost the Rock Island $875,000 for nine month's work, and the railroad supposedly had also enticed him with a million-dollar bonus to leave the Baltimore & Ohio. Both sums were scandalous in 1904 when a worker's average annual salary was approximately $500.†

Loree's boldest Missouri ploy took place during the 1920s when in mid-decade he attempted to forge a new "Southwestern System" that combined the Kansas City Southern, Cotton Belt, and Missouri–Kansas–Texas. The name suggested the original "Southwestern System" that Jay Gould assembled during the 1880s to connect St. Louis with Texas. Bolder still was Loree's quest in 1925 to forge an entirely new transcontinental rail system by combining five railroads that stretched diagonally across the United States from Montreal, Canada, via St. Louis to the heart of Texas. It would have served as a forerunner of the Canadian National and Canadian Pacific systems that a century later took advantage of the newly implemented North American Free Trade Association, but the Interstate Commerce Commission checkmated Loree when it claimed his proposed combination was a trust, illegal under federal law. Thus, nothing came of his daring attempts to redraw the railroad landscape of the United States.‡

FIGURE 2.2.1. The bewhiskered face of Leonor Fresnel Loree appeared frequently in Missouri newspapers during the 1920s, and at the time he was probably the best-known railroad executive around the state. Schwantes-Greever-Nolan Collection.

More than anything, when federal regulators blocked Loree they revealed how much the familiar prewar world of American railroads had been altered forever by the conflict and its immediate aftermath, tumultuous years that included federal operation of the nation's rail network. No longer would any large new railroads or systems be constructed, and until the modern merger movement that dates from the early 1970s, the configuration of rail carriers in place in the 1920s remained basically unaltered for the next half century.

For the remaining years of his long railroading career, Loree was content to oversee the Delaware & Hudson, a New York and Pennsylvania line that would have formed a vital link in the transcontinental chain he dreamed of forging across the United States by way of St. Louis. He joined the railroad in 1907, and thirty-one years later he retired in 1938. As for his legacy in Missouri, "energy, dominant will power, and concentration have enabled L. F. Loree to restore more ailing roads to health than any other man alive today."§

FIGURE 2.2.2. This map of Leonor Loree's proposed "New Southwestern System" appeared in newspapers across Missouri in the mid-1920s, but the Interstate Commerce Commission thwarted his ambitions. Schwantes-Greever-Nolan Collection.

* *St. Louis Republic*, October 5, 1904. Loree, a civil engineer by training, served as president of the Baltimore & Ohio from 1901 to 1904, was president of the Rock Island in 1904, was president of the Kansas City Southern from 1918 to 1920, was chairman of the Missouri–Kansas–Texas from 1926 to 1928, and was president of the Delaware & Hudson from 1907 to 1938. See also H. Roger Grant, *A Mighty Fine Road: A History of the Chicago, Rock Island & Pacific Railroad Company* (Bloomington: Indiana University Press, 2020).

† *Kansas City Star*, October 5, 1904; *St. Louis Post-Dispatch*, October 5, 1904.

‡ The five railroads included in Loree's grandiose consolidation proposal were the Delaware & Hudson; Delaware, Lackawanna & Western; Wabash; Missouri–Kansas–Texas; and Kansas City Southern. *Kansas City Star*, April 14, 1925.

§ Jim Shaughnessy, *Delaware & Hudson* (Berkeley, CA: Howell-North Books, 1967); *Kansas City Star*, January 24, 1926. Numerous Missouri newspapers lauded Loree's role as "the doctor of sick railroads" or as "the world's most masterful genius in the field of transportation." *Jefferson City Post-Tribune*, August 30, 1926.

Missouri's scattering of electric traction roads were particularly vulnerable. In 1920 the Joplin-Pittsburg Railroad ("Rock Ballast—No Dirt—No Cinders") carded fifteen passengers' movements daily between Joplin, Missouri, and Pittsburg. Kansas—a distance of twenty-six miles. Two decades later the interurban was operated for freight service only, and not out of Joplin but from Waco, Missouri, to Croweburg, Kansas. Others clung to precarious life, atrophied, and finally perished: St. Louis, St. Charles & Western (1932); Kansas City, Clay County & St. Joseph (1933); Kansas City, Lawrence & Topeka Electric (1934); Kansas City, Leavenworth & Western (1938); and Southwestern Missouri Electric (1939).[14]

Fair-minded observers logically could have concluded that vicissitudes of the Great Depression would cut evenly against all modes of transport, but various New Deal and other state and local "make work" programs served unfairly to aid greatly the motor vehicle sector against the country's investor-owned railroads. Gravel replaced mud, blacktop replaced gravel, and roadways improved dramatically. All of this pleased the auto-minded public, of course. Domestic manufacturers produced the fifty millionth automobile early in the 1930s, and during the decade nationwide auto registrations increased from 23,059,000 in 1930 to 26,201,000 in 1939—hard times notwithstanding. Indeed, in 1936, automobile companies sold more cars than in any year, except for 1928 and 1929. Americans clung almost wistfully to their motor vehicles. They praised the 614 Durant for its "hill climbing ability and quality seating that withstand hard everyday usage" and extolled the value and utility of Studebaker's "Big 6-Passenger Cruising Sedan"—"Surprising Gas Economy" available for only $665. The surge in automobile ownership cast a dark shadow over the nation's passenger-carrying railroads—not just the short-haul interurbans.[15]

Rock Island managers put the matter starkly before that company's shareholders in 1931: "We have advised you how seriously the railroads are affected by the loss of their passenger traffic to the automobile. In order to illustrate this, we call your attention to our figures, which we believe are typical of railroads in general."

TABLE 2.1

Year	Passengers carried (noncommuter)	Revenue
1920	15,620,116	$34,311,423
1929	3,839,498	$17,870,894
1931	1,734,945	$9,475,460

"The figures show that the short haul passenger has gone to the motor bus or the private automobile, and that those facilities are gradually extending their area of competition."[16]

FIGURE 2.6.
Quanah, Acme & Pacific joined with parent St. Louis–San Francisco to offer through passenger operation all the way from the High Plains of West Texas to Kansas City and St. Louis. The *Plainsman* would not survive the Great Depression. Don L. Hofsommer Collection.

Railroad companies did what they could to stem the tide. Passenger departments advertised attractive destinations for patrons who still had discretionary income, argued for enhanced equipment, implemented faster schedules, lowered rates, and targeted specific constituencies. Missouri Pacific put on a twice-weekly sleeper to New Mexico's Carlsbad Caverns (automobile from Van Horn, Texas) and, with Denver & Rio Grande Western and Western Pacific, sped up the crack *Scenic Limited* from St. Louis through the Rockies and Sierra Nevada to San Francisco.

Burlington advertised escorted tours from St. Louis to the Black Hills of South Dakota, and Chicago & Eastern Illinois joined with Michigan's Pere Marquette to run seasonal through cars to "Holiday Land," the resorts of northern Michigan at Petoskey and Bay View. Katy continued to promote the "sunny days and old-world atmosphere of San Antonio," and, for its part, New York, Chicago & St. Louis placed coaches "of the

58   Missouri Railroads

FIGURE 2.7. Competition for passengers between St. Louis and Chicago was vigorous and pitted the Alton against its Illinois Central, Wabash, and Chicago & Eastern Illinois competitors. Alton was among several railroads that introduced "all air-conditioned" trains during the 1930s. Schwantes-Greever-Nolan Collection.

latest all-steel construction" on its Cleveland–St. Louis train. Cotton Belt would institute new train service, the *Lone Star*, with drawing-room sleeping cars from St. Louis to Houston via Dallas. Pennsylvania placed two of its trains, *Spirit of St. Louis* and the *American*, on twenty-three-hour schedules.

All four roads on the Chicago–St. Louis route (Alton, Chicago & Eastern Illinois, Wabash, and Illinois Central) agreed in 1933 to coordinate service to reduce duplicative train miles—each road reserving for itself, however, midnight service northbound. To retain business between St. Louis and Des Moines, Iowa, Wabash in 1932 reduced lower berth fares to $3.75, or to $13.50 for the drawing room aboard the Pullman standard sleeper assigned to that run.

Those roads with lines from St. Louis to Chicago and to the East eagerly sought business from baseball teams. The American League's St. Louis Browns typically used the Wabash to Chicago and Detroit, New York Central to Cleveland and Boston, and Pennsylvania to Washington, Philadelphia, and New York. In the National League, the St. Louis Cardinals used Chicago & Alton or Wabash to Chicago, Baltimore &

The Dark Decade   59

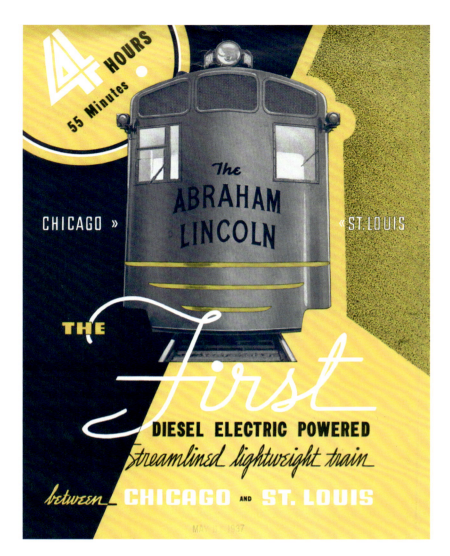

FIGURE 2.8.
Chicago & Alton inaugurated a "new lightweight steam train reflecting new principles in streamlined trains"— the *Abraham Lincoln*—on July 1, 1935, replaced steam with diesel for that train on May 17, 1936, and announced a four-hour-and-fifty-five-minute schedule between St. Louis and Chicago. Schwantes-Greever-Nolan Collection.

Ohio to Cincinnati, New York Central to Boston, and Pennsylvania to Pittsburgh, Philadelphia, and New York. Roads usually added two sleepers for overnight runs required by the teams, coaches for day runs, and in all cases a baggage car for equipment.[17]

Air-conditioning was one area in which rail carriers gradually, if often grudgingly, made service improvements during the 1930s. It was not so much that carriers wanted to maintain the status quo as that the dollars required to air-condition cars during the Great Depression seemed a questionable use of precious capital. But they had no choice, else risk even more empty seats. Of the roads serving Missouri, Baltimore & Ohio led the way, boldly proclaiming its marvelous *National Limited* fully air-conditioned as early as May 1932. New York Central and Pennsylvania could respond only meekly, noting that their trains from New York would be "pre-cooled." Missouri Pacific added air-conditioned diners to

60   Missouri Railroads

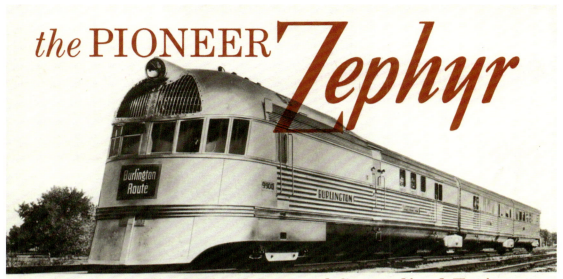

ABOVE, FIGURE 2.9. The Chicago, Burlington, and Quincy issued a commemorative brochure to salute its mid-1930s introduction of America's first diesel-powered passenger train. Schwantes-Greever-Nolan Collection.

LEFT, FIGURE 2.10. Burlington introduced a fleet of *Zephyr* streamliners during the mid to late 1930s, several of which burnished the rails of Missouri. Don L. Hofsommer Collection.

Show Me Rail Depots

FIGURE 2.3.1.
The Wabash depot at Elmo was typical of Missouri small-town rail stations. The railroad company held title to the building, but the depot belonged emotionally to the townspeople. The company's agent was viewed as a pillar of the community. Don L. Hofsommer Collection.

The nature, circumstance, and culture of railroad stations across rural Missouri were essentially the same everywhere. The depot was one of the few buildings in which lights burned all night. In fact, it set the tempo for the entire community. Yes, the railroad company held the title to the building, but the depot belonged emotionally to the townspeople. The company's agent—the "depot agent" as he was universally called—was a pillar of the community, and the fact that he was also a telegrapher only added to his stature. He was, in the days before long-distance telephones, the first person in town to get the "latest news," and he was the keeper of "standard time" courtesy of Western Union.*

its *Scenic Limited* and *Sunshine Special* in 1933, and a year later Illinois Central air-conditioned its lounges and diners to and from St. Louis.[18]

If railroads had been lethargic in the face of determined competition throughout the 1920s and into the next decade, they were fully alert by the mid-1930s—at least in terms of protecting long-distance travel. Locals and branch services were trimmed when regulatory restrictions permitted, and carriers consolidated their head-end business as much as possible on secondary trains. But, strapped as they were for cash, several railroads turned their attention to high-speed service with streamlined trains drawn frequently by new internal combustion engines, most notably diesels. On the national level, Union Pacific and Chicago, Burlington & Quincy showed the way in 1934 with whirlwind tours of their *M-10000* and *Zephyr* trains, respectively.

Atchison, Topeka & Santa Fe responded with its *Chief* and then *Super Chief* in Chicago–Kansas City–Los Angeles service. And Rock Island

There certainly was a mystique about the depot, with its tobacco-smelling office, its clattering telegraph instruments, and its dark and dingy freight house. And there was an excitement about the place—a great lure for those who saw that "city life" began at the ticket window and a fear for those who likewise recognized that fact but were appalled by it. "Train time" always meant considerable milling about, hack drivers and draymen appearing as if by command, passengers heading for the platform, and always some curious onlookers taking it all in.

FIGURE 2.3.2. The depot agent was the busy master of his or her domain. Don L. Hofsommer Collection.

* H. Roger Grant and Charles W. Bohi, *The Country Railroad Station in America* (Boulder: Pruett, 1978), 3–10.

acquired a fleet of *Rockets* for deployment across the midcontinent. Chicago & Alton inaugurated a "new lightweight steam train reflecting new principles in streamlined trains"—the *Abraham Lincoln*—on July 1, 1935, replaced steam with diesel for that train on May 17, 1936, announced a four-hour-and-fifty-five-minute schedule between St. Louis and Chicago, and added a sister train, the *Ann Rutledge*, during the summer of 1937. A few months earlier, on May 17, 1936, Illinois Central placed its *Green Diamond* in service. Diesel-powered and air-conditioned throughout, the *Green Diamond* boasted "a radio in every car," a nurse/stewardess, and a four-hour-and-fifty-five-minute prance between Chicago and St. Louis. Near the end of the year, on December 20, the Chicago, Burlington & Quincy introduced its *Ozark State Zephyr* between St. Louis and Kansas City.[19]

Other developments were less dramatic but important nevertheless. Eastern roads in 1936 reduced rates to two cents per mile in coaches and

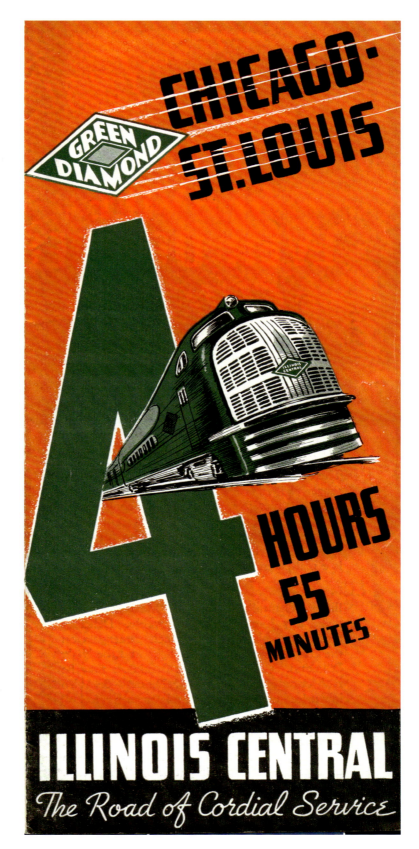

FIGURE 2.11. Illinois Central saluted its newly inaugurated St. Louis–Chicago speedster, the *Green Diamond*, one of several internal-combustion trains American railroads introduced during the mid-1930s. Schwantes-Greever-Nolan Collection.

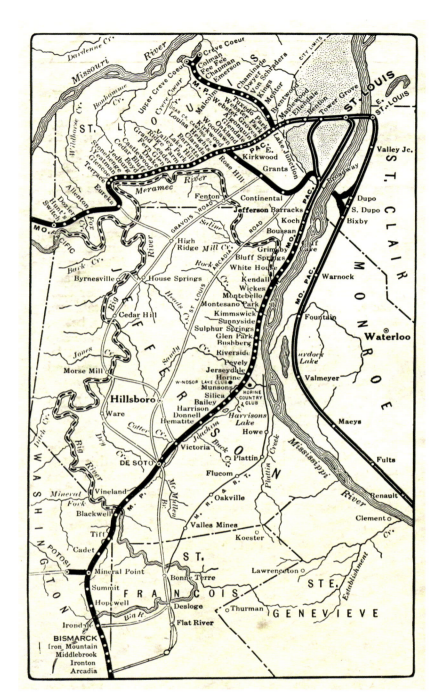

FIGURE 2.12.
During the early twentieth century, railroads operated a modest network of commuter trains in the St. Louis area. Emphasized on this detailed map are Missouri Pacific's several local lines. Schwantes-Greever-Nolan Collection.

three cents per mile in Pullman cars. On the equipment front, the industry proudly noted in 1937 that it had over eight thousand air-conditioned cars in operation. Similarly equipped cars were assigned to the *Blue Bird*, a new train acquired by Wabash in 1938 for afternoon operation in the Chicago–St. Louis corridor. Meanwhile, Frisco introduced snack cars on the St. Louis–Memphis circuit and hired Filipinos as attendants in lounge cars assigned to the *Meteor* that sprinted through the Missouri Ozarks from St. Louis to Springfield and Oklahoma City. During the second half of the 1930s, Baltimore & Ohio extended stewardess nurse assignments to its *National Limited* but discontinued secretary service on that train, and the Louisville & Nashville and Cotton Belt both advertised air-conditioned sleepers on runs into and out of St. Louis.[20]

Despite the terrible economic dislocations of the 1930s, Chicago, Dallas, New York, and San Francisco all staged marvelous extravaganzas calculated to attract large numbers of visitors. Many Missouri residents would attend those celebrations, and many more would pass through the gates of Kansas City Union Station and St. Louis Union Station en route. Chicago hosted the Century of Progress Exposition in 1934, and Dallas welcomed the Texas Centennial Exposition in 1936. Missouri Pacific prepared for the Texas event by air-conditioning its *Sunshine Special* and the Texan and by improving track to "quicken the schedule" of each train, while Frisco and Katy polished and speeded up their joint *Texas Special*, *Bluebonnet*, and *Texas Limited*. Katy also publicized its own train, the *Katy Flyer*, temporarily dubbed the *Katy Centennial Flyer*. The centennial sequel, the Greater Texas and Pan-American Exposition of 1937, promised to attract several million guests, but by that time plans were abroad elsewhere for the Golden Gate International Exposition at Treasure Island in San Francisco Bay and for the New York World's Fair—both in 1939. The country's railroads advertised maximum ninety-dollar rates (in coaches) to either event from any location in the country. Of St. Louis roads, Pennsylvania, Baltimore & Ohio, and New York Central were predictably enthusiastic in boosting the New York fair—Baltimore & Ohio pointing out that its route from St. Louis passed through Washington and that liberal stopovers were "accorded passengers desiring to stop at the Nation's capital for a sight-seeing visit."[21]

Passenger business staggered and then stabilized. Passenger miles for combined modes dropped from mid-1930 to mid-1933 but then turned upward. Rail passenger miles stayed constant from 1931 through the decade—claiming about 8 percent of America's total transportation miles, with automobiles taking a whopping 88 percent and intercity buses picking up the remainder. Such statistics could hardly give railroaders reason to rejoice; the erosion of passenger miles on a comparative basis during the 1920s and especially during the 1930s was truly monumental.

But exciting equipment, faster train speeds, new marketing approaches, and a moderately improved economy had at least yielded stability.[22]

Not surprisingly, the nature and volume of commuter train operation into and out of St. Louis Union Station changed substantially over time. At the dawn of the twentieth century, several roads—Chicago, Burlington & Quincy; the Terminal Railroad's Merchant Bridge Terminal; some of the eastern roads; and even Chicago, Peoria & St. Louis—operated commuter trains to points across the Mississippi River from St. Louis, but these disappeared as a result of automobile competition and as interurban rail service was established. Consequently, the focus centered on western suburbs. As early as 1875, Missouri Pacific advertised six weekday trains over its line to and from Kirkwood, fifteen miles from downtown. Frisco also offered service on its roughly parallel line; in 1904, it scheduled seven trains in each direction to and from Valley Park, eighteen miles west of St. Louis, and another three trains to and from Pacific, thirty-four miles from Union Station. In the same year, Wabash carded several trains to Ferguson and Kinloch Park, with two runs continuing to St. Charles, twenty-two miles removed. Some of these trains served Union Station, but for the most part Wabash used an independent stop on the riverfront at Olive Street. At one time, Missouri Pacific also had scheduled service on its Creve Coeur and Carondelet lines, and even Rook Island's local predecessor had been part of the parade, but commuter business proved especially susceptible to competition from streetcars, interurbans, automobiles, and buses. Declining train numbers reflected this. In 1929, Missouri Pacific and Frisco ran

FIGURE 2.13.
Pennsylvania advertised "Air-Rail Coast-to-Coast Service." Commercial air travel across the United States in 1929 was feasible only with overnight assists from two railroads, the Pennsylvania and Atchison, Topeka & Santa Fe, because flying during hours of darkness was not yet considered safe. The trip between New York and San Francisco served the St. Louis market along the way. Schwantes-Greever-Nolan Collection.

The Dark Decade 67

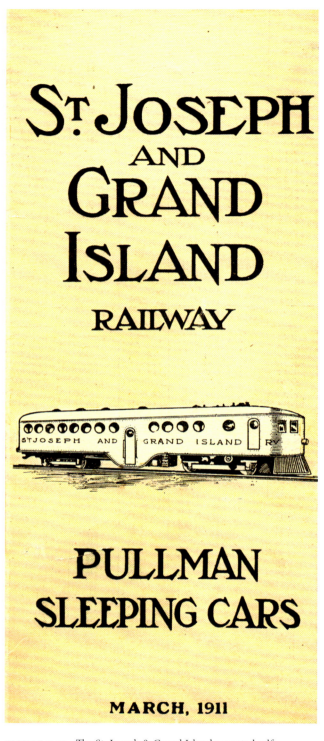

FIGURE 2.14. The St. Joseph & Grand Island operated self-propelled rail cars between its namesake cities. Among the most famous makers of these vehicles was the McKeen company of Omaha, Nebraska. One of their distinctive "windsplitters" is pictured on the cover of a 1911 timetable. Schwantes-Greever-Nolan Collection.

only twenty-three commuter trains combined; Wabash dropped out in 1933; and with the dawn of the next decade, only Missouri Pacific remained in the trade—and barely, with but a single commuter train daily each way between St. Louis and Pacific.[23]

Although it had no impact on commuter operation, commercial aircraft posed a distinct threat to intercity rail passenger business. "Flying Machines" were not taken seriously at first, but their utility was proved quickly. As early as 1924, the Post Office Department announced thirty-four-hour airmail service between New York and San Francisco. Six years later airmail had expanded greatly and included Chicago to St. Louis and St. Louis to Omaha, with connections at Chicago and Omaha to the national airmail network. In 1929, Pennsylvania joined Santa Fe and Transcontinental Air Transport-Maddux Air Line to operate rail-air service between New York and San Francisco along a route that included St. Louis. Through passengers changed transport modes at Columbus, Ohio; Waynoka, Oklahoma; and Clovis, New Mexico. Patrons used rail sleeping cars only on the relatively short stretches between New York and Columbus and between Waynoka and Clovis. In 1930, Robertson Aircraft advertised "Boeing four-passenger cabin planes, carrying mail in separate compartments" on its twice-daily Chicago–St. Louis assignments. At mid-decade United Air Lines claimed a world record for air travel—18,577 revenue passengers in a single month on its New York–Chicago–Pacific Coast system. Especially attractive was United's seventeen-hour coast-to-coast

FIGURE 2.15. St. Louis & Hannibal was among several Missouri carriers that opted for rail motor cars, or "doodlebugs." One is seen here in Hannibal, June 20, 1933. Conrad Cheatham Collection.

schedule. Transcontinental & Western, a predecessor of Trans-World Airlines, pointed to its own Douglas Luxury "Skyliners" and "Skysleepers." Railroaders brooded because they feared commercial aviation might threaten their remaining primary sources of passenger revenue—long-distance travelers and letter mail. They were right to brood.[24]

Missouri railroad managers likewise were forced to brood over the issue of branch-line or local passenger trains that typically catered to short-haul customers and suffered from marginal profitability. Petitioning for discontinuance almost always proved a public relations nightmare, and regulators were often unsympathetic. In an effort to solve or at least alleviate the problem, several Missouri railroads acquired "motors," or gas-electric "puddle jumpers" or "doodlebugs," as they were often and derisively labeled.

In some cases, they were self-contained units (engineer's compartment in the power section, Railway Post Office apartment, baggage/express section, and a few passenger seats shoehorned in at the rear). In other cases, they featured power units with a Railway Post Office apartment and storage for mail, express, and baggage fully capable of pulling coaches.

As early as 1930, Missouri Pacific assigned a gas-electric train to the St. Louis–De Soto circuit, among many steam trains; Rock Island

The Dark Decade   69

FIGURE 2.16. Missouri–Illinois employed motor car #625 and trailer between St. Louis Union Station and the mining community of Doe Run during the 1930s and elsewhere later. When Missouri–Illinois vacated the passenger-carrying trade, the railroad dispatched this pair to Bonne Terre, where they reposed in 1954—"all dressed up and nowhere to go." Missouri Pacific Historical Society Collection.

deployed similar "doodlebug" units on its St. Louis–Eldon and Eldon–Kansas City runs; Santa Fe advertised a similar arrangement on its St. Joseph to Topeka leg; and Milwaukee Road dispatched motors between Mystic, Iowa, and Kansas City. Six years later Chicago & Alton boasted of a 356-mile motor-train assignment across northern Missouri between Bloomington, Illinois, and Kansas City. In 1938 Burlington assigned a gas-electric train to the ten-hour sojourn between Burlington, Iowa, and Carrollton, Missouri, with thirty-seven station stops en route. Many of these rail-motor cars were constructed by the St. Louis Car Company and featured "powerplants" manufactured by Electro-Motive.[25]

There was another opportunity to deal with the short-distance passenger dilemma—an "if ya, can't beat 'em, join 'em" approach. Several Missouri railroads established motor transport subsidiaries that put intercity buses on branch-line routes and in some cases even on highways than ran parallel to the main rail routes. As early as 1930, Missouri Pacific Transportation Company had a fleet of 185 motor coaches serving four thousand route miles that tapped St. Louis, Charleston, Poplar Bluff, Sedalia, Jefferson City, and various Kansas communities, among other places. Chicago, Burlington & Quincy acted similarly, incorporating Burlington Transportation Company in 1929 and operating more than eight hundred route miles, eventually with Omaha–Kansas City and Chicago–Kansas City service. Chicago & Alton put forward its Alton Transportation, which advertised bus service between Louisiana, Missouri, and the state capital, Jefferson City.[26]

Railroaders everywhere looked on with growing alarm as motor trucks scampered off with more and more freight—aided as they were by publicly funded and maintained streets, roads, and highways. Ironically,

Missouri Railroads

FIGURE 2.17. During the early 1920s, it grew increasingly obvious that a transportation newcomer, the intercity motor coach, attracted cost-conscious patrons from the railroads. During the second half of the decade and into the 1930s, numerous railroads, including Burlington, Santa Fe, Pennsylvania, and Missouri Pacific, joined the ranks of bus operators, a defensive move that resulted in the creation of regional networks of rail-owned highway vehicles that frequently included trucks as well as buses. Schwantes-Greever-Nolan Collection.

hard times accelerated the growth of over-the-road trucking. As better roadways beckoned, truck competitors gained greater capacity, reliability, and speed, and it was so easy to join the trucking business. With the Depression Decade's high unemployment, many men sought to support

FIGURE 2.18.
St. Louis Southwestern was an early promoter of highway vehicles to supplement its trains, both passenger and freight. Don L. Hofsommer Collection.

themselves by becoming "gypsy" truckers or working for other trucking concerns at wages far below those afforded railroad employees. For back hauls, some truckers even accepted freight simply for "gas money." Less-than-carload (LCL) freight was especially susceptible. Traditionally, high-rated commodities such as merchandise and miscellaneous manufactured goods had moved in carload lots to distribution centers and then by LCL to local wholesalers, retailers, and other consignees. Now, because many orders were small and trucks easily handled door-to-door shipments, railroad LCL billings declined precipitously.[27]

What could be done to stem the tide? In 1932, Cotton Belt's J. R. Turney had suggested a new package car system that embraced a multi-modal approach. The current system, Turney argued, was "as out of place as a corset at the seashore." Railroaders, he groused, had not listened to him and instead had clung to old ways of handling small lots and package shipments—much to their collective detriment as that business floated away to truckers. Four years earlier, on its own, Cotton Belt had promoted incorporation of the Southwestern Transportation Company to operate buses and trucks along several routes that paralleled the railroad—all part of a program of coordinated railway and highway service in all parts of the railroad's service area. Early operation included a route from Malden, Missouri, to Jonesboro, Arkansas, with, as the company said, "motor trucks of various sizes . . . [and] . . . several tractors . . . and semi-trailers." Others were slower to follow the Cotton Belt's example.

Chicago, Burlington & Quincy in 1935 inaugurated a truck division of its Burlington Transportation Company satellite. A year later truck

FIGURE 2.19.
Cotton Belt advertised its *Blue Streak Merchandise* from St. Louis with "through connections to and from all eastern cities." The train commenced operations on October 1, 1931. Don L. Hofsommer Collection.

service was available over 1,306 route miles, and before the decade was out, it extended to 3,998 route miles, including those reaching both St. Louis and Kansas City.[28]

Managers responsible for gaining and retaining carload freight along Missouri's rail network during the first half of the 1930s seemed utterly frozen and consumed by the harsh economic reality of the Great Depression and the vigorous assault by truckers on what had been the rail's historic near modal monopoly. They watched grimly as freight billings plummeted. At Rock Island, for instance, tonnage handled in 1929 reached 37,971,933, but it dropped to a dreary 19,949,383 in 1935. Revenues sagged accordingly. Some of this was directly attributable to the economic malaise, but trucks had siphoned traffic well beyond the LCL business. As early as 1929, a full 23 percent of livestock received at the nation's primary markets arrived by truck, which meant a loss of

The Dark Decade

FIGURE 2.20. The "Go Katy" map advertisement appeared in 1934. Maps such as the one prominently displayed in this Katy advertisement were a common feature of rail publications intended for public consumption. System timetables typically included one or more maps, but usually drawn in a creative way intended to emphasize the geographic advantages of their rail issuer. Schwantes-Greever-Nolan Collection.

232,000 single-deck carloads to railroads. By 1938, trucks carried 71.4 percent of hogs and 59.1 percent of cattle to market.[29]

It was not all doom and gloom, however. In 1930, Wabash dispatched a "poultry demonstration car" over its lines in Missouri where 4,630 persons came to learn about "correct chick housing equipment." Frisco and its Quanah, Acme & Pacific puppet inaugurated through package cars from St. Louis and Kansas City all the way to distant Quanah, Texas. Missouri Pacific upgraded its line from Pueblo, Colorado to Kansas City so that perishables from Colorado (cabbage, cauliflower, carrots, broccoli, onions, and melons) could be delivered over the 623-mile route in just under twenty-four hours. A change in public policy also benefited the rails when ratification of the Constitution's Twenty-First Amendment on December 5, 1933, ended Prohibition. Even before, in March, Congress had changed the legal definition of an intoxicating beverage from 0.5 to 3.2 percent alcohol, and with that decision breweries had reopened, at least some of them. On March 23, 1934, a train of twenty-seven carloads of beer from the Anheuser-Busch Company in St. Louis rolled into Chicago over Illinois Terminal and Chicago & North Western tracks. Inbound lading to Anheuser-Busch and other breweries included barley, hops, kegs, cases, and bottles—all welcome business.[30]

By the mid-1930s several Missouri railroad companies bestirred themselves and initiated vigorous campaigns to hold or gain freight traffic of all kinds. St. Louis–San Francisco in 1936 inaugurated overnight merchandise service between St. Louis and Oklahoma City. *The Flash*, said Frisco, was the "symbol of FFF—Frisco Faster Freight—Superior Service." Katy countered with its *Bullet*, "fast, dependable freight service" between St. Louis/Kansas City and Oklahoma and Texas points. Illinois Central promised overnight delivery of Chicago–St. Louis carload freight in each direction. The railroad also offered free pickup and delivery of LCL shipments and assured customers that merchandise delivered to its South Water Street freight house in Chicago before 5:00 p.m. would reach East St. Louis by 1:00 a.m. the following day. "Up-to-date equipment, smooth roadbed, and alert personnel" allowed Burlington to offer 29-hour freight service between St. Joseph and Chicago, 16½-hour service between Kansas City and St. Louis, and 36½-hour schedules between St. Joseph and Minneapolis.[31]

Rock Island and Wabash established *Redball* trains, but neither these nor other expedited trains serving Missouri or the Southwest could match the allure, pizzazz, or longevity of Cotton Belt's *Blue Streak Merchandise*. This train, insisted St. Louis Southwestern, would "jettison conventions and taboos of railroading." It would do so by being carded as "first class," by assigning passenger locomotives to it, by dispatching only carloads of LCL merchandise on it, and by coordinating its schedules with connecting trains plus pickup and delivery by Southwestern Transportation Company. In that way merchandise purchased in St. Louis on one day would be "ready for sale before the next day over store counters . . . [at] . . . all points served by Cotton Belt in Missouri, Arkansas, and Louisiana." The *Blue Streak* was St. Louis Southwestern's

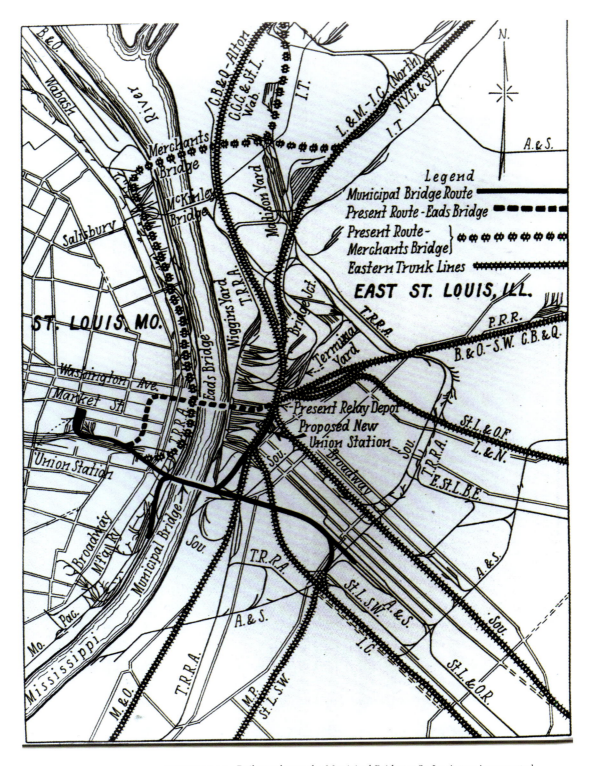

FIGURE 2.21. Rail travel over the Municipal Bridge at St. Louis was inaugurated in 1930, but it would require the remainder of the decade to prepare the structure for its greatest utility. Don L. Hofsommer Collection.

answer to "the demand of modern business," and the company predicted it would "prove to be the forerunner of a new breed of freight train." Service began between East St. Louis and Pine Bluff, Arkansas, on October 1, 1931, with much publicity—and much gnashing of teeth by Cotton Belt's rail competitors, particularly Missouri Pacific and Frisco, both of which considered the expedited service both wasteful and unnecessary. Nevertheless, the *Blue Streak Merchandise* was an immediate success, capturing, as it did, new business. "Cotton Belt Shows the Way!" was the bold assertion made by the company when the train took to the rails. That was no idle boast.[32]

* * *

Gas-electric rail motor cars, the humble "doodlebugs," served as precursors to diesel-electric locomotives, which, of course, were soon celebrated as modern motive power for the streamlined passenger trains introduced during the 1930s. Rock Island and all other major roads were at the same time more or less receptive to the efficiencies of internal combustion over steam power as demonstrated by their earlier experience with gas-electric rail motor cars and with diesels on passenger runs. Indeed, Rock Island purchased its initial diesel-electric switch engines in 1930. Others followed with their acquisition of switchers—Burlington in 1933, Chicago Great Western in 1934, and Milwaukee Road in 1939. Substantial employment of diesel-electric power for the movement of freight in road service would have to wait, however, until the following decade.[33]

FIGURE 2.22. The Bevier & Southern was typical of Missouri's several short rail lines and their modest motive power. In this photograph taken on September 15, 1952, one of its steam locomotives hauls cars of coal from a mine near Bevier, Missouri, to an interchange with the Chicago, Burlington & Quincy. Don L. Hofsommer Collection.

The Dark Decade   77

Steam Motive Power

What was the motive power for these and other freight assignments? During 1929, American manufacturers built 926 steam locomotives. This number included eight brawny 4-8-4s for Chicago, Burlington & Quincy; sixty-four 4-8-4s for Chicago, Rock Island & Pacific; five 4-8-2s and twenty-five 2-8-4s for Missouri Pacific; twenty 2-8-2s for Frisco; twenty-five 4-8-2s and twenty-five 4-8-4s for Wabash; two 0-8-0s for Manufacturers; and five 0-8-0s for the Terminal Railroad. Chicago Great Western in 1929 took delivery of fifteen 2-10-4s, and a year later St. Louis Southwestern received ten 4-8-4s. By then, the year 1930, a paralyzing economic depression had swept across the American landscape. In 1933, Baldwin took orders for only fourteen locomotives, Alco sold one, and Lima received no orders. During the six-year period 1931-1936, Rock Island purchased no locomotives. It was much the same story elsewhere. Toward the end of the 1930s, however, a few more orders reflected a slightly improved economy. Chicago, Burlington & Quincy, for example, in 1936 acquired three more 4-8-4s, Kansas City Southern placed in service ten giant 2-10-4s, and Cotton Belt added ten more 4-8-4s in 1937, as did Burlington in the same year.*

FIGURE 2.4.1.
Steam locomotive wheel arrangements varied widely. Large driving wheels provided power to pull the trains (such as this Cotton Belt freight near Dupo, Illinois) with additional drivers added as trains grew heavier and steam locomotives became larger. Don L. Hofsommer Collection.

* *Railway Age*, January 4, 1931, 80–82; Richard J. Cook, *Super Power Steam Locomotives* (San Marino: Golden West Books, 1966), 44–45; Chicago, Burlington & Quincy, *Annual Report, 1936*, 10–11; Chicago, Rock Island & Pacific, *Annual Report, 1936*, 39.

Given the gloomy nature of the economy during the 1930s, it was hardly surprising that Missouri's railroads were spare in their capital expenditures for plant and rolling stock. As Rock Island management put it starkly in 1931, "No new equipment was purchased." Milwaukee Road announced in 1930 that it had cut its maintenance-of-way and structures expenses by nearly 20 percent. However, both the Rock Island and Milwaukee Road took pride in announcing their commitment to $11.3 million in improvements along the thirty-seven-mile route from Polo to Birmingham, Missouri, joint operation of what now was a "double track railroad, and vast improvement of train operation into Kansas City from the north." Across the state to the east, a long-slumbering debate over what became the "Municipal Bridge" issue inched toward final resolution.

A Manufacturers Railway train rumbled over that fine new structure from St. Louis to East St. Louis on September 24, 1930, to inaugurate service. It would require the rest of the decade to finish new approaches and otherwise prepare the Municipal Bridge for its fullest utility. By 1940 nearly one-quarter of all passenger trains reaching St. Louis over the Mississippi River would use that bridge. Elsewhere, Katy completed a bridge renewal at Boonville, as did Wabash at St. Charles. Kansas City Southern opened a new 13.3-mile line from Grandview to Leeds to perfect its Kansas City connection. Missouri Pacific announced plans for a $1.8 million grain elevator with eight miles of support track at Kansas City, while the Milwaukee Road authorized a new water treatment plant at Lawson and "alterations and improvements" to its Kansas City freight house.[34]

Missouri's short-line railroads proved surprisingly resilient during the Great Depression. Missouri & Arkansas offered passenger service and scheduled a "manifest freight" train over its entire 368-mile route between Neosho, Missouri, and Helena, Arkansas. Bevier & Southern lugged coal to its Burlington connection at Bevier; St. Louis & Troy operated over five miles of line that once had been part of St. Louis & Hannibal; the financial health of Manufacturers Railway seemed well assured with the end of Prohibition; Cassville & Exeter delivered to and picked up lading from Frisco at Exeter; Kansas City, Kaw Valley & Western provided carload and LCL service to and from the six stations along its thirty-seven-mile Kansas City, Missouri, to Lawrence, Kansas, route; and Missouri Southern advertised a daily passenger turn over its route between Leeper and Bunker, advising, however, that it provided "minimum freight service tri-weekly . . . not operated on schedule." Indeed, early in the 1940s, Missouri Southern filed for abandonment of its entire fifty-four-mile system. The Terminal Railroad Association of St. Louis remained vibrant, however, as did Kansas City Terminal. Intermediate carriers such as Kansas City Connecting, St. Joseph Belt,

FIGURE 2.23.
Chicago, Rock Island & Pacific enthusiastically celebrated the first birthday of its late 1930s fleet of Rockets. Don L. Hofsommer Collection.

St. Joseph Terminal, and Union Terminal at St. Joseph continued in their useful endeavors.[35]

The economy followed a jagged path during the 1930s, and the pattern was reflected by the fortunes of Missouri's railroads. "The outstanding feature of the traffic situation in 1935," said Burlington management, "was the loss of livestock, feed and grain products, as a result of the drought in 1934," but in the next year the road reported a pleasant increase in nearly all commodity classes. It was much the same elsewhere. Santa Fe handled 31,236,481 tons of freight in 1931 and only 20,082,828 in 1933, but it rose to an impressive 29,865,519 tons four years later.[36]

Near the end of 1937, the stock market experienced a shudder, and business across the country showed signs of slackening. By fall the market was demoralized; prices would not bottom out until April 1938, and then only after erasing about two-thirds of the gains registered since their low point in early 1933. Business tumbled off the same precipice. Industrial production declined by one-third in only nine months and showed no sign of recovery until May 1938. Mild optimism that had been voiced throughout the land during the last few years reversed direction. The "recession within the Depression" of 1937–38 was one of the sharpest short-term economic downturns in national history.[37]

The performance of the nation's railways during the Great Depression was, on one hand, a mirror image of the greatly distressed national economy and, on the other hand, a reflection of significant inroads made by alternate means of transportation against what long had been a near modal monopoly by rails. In 1930, rail carriers had moved 703,598,000 passengers; in 1939, they moved only 451,089,000 passengers. In 1930, rail carriers handled 45,717,000 carloads of freight; in 1939, they handled 34,103,000 carloads. The loss of business was catastrophic for some roads—a total of 110 railroads across the United States entered receivership during the Depression Decade. The operating ratio (ratio of operating expenses to operating revenues) for Missouri railroad companies during the "Dirty Thirties" pointed to general financial distress but also to the dreadful drag of passenger operations on overall performance.

TABLE 2.2

Passenger Operating Ratio	1931	1939
Chicago Great Western	143.6	176.5
Chicago, Rock Island & Pacific	125.0	141.4
Kansas City Southern	157.2	160.0
Missouri–Kansas–Texas	127.9	144.5
Missouri Pacific	129.5	144.7
St. Louis–San Francisco	133.6	159.4
Wabash	130.8	134.5
Freight Operating Ratio	**1931**	**1939**
Chicago Great Western	66.4	63.7
Chicago, Rock Island & Pacific	64.6	66.5
Kansas City Southern	60.2	56.2
Missouri–Kansas–Texas	59.4	64.9
Missouri Pacific	65.3	68.0
St. Louis–San Francisco	63.3	70.8
Wabash	78.9	69.9

Source: *Moody's Manual* (1941), a27, a39, a77–a80, a104–a105.

There could be no doubting the destructive financial headwinds the Great Depression created. Neither was there doubting powerful competition in the form of automobiles, buses, and even airlines that claimed more than 50 percent of railroad passengers compared to the

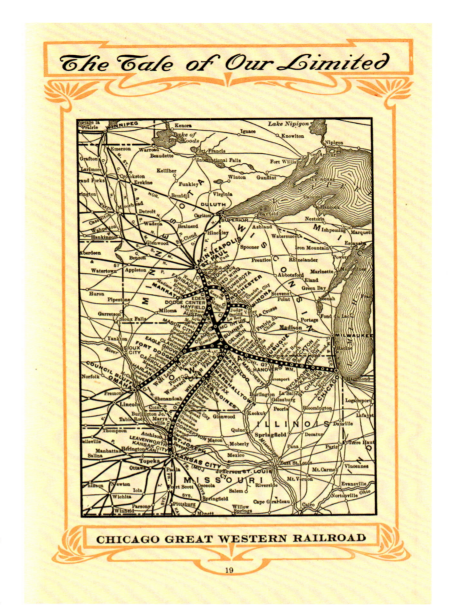

FIGURE 2.24. Creative publicists for the Chicago Great Western once portrayed its system map as the veins of a maple leaf. Here is a more conservative 1920s visualization of its track layout across the Midwest. Schwantes-Greever-Nolan Collection.

1920s. Trucks, pipelines, and government-subsidized inland waterways diverted high-rate traffic as well as petroleum products from the rails. And there were factors beyond the economic depression and competition that had had a negative impact on the carriers. In some instances, industries relocated factories to be closer to sources of raw materials, which in the process lessened demand for transport. In other cases, factories and generating plants installed more efficient boilers to reduce demand for coal. The development of high-tension electric transmission lines likewise reduced demand for coal that typically had moved by rail. Finally, there was slack demand for exports—this being, after all, a worldwide slump.[38]

Passenger Solicitation

During the spring of 1929, Chicago Great Western inaugurated combined rail and air service to St. Louis in conjunction with Universal Air Lines, using trimotor planes. As an example, passengers could board Chicago Great Western's *Legionnaire* in Minneapolis at 7:45 p.m., arrive in Chicago at 8:15 a.m., ride a motor coach from Grand Central Station to the municipal airport, and depart Chicago at 9:45 a.m. for a 1:00 p.m. arrival at St. Louis.*

During the next year, Chicago Great Western advertised "tours to the tropics" at "moderate cost" from "all points on its railroad." All of this was in cooperation with United Fruit Company and its "Great White Fleet" that cruised the Caribbean to carry bananas from Central America to the United States: "You can buy a round trip ticket from your hometown on Chicago Great Western to Cuba, Jamaica, Panama, Costa Rica, Columbia, or Honduras—the Golden Lands of the Caribbean." Passengers from Chicago Great Western locations would be taken by "fast, all-steel, splendidly appointed" trains to either Kansas City or Chicago, with connections to New York City or New Orleans to board vessels of the Great White Fleet at either location.

And, reminded an immodest Chicago Great Western, those vessels boasted "all outside rooms, an unsurpassed cuisine, only one class—FIRST CLASS." In Kansas City, tickets could be purchased from the railroad's passenger agents at 715 Walnut Street, at St. Joseph from the road's representatives at 505 Francis Street.†

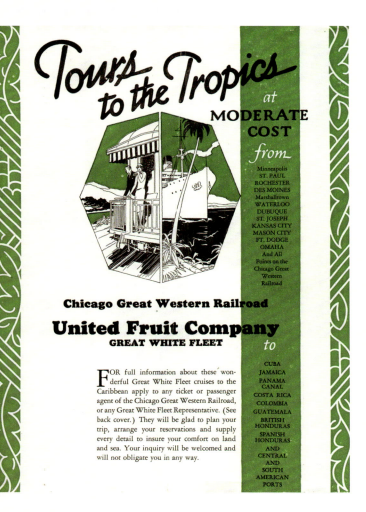

FIGURE 2.5.1. The tie between a Midwestern railroad of modest size and tropical vacations resulted in an unusual promotional brochure. Don L Hofsommer Collection.

* "CGW Sells Airplane Tickets," *Railway Age*, April 13, 1929, 864.
† "Tours of the Tropics," CGW promotional brochure (1930).

The state of America's railways in 1939 was predictably different from what it had been in 1930. Mileage was down from 242,391 in 1930 to 233,468 (Missouri's rail mileage dropped from 7,897 to 7,042), and locomotive numbers declined from 56,130 in 1930 to 39,309 in 1939. Companies also reduced rolling stock inventories to match curtailed demand. Passenger car numbers were reduced by 12,821 and freight cars by 46,800 over the 1930s. Average freight car capacity had risen, however, and newer locomotives had greater tractive effort, with the result that total freight capacity was down only 7 percent and the locomotive fleet's aggregate tractive effort actually was a bit higher than it had been a decade earlier. The picture was not rosy, but neither was it desperate.[39]

What did the future hold? The past seemed an inconclusive prognosticator. Small wonder Missouri railroaders faced the 1940s with more than a bit of nervousness. Yet there were glimmers of hope. Weather conditions had moderated, and demand for agricultural products trended upward to bring hope not only for farmers but also for those who lived in towns and cities. Demand for manufactured goods tended to perk up with collateral demand for raw materials. The National Industrial Conference Board estimated that 9.5 million Americans remained out of work in 1939, but that did not dampen the mood in New York City, where on April 30 gates to the World's Fair swung open to a vast enclosure called the "Court of Peace." The extravaganza was a monumental success and prompted a decision for a repeat performance in 1940—the "Forty Fair," to be "bigger, better and more fun in every way." The Railroad Building, designed as a roundhouse, occupied 140,000 square feet of space—adequate for performances of "Building the Railroad," "Railroads in Action," and "Railroads on Parade." More than a third of the Railroad Exhibit acreage was devoted to exhibits of modern locomotives and rolling stock. The entire enterprise oozed pride in the past and optimism for the future. Missouri railroaders could only applaud.[40]

"Yes, It's polite to 'Eat and Run'—these days!"

—Title of a World War II brochure issued by the Atchison,
Topeka & Santa Fe Railway to encourage dining car patrons
to clear space for others as rapidly as possible on their overly
crowded wartime trains, to forego comfort for victory

3

Of War and Peace

Deep-snow winters, glare-sun summers, and hard times of the "Dirty Thirties" etched deep furrows into mahogany faces of Missouri railroaders. Those grim days of the Great Depression had greatly tested all of them. They had withstood much and could take pride in that, but they also had reason to be skittish. Yet there were glimmers of hope. Weather conditions had moderated, and demand for agricultural products trended upward to bring hope to farmers as well as to residents of Missouri's towns and cities. The National Industrial Conference Board estimated that 9.5 million Americans remained out of work in 1939, but that did not darken the mood in New York City, where on April 30 the gates to the World's Fair opened to a vast enclosure called the "Court of Peace." That was the great hope of 1939.[1]

That hope was dashed a few months later when Nazi Germany invaded Poland in September and set Europe ablaze with yet another war. The year 1940 proved a watershed. Adolph Hitler's troops occupied a huge swath of Europe from Norway through France while a monumental air war raged over England. Instincts of isolation tugged mightily on American heartstrings, but President Franklin Roosevelt did all he could to prepare the country for a war he thought inevitable. Congress grudgingly concurred, authorizing major military appropriations, enacting the first peacetime draft, and calling the National Guard into federal service.[2]

Railroad managers, greatly traumatized by hard times and by recurring threats of nationalization during the Depression, mostly took defensive positions as demand for transportation increased. They rightly had allowed equipment inventories to sag during the 1930s to match reduced need and now were reluctant to place orders for power, rolling stock, and plant improvement, unconvinced that recovery was genuine

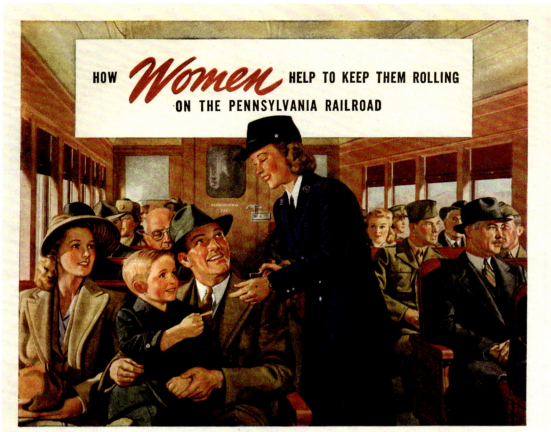

FIGURE 3.1. Women employed aboard Pennsylvania's passenger trains during World War II to ease a labor shortage earned praise in this widely distributed advertisement. Schwantes-Greever-Nolan Collection.

and long-term. Railroads serving Missouri had taken delivery of 184 new locomotives in 1929 and placed orders for an amazing 532 machines—everything from humble 0-8-0 switchers to broad-shouldered 4-8-4s capable of handling either freight or passenger assignments. Change came quickly. American Locomotive Company had erected an average of six hundred locomotives annually during the 1920s; in 1932 it sold but one. It was much the same in terms of freight car inventory.

Carriers nationwide placed orders for 111,218 cars in 1929—the highest number since 1924. Then the bottom dropped out. Optimism from the 1920s was also reflected by investment in plant. Milwaukee Road and Rock Island united to place in service a thirty-eight-mile joint operation between Polo and Birmingham in 1930—this to maximize efficiency into and out of Kansas City. (Rock Island's portion was a new line costing $11,300,000; Milwaukee Road relocated and otherwise updated its adjacent line.) But as the Depression deepened, receivership claimed both Rock Island and Milwaukee as well as other Missouri roads. Capital expenditures suffered accordingly.

Compared to 1917 when the United States became involved in World War I, the nation's carriers in 1942 had 31 percent fewer locomotives, 24 percent fewer freight cars, 35 percent fewer passenger cars, and 27 percent fewer employees. (Newer freight cars had greater carrying capacity, however, and newer locomotives had greater tractive effort.)[3]

The pall of the Great Depression clung to railroad owners and managers. They hesitated even as the industry in 1940 rang up higher operating revenues than in any year since 1930—much of it war-related. Railroad leaders pondered and fussed, also recalling unpleasant consequences of the United States Railroad Administration during the Great War and after. Yet the events of 1914–18 had shown, in fact, that some sort of centralized planning was essential in times of war. With this in mind, President Roosevelt appointed a War Resources Board in September 1939 and a National Defense Advisory Commission shortly thereafter. For the latter group, he chose Burlington's talented and respected Ralph Budd to represent and oversee transportation.[4]

Change was afoot. Events of 1940—Lend-Lease, the first peacetime draft, calling up of reservists, and simultaneous orders for war material—resulted in a huge surge of business for the nation's railroads. Then came startling news from Pearl Harbor in Hawaii: "UNITED STATES AT WAR," screamed newspaper headlines following the Japanese attack on December 7, 1941. The day that President Franklin Roosevelt said would live in infamy brought immediate and dramatic change to the very fiber of the country.

Japanese incursions in the Pacific cut off the major supply of cultivated rubber, and German submarines viciously attacked and sank tankers carrying crude oil from the Gulf Coast to refineries on the eastern seaboard. Total war enveloped the United States. The federal government quickly imposed strict rationing of rubber tires across the domestic sector—husbanding rubber stock for planes, tanks, and other implements of war—and then extended rationing to gasoline. The nation finally threw off the awful trauma of the Great Depression, converting with amazing swiftness to a wartime footing. By September 1942, the American economy had achieved full employment—indeed, there was a labor shortage. The change was especially dramatic in Detroit and elsewhere in the motor vehicle industry. Manufacture of all civilian passenger cars and trucks ended in early 1942, with Ford, for example, rolling out its final automobile on February 20. Thereafter Ford churned out B-24 bombers, gliders, and Jeeps; General Motors produced 75-millimeter shells, Howitzers, and army trucks; Packard rolled out Rolls-Royce Merlin V-12 aircraft engines; Hudson supplied frames for B-26 bombers; and Chrysler delivered M3 Sherman tanks and ambulances. Missouri agriculture, mostly in the doldrums for the previous two decades, now would be waging a gigantic battle to increase food production. All of it reflected the national defense emergency—total mobilization.[5]

The Japanese attack on Pearl Harbor and the hysteria that followed had an immediate effect on the entire rail industry. Railroaders everywhere were sternly directed by the army not to disseminate information regarding the location of troop staging areas. Managers ordered that "no information be given out or the subject discussed at any time as to the handling of freight or anything else connected with the operation of the Army." The government further suggested that "suspicious persons" loitering about the "vicinity of telegraph offices be duly reported," that safeguards to property and equipment be undertaken, and that critical material be conserved.[6]

Demand for freight transportation grew exponentially. The success of German submarine activity along the eastern seaboard and Gulf Coast forced movement of crude oil and refined petroleum products to rail. This was reflected at Illinois Central, as an example, where oil shipments in 1942 made up 12 percent of that road's total freight volume. The same was reported at Gulf, Mobile & Ohio, but that company also noted that the submarine threat additionally had the negative impact of drying up shipments of bananas from Central and South America. Chicago & Alton noted a rise in freight tons handled of 12.6 million tons in 1942, up from 7.2 million tons in 1940—much of it war related, including ordinance as well as half-tracks, tanks, and Jeeps from on-line manufacturers. A heavy volume of traffic moved from east to west through St. Louis: fifty-six carloads of trucks moving in fifty-foot automobile cars from Fort Wayne, Indiana, to San Diego, California; sixty-three carloads of dump trucks built by Galion All Steel Body Company of Galion, Ohio, and destined for Port Hueneme, California; two thousand carloads of fabricated houses from points in Ohio to a California port; seventy-eight cars of cargo for the Soviet government billed from Terre Haute, Indiana, to the port of San Francisco; and two trainloads of Studebaker trucks, lend-lease material for the Soviets—all of these routed west from St. Louis via St Louis–San Francisco, Quanah, Acme & Pacific, and Atchison, Topeka & Santa Fe.[7]

Kansas City, of course, was another primary entrepot, and, given its marvelous single-line thoroughfare linking Chicago with Southern California and the Texas Gulf Coast, the Santa Fe was a major player. The company's sprawling Argentine Yard across the river in Kansas hummed with round-the-clock classification of thousands of cars per day—some moving on to Santa Fe destinations and others interchanged with other roads.[8]

Given government rationing of rubber tires and gasoline coupled with escalating demand for military movements, it was hardly a surprise that

FIGURE 3.2.
Countless implements of war traveled by train. Don L. Hofsommer Collection.

passenger numbers skyrocketed. Moving one army division required fifty-five Military Authorization Trains totaling twenty-two miles of cars. Faced with a depressing decline in passenger boardings during the previous two decades, carriers had trimmed their inventory of passenger equipment to match a much-slimmed-down offering of trains. Gone were services such as that provided earlier by Chicago Great Western's "shopper train" from the north that had arrived at St. Joseph around 10:00 a.m. and taken those same customers back home late in the afternoon after a day of purchasing their needs in the city. New to the Missouri scene, however, were sixteen "streamliners," including Santa Fe's *Chief* and Missouri Pacific's *Missouri River Eagle* among others. Nevertheless, in the end railroads retrieved obsolete equipment from scrap lines and painted and patched in a campaign to "make do."[9]

World War II sent predictable surges of adrenaline into the lifestream of the American economy. The nation's railroads reflected as much. The army opened Fort Leonard Wood, an eighty-five-thousand-acre training center along Frisco's main line near Newburg, Missouri, in 1941; the railroad responded quickly with a new train, the *General Wood*, providing "convenient daylight service for passengers destined to and from" the post (connecting bus from Newburg). Passenger business was vigorous as new inductees and National Guard troops flowed to Leonard Wood

Of War and Peace   91

FIGURE 3.3.
Endless military special trains popped up across the nation's rails. Here a seemingly underpowered Cotton Belt 4-6-0 lugs a long string of cars into Valley Junction, Illinois, across from St. Louis, in December 1942. Harold Volrath photograph, Don L. Hofsommer Collection.

and other installations around the country. Pennsylvania announced that in the first eight-and-a-half months of 1941, it moved 380,000 selective service men in special trains and in cars added to regular trains. Collectively, the carriers agreed to 1.25 cents per mile furlough fares for all military personnel.[10]

Volumes mushroomed. A total of 38,695 passenger trains rumbled over the three bridges to and from St. Louis Union Station during the fiscal year ending June 30, 1942. To handle these as well as other trains to and from the west required about forty switch crews daily at the increasingly busy passenger terminal. The response to war took many forms. The shiny aluminum-painted tops of Railway Express Agency trucks were covered in "war paint"—olive drab; full-length observation cars were shopped to emerge with sleeping accommodations; schedules for crack trains—such as Baltimore & Ohio's *National Limited* and New York Central's *Southwestern Limited*—were lengthened; and Americans were urged, as a patriotic gesture, to vacation at home. "When the war is over and we've put the ax to the Axis for good and all, we'll return to our former ways of get up and go," said the Office of Defense Transportation. Some service was expanded, however. Chicago & Eastern Illinois, late in 1942, joined with Frisco to establish a Chicago–Tulsa sleeping car route using C&EI's *Zipper* and Frisco's *Will Rogers* via St. Louis. And, of course, the 1942 World Series went on as scheduled—the Cardinals

Troubles on the Tracks

Of the several receivership proceedings involving Missouri railroads, none was more complicated and none drew more attention than the tedious and extremely acrimonious financial reorganization of Missouri Pacific.

In 1929, Oris Paxton Van Sweringen and James Van Sweringen along with others associated with the brothers formed the Alleghany Corporation, a holding company with large capital coming from bonds and nonvoting stock. A year later Alleghany gained control of Missouri Pacific, and shortly thereafter it had Missouri Pacific use its own funds to acquire $4 million of its own securities. But the Great Depression was abroad the land, and the market value of this new investment quickly shrunk to a mere $200,000—a dramatic loss of $3,800.000. On March 31, 1933, Missouri Pacific became the first major railroad to file for reorganization under the federal government's recently enacted Bankruptcy Act.*

Critics were numerous and vocal, charging, among other things, that Alleghany had "questionable motives," that it engaged in "mystery and concealment," that its accounts were "juggled," that it dealt in "fraud"—that it "followed a policy of intercompany dividends, loans, and advances whose effect was to strip subsidiaries of system for the benefit of higher units in the corporate pyramid." Indeed, the $3,800,000 loss was hardly the only sin of Alleghany.†

Missouri Pacific eventually turned to the Reconstruction Finance Corporation for a loan of $12 million—a loan that was granted but, as it developed, based on "false accounts and balance sheets . . . overstating the railroad's current assets and income account, and understating its liabilities." The federal government sought redress; the statute of limitations denied satisfaction.‡

The Missouri Pacific case bounced along on a thoroughly uneven path. Reorganization committees were formed; they fussed, fumed, and fizzled. The hard times of the 1930s consumed the Van Sweringen brothers, but the Alleghany Corporation survived and would continue to be a player on the American railroad landscape for many years. Missouri Pacific? It would emerge from the courts only in 1956.§

---

* Investigation of Railroads, Holding Companies and Affiliated Companies, United States Senate, 75th Congress, First Session (1939), 37–40.

† Ibid.

‡ Ibid.

§ *Poor's Railroad Volume 1938*, 1203–4; H. Craig Miner, *The Rebirth of the Missouri Pacific, 1956–1983* (College Station: Texas A&M University Press, 1983), 3–17.

---

against the Giants, with the Cardinals winning in five games and with New York Central supplying special trains to St. Louis and to New York for each team.[11]

As it developed, 1942 traffic was merely a warm-up for 1943. Formal policies such as tire and gasoline rationing reduced automobile

FIGURE 3.4.
Demands of war resulted in some passenger trains adding cars or in some instances having consists shortened. The *Wabash Cannonball* racing for St. Louis in 1945 is surprisingly abbreviated. Don L. Hofsommer Collection.

passenger miles, and unofficial advertising campaigns asked pointedly, "Is this trip necessary?" The result was diversion of passengers from highways to rail even as government demands increased. Rail passenger miles rose to about 32 percent of the total for 1943—53 million passenger miles, 13 percent over the previous record of 1920 and fully 80 percent over 1941. Early in 1943, American railroads moved two million troops monthly, requiring 15 percent of the industry's coaches and fully half of all sleepers. Pullman reported boarding one sleeping car with troops on the average of every two minutes and forty-eight seconds. All of it was reflected in frenetic activity at St. Louis Union Station, where in 1943, 1.3 million tickets were purchased.[12]

Demand was insatiable, but capacity was inelastic. A tight-fisted War Production Board routinely turned down carrier requests for new passenger cars as part of the war effort; the fleet would increase by only a paltry 1 percent during the traffic-flooded war years. Illinois Central, for example, had something over a thousand cars for passengers, mail, express, and baggage service, and, with no new equipment in sight, these were loaded to capacity (and often beyond) and patched hurriedly by weary carmen to maintain maximum availability. The government refrained from formal travel restrictions, but increasingly the government and the carriers urged Americans to stay home. Vacation and holiday travel was discouraged, and Joseph B. Eastman, director of the Office of Defense Transport, called on his countrymen to "hold the line against conventions, trade shows and other gatherings as a means of curtailing travel." Nevertheless, in 1944, railroads established a record

FIGURE 3.5.
Demand for the nation's passenger service increased as America pressed a two-front war. These young men are headed for embarkation and possibly to frontline positions. Don L. Hofsommer Collection.

of 95.5 billion passenger miles employing an aging fleet of equipment over a support structure that was painstakingly maintained under heavy traffic.[13]

Demand for the nation's rail passenger service increased as America pressed its two-front war. Now trains moved not only troops for embarkation but also troops on leave and, sad to say, casualties of battle moving to military hospitals or finally going home. Military transportation requirements would be greater in the next year than at any time since Pearl Harbor, said a spokesman in 1945. "Civilian travel in the Pacific Coast area will become nigh impossible at times during the coming months," he forecast in anticipation of Allied victory over Germany and subsequent massive redeployment of men and material to the Pacific thereafter. Railroads were obliged by government order to cancel all service to resort, recreational, or vacation areas; light-density trains across the country were discontinued; and in mid-1945, all sleeping car lines of fewer than 450 miles were suspended. Among other things, this resulted in terminating all overnight sleeper service along the Chicago–St. Louis corridor, which resulted in cars usually assigned to Alton, Chicago & Eastern Illinois, Illinois Central, and Wabash trains being

Of War and Peace 95

FIGURE 3.6.
Some wartime special trains consisted entirely of hospital cars. Don L. Hofsommer Collection.

freed for troop movement elsewhere. These orders dampened domestic demand a bit, but early in 1945, seventy to eighty thousand persons per day still passed through St. Louis Union Station.[14]

During the spring of 1943, when troop movements were especially heavy, the Armed Forces at times consumed as much as 50 percent of sleeping car equipment and 30 percent of coaches. A decision was then made to build twelve hundred troop sleepers and four hundred troop kitchen cars. Although lightweight and of very simple design, the military sleepers were well equipped. Each car provided thirty berths in tiers of three, and they were turned over to the Pullman Company for operation. A later order included another twelve hundred sleepers and four hundred kitchen cars.[15]

Troop trains added much to the hectic comings and goings at St. Louis Station. In 1944, the peak year, 71,744 trains, which carried more than twenty-four million passengers, used the facility. Many were filled with soldiers, sailors, marines, and fliers, who were commonly headed to area military bases or for assignments in the Atlantic and Pacific theaters. This was really a different war. While Armed Forces personnel averaged three moves by train from induction to embarkation during World War I,

96   Missouri Railroads

FIGURE 3.7. St. Louis Union Station opened to passengers in 1894, and its Romanesque design was modeled after the walled French city of Carcassonne. Schwantes-Greever-Nolan Collection.

they made eight in World War II. Later mingling with departing troops were returning ones, some of whom were on crutches, in wheelchairs, or confined to stretchers. Even German and Italian prisoners of war, well guarded and headed to regional internment camps, joined the war-generated throngs. "I can remember during the war that the midway was so crowded with people that when several trains were arriving or departing one had to 'inch' his way along," related a longtime Terminal Railway Association employee.[16]

Not all workers at the St. Louis Union Station received remuneration. Volunteers joined the labor force as well. Travelers' Aid commonly had both paid and unpaid personnel, but the size of its volunteer corps grew substantially during World War II. Scores of area women, for example, contributed to the St. Louis unit of the American Women's Voluntary Services, an affiliate of Travelers' Aid. These public-spirited individuals maintained the station's nursery, which catered to the infants of military parents. Many families relocated or traveled extensively when husbands entered the service, and these journeys often involved rail trips via St. Louis. The American Red Cross also had a volunteer contingent at the station. Although its Home Service Division, based at Red Cross headquarters on Olive Street, employed more than two hundred professional caseworkers, it recruited volunteers to help Travelers' Aid. Their duties mostly involved assisting military personnel and their dependents.[17]

Volunteers other than ones associated with Travelers' Aid and the Red Cross also came to Union Station during the war. The best known were

Of War and Peace   97

FIGURE 3.8.
The capacious waiting room of St. Louis Union Station accommodated World War II travelers. Don. L. Hofsommer Collection.

surely those affiliated with the United Service Organization (USO). This group, launched in 1941, relied heavily on unpaid personnel to staff its Service Men's Center on the second level west of the Grand Hall. The USO in St. Louis and nationally, too, provided leisure-time activities for military personnel. It supplied reading materials, comfortable chairs, and the like, and operated an adjoining canteen that made available food and soft drinks, always free of charge. (The latter functioned between September 1942 and April 1946.) In the case of its station operations, USO volunteers tapped the generosity of others. For instance, the St. Louis Terminal Boosters Club, a Missouri Pacific–sponsored organization, gladly contributed twenty-five dozen cookies in June 1943 to the "inexhaustible cookie jar" in the USO lounge.[18]

The Railway Express Agency likewise served as a major player in the war effort. Indeed, by late 1943 perhaps 65 percent of its volume was war-related—everything from aircraft engines to serums, antitoxins, and vaccines was expedited by Railway Express. Blood collected by the Red Cross was especially time sensitive. Inductees often sent their civilian clothes home by express, and the army's famous K-9 Corps similarly

Golden Anniversary

St. Louis Union Station celebrated its golden anniversary in subdued fashion on September 1, 1944. While some St. Louisans enjoyed an eighteen-footlong birthday cake placed in the Midway or watched a student presentation that depicted the station's history in tableau form, probably more heard a special radio program, "Gateway of the Nation: A Romantic Story of Railroading," which aired two days later. The copy in a newspaper announcement read, "Do you know . . . the exciting, real-life dramas that take place in St. Louis Union Station every day? Hear about them at 6:00 p.m. Sunday on KMOX." Surely many did over this popular fifty-thousand-watt clear-channel radio station.*

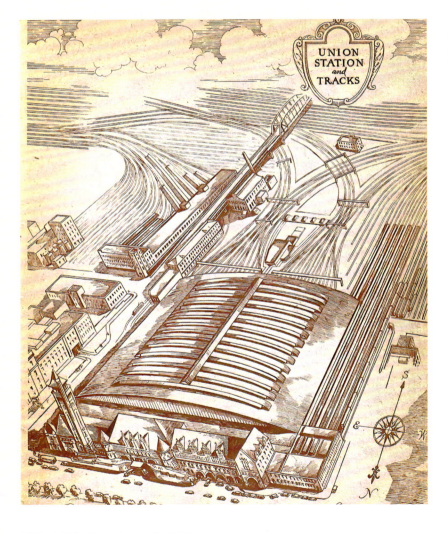

FIGURE 3.2.1. Providing an unusual perspective on the St. Louis Union Station and its maze of tracks is this aerial view. Schwantes-Greever-Nolan Collection.

* *St. Louis Globe-Democrat*, September 1, 1944.

FIGURE 3.9.
Railroad companies scrambled to improve efficiency during World War II. Don L. Hofsommer Collection.

moved aboard express cars. Baby chicks often were part of the mix. So were used tires, turned in by patriotic citizens and stacked along depot platforms awaiting movement. Railway Express also played an important role in bolstering morale on the home front by faithfully relaying movie films to the more than seventeen thousand theaters around the country, which thronged with upward of eighty-five million attendees weekly.[19]

Railroad companies scrambled to improve efficiency even as their lines shouldered a heavy load of traffic. For some, like the Santa Fe, an answer was to install centralized traffic control, which would include track circuit-controlled signals and power machines to operate passing track switches—all of it with the purpose of accelerating movement and cutting down on the need for telegraph operators at wayside stations. Another important avenue was replacement of elderly motive power. The

FIGURE 3.10.
The nation's rail carriers turned in an astonishing performance. It was their finest hour. Don L. Hofsommer Collection.

diesel locomotive revolution had begun earlier and would have accelerated rapidly but for the fact of War Production Board decisions limiting availability. As a consequence, several carriers—Missouri Pacific, New York Central, and Baltimore & Ohio among them—acquired modern steam locomotives instead. Yet there were exceptions. Burlington took delivery of forty-three diesel locomotives in 1943—sixteen fifty-four-hundred-horsepower freighters and twenty-one thousand-horsepower switchers—and the Rock Island, Milwaukee Road, and Santa Fe expressed pleasure in the performance of their four-unit FT locomotives from the Electro-Motive Division of General Motors.[20]

Suddenly, it seemed, America had gone from unemployment of approximately 25 percent of its nonagricultural work force to full employment. Workers furloughed during the Depression were called back to run trains or improve property, but many of them were subject to the draft. During the four years of war, nearly one-quarter of Illinois Central's total work force found themselves wearing new military uniforms. "Shortages of manpower and lack of materials prevented as much work being done as the heavy traffic would justify," complained Burlington in 1943. Rock Island, too, deferred "a certain amount of maintenance . . . on account of the manpower shortage and the difficulty of obtaining

Of War and Peace   101

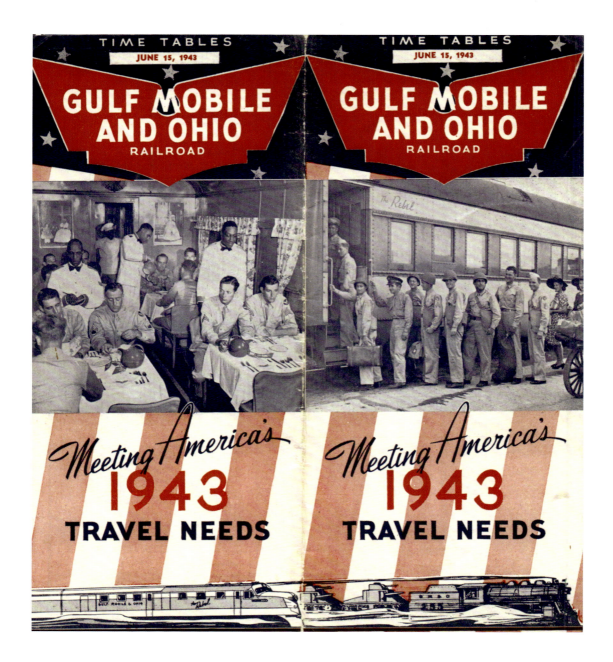

FIGURE 3.11. Military traffic was prominently featured on the cover of Gulf, Mobile & Ohio's public timetable in 1943. Schwantes-Greever-Nolan Collection.

materials." Older personnel postponed retirement, retirees went back to work, and women entered the workforce as never before. More than 350,000 railroaders were called into military service; more than 10,000 of them made the ultimate sacrifice.[21]

The nation's rail carriers turned in an astonishing performance; it was their finest hour. In 1943 they registered 725 billion revenue ton miles of freight, 14 percent over 1942, and 72 percent of all freight transportation in the United States. Passenger volume leaped from 452,921,000 riders in 1940 to 910,295,000 in 1944. All of it was reflected on the balance sheets of the various companies. At Chicago & Alton a deficit of $1.7

FIGURE 3.12.
Chicago, Burlington & Quincy boldly proclaimed that it was ready and prepared to serve in "Defense or Peace." Don L. Hofsommer Collection.

million in 1940 turned to a profit of $2.1 million in 1942. Revenue at Illinois Central in 1944 was nearly three times greater than that of the early 1930s and nearly half again as much as the average for the prosperous 1920s. Rock Island happily announced that operating revenues in 1942 had increased by $40,104,639 over 1941, while Milwaukee Road in 1943 recorded the largest gross revenue in the company's history; and the Burlington Route in 1944 provided more transportation than in any previous year—about 60 percent of it tied in some way to the war effort.[22]

Railroad companies wanted the public to know the job they were doing as part of the national war emergency; they wanted to create an understanding of the industry's wartime problems, hoped to sow goodwill for themselves during the war and thereafter, and pledged to a policy of patriotism as a matter of routine. These collective impulses were reflected in the advertising of the era. "Designed for peace, but a mighty instrument of war," intoned the Milwaukee Road. "Modern as Uncle Sam's battleships, Planned Progress has made Rock Island one of America's great railroad systems," exclaimed the Chicago, Rock Island & Pacific. "We're on active duty on an 11,000-mile front in thirteen states," enthused the Burlington, while the Association of American Railroads sternly admonished Americans not to "waste transportation." Santa Fe declared that its "Iron Horses" had been transformed into "War Horses"—"Hauling tens of thousands of troops and millions of tons of war material and foodstuff." "Daddy, don't you have a uniform?" plaintively inquired one young lad. "Yes, son, this is my uniform," replied his father, a Union Pacific trainman. "Railroads are the first line of defense."[23]

Nearly overwhelmed by demand for passenger service, the carriers found themselves in the curious position of saying, "Don't travel—unless your trip helps win the war." A program to "keep 'em rolling," said Burlington, meant that "nothing can be allowed to interfere with the swift, sure movement of troops and war supplies"—"even though it entails an occasional inconvenience to civilian traffic." Rock Island took a similar position. "Until victory is won, the requirements of our fighting forces must, of course, come first." Make travel plans early, counseled Rock Island, pick up reservations promptly, cancel reservations at once if travel plans change, travel at midweek if possible, and carry minimum baggage. In another ad, a male civilian wearing a finely tailored suit stood back, allowing a soldier to board a sleeping car. "After you soldier," said the businessman. Indeed, Pullman Company handled twenty-five thousand troops per night early in the war—a figure that escalated greatly in 1944 and 1945. That same escalation was mirrored in dining cars. Carriers urged patrons to eat only two meals a day on diners. "In ordinary times," explained Rock Island, "this situation would be immediately corrected by adding dining cars to regular trains when necessary," but that was not possible now because "many diners are needed for troop trains, and new ones cannot, of course, be constructed."[24]

Washington's Office of Defense Transportation warned that 1945 would be the toughest year of all. By March it was clear that Germany would soon fall, and the nation's railroads braced for an accelerated east-to-west movement of men and material as the war focused on Japan. But even as victory in Europe approached, the nation was stunned on April 12, 1945, when news came from Warm Springs, Georgia, that President Franklin D. Roosevelt had died there of a cerebral hemorrhage. That evening his body was put aboard a special train for the somber trip to the nation's capital and then on to Hyde Park, New York, for burial. The date, April 14, that of Abraham Lincoln's assassination in 1865, did not go unremarked. "Dr. New Deal" had become "Dr. Win the War," but on the eve of victory in Europe, he was gone, replaced as president by Harry S. Truman of Missouri. Germany did finally surrender several days later. News of victory in Europe was received gratefully by a subdued citizenry, who realized war in the Pacific would continue long and deadly. Business houses closed for the day; individual churches held services of thanksgiving. The mood was the same everywhere.[25]

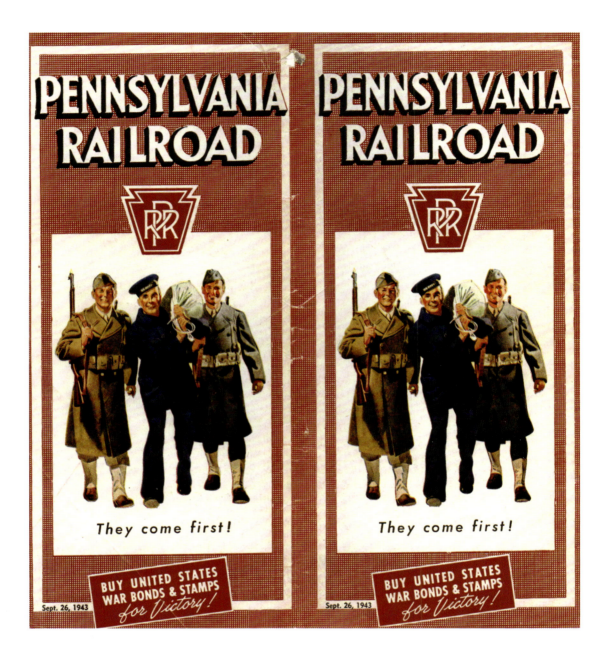

The grim business of war continued. There was no time to celebrate. Food, clothing, medical goods, and general subsistence materials still flowed eastward to supply the army of occupation in Europe, but the bulk of the nation's energies were now riveted to the Pacific theater. The War Department advised the railroads that about two-thirds of the force in Europe would return to this country for furloughs before heading to the Pacific. The plan would put even greater pressure on the carriers to move men and material to the West Coast for embarkation. Pentagon predictions of a travel crunch came true as Japan attracted the full military might of the United States following victory over Germany

FIGURE 3.13. Pennsylvania used the cover of a 1943 system timetable to salute members of America's armed forces. Given that the railroad's typical print run for its public schedules was in the millions, the patriotic image enjoyed widespread attention. Schwantes-Greever-Nolan Collection.

Of War and Peace   105

FIGURE 3.14. Sad to say, casualties of war moving to military hospitals or finally going home after discharge were part of the traffic mix. Don L. Hofsommer Collection.

FIGURE 3.15. WAVES, navy women: total mobilization meant that every person was bound to tight patriotic responsibility. The grim business of war continued; there was no time to celebrate even after Germany capitulated in May 1945. There remained three months of awful hostilities in the Pacific. Don L. Hofsommer Collection.

in May 1945. Units of all types were removed from Europe and readied at home for a final push in Asia.[26]

Then, with astonishing swiftness, it was over. Atomic bombs dropped on Hiroshima and Nagasaki were followed by Japan's surrender on August 14. "Shouting throngs" filled the streets of tiny villages and great cities.

Confusion followed euphoria. An average of ten thousand men per day had been swarming into West Coast embarkation ports for trans-shipment to the Pacific in preparation for an invasion of Japan. Now, however, trains all over the country were shunted onto sidings as officials sorted out what to do with men and materiel no longer necessary for war. Nobody had anticipated that the fight would end so quickly. Plans in the short term were ad hoc, but they gradually evolved into a generally orderly demobilization. Redeployment of units from Europe to Asia stopped, and cutbacks in military procurement were followed by cancellation of contracts. Retooling of the economy from a wartime footing commenced. But demobilization and converting the economy would prove a slow process against which could be heard anguished cries to "bring the boys home" and civilian demands to immediately end price, wage, and transportation controls.[27]

For railroads, the peak movement of passengers was yet to come. The military expected to reduce about five hundred thousand personnel per month by year's end. Given the movement of replacement troops headed for Europe and Asia plus the glut of returnees and the need to return prisoners of war, American railroads would face the need to carry 1.25 million military passengers per month for a least half a year. These involved dedicated military trains as well as individual men and women in the military moving from place to place on orders, on furloughs, or returning to their homes around the country upon separation from the services. And it said nothing of domestic needs. Rails everywhere were glutted, especially the primary routes.[28]

Holiday travel in late 1945 would be grim. In the West, giant Southern Pacific anticipated that 94 percent of its carrying capacity would be given over to the military in December, with civilians picking up the scant remaining seats. What explained this unprecedented demand? "The spirit of Christmas itself," said the *New York Times*. "The feeling that it [Christmas] is the day of days to be spent at home." This year, loosed from the bonds of war, the impulse was blind, overwhelming, and disorganized. Demand greatly exceeded capacity. Military authorities made every effort to discharge personnel before Christmas. That had the predictable impact of producing the heaviest concentration of government travel for the entire war period. Railroads staggered uncontrollably under the strain of combined military and pent-up civilian demand during the Christmas holidays of 1945. Eastern roads—the Baltimore &

Ohio, New York Central, and Pennsylvania—rushed a thousand empty coaches through St. Louis to aid congested western carriers, and Union Station was jammed on December 22 and again the next day when trains "crammed to the aisles" left additional throngs of disappointed passengers to await later departures. One gate attendant likened the scene to "holding a flood back." Complaints were predictable, mixed as they were with disappointment among those who could not purchase tickets at all and those who were delayed or missed connections. Nevertheless, concluded the *New York Times*, "this year there is some approximation of peace on earth even on a railroad siding."[29]

When railroad accountants finally got around to closing the books on 1945, they discovered that carriers had turned in about ninety-one billion passenger miles. For that matter, during the war years rail carriers had moved 90 percent of the military freight and 98 percent of all organized group travel of servicemen within the continental United States.[30]

"Nineteen forty-five was a year of war, of victory and of transition to the tasks of peace. Throughout all those memorable twelve months the Illinois Central Railroad rendered our nation and our allies vitally important service of which every member of our organization can well be proud," reported the company's president. The editor of the *Baltimore & Ohio Magazine* was more expansive in his assessment of the final victory. "In this story," he argued, "no small portion of glory will be assigned to the railroads. . . . It would be difficult indeed to find a single agency that contributed more to the success of allied arms."[31]

*   *   *

The railroad industry, like the country itself, had been on a roller-coaster ride for a decade and a half. The carriers had experienced the darkest days of their existence during the Great Depression and their finest hour during World War II. Owners and managers could but wonder what the future might bring. Some worried that the country would slip back into depression; others forecast a rosy future based on the nation's vibrant performance during the war. There was reason for sober reflection and analysis. The years 1939–45 brought spectacular increases in railway revenues, but net operating income for the industry before interest and taxes in 1945 was approximately 23 percent less than in 1944. And at the end of 1945, the nation's carriers were hauling freight at general rates no higher than in 1941 despite wage increases of 28 percent over the same period. A writer for *Railway Age* pointed out that "railroad prosperity depends on national prosperity and a high rate of productivity." While concerned by uncertainty "due to transition from war to peace," by the possibility of "labor disputes and by prevailing and threatened government policy," *Railway Age* was essentially upbeat nevertheless "because of the increase in population, and of the enormous accumulation of unsatisfied needs during the depression and the war." To be sure, the nation had "the most extreme shortage of housing in history—shortages of houses, of apartments, of hotels—due to lack of building for a decade and a half, millions are without homes and many thousands can hardly find lodging on necessary business trips." Moreover, "there are shortages of everything—shirts, washing machines, candy, paper, printing capacity, furniture, whatever you desire, whether for personal or business purposes." Against this "there are huge amounts of purchasing power accumulated during the war in the hands of both the consuming public and of business." In the end, the industry's leading trade publication considered that economic conditions were favorable for a "prolonged period of high-level construction, production, transportation, employment and prosperity."[32]

The conversion from a war economy was surprisingly quick and featured little unemployment. The primary reason for the painless transition was the dramatic surge in consumer demands, especially for durable goods, and residential construction, especially in the suburbs. Financing for this package came from savings and war bonds, as well as accumulated profits in industry now available for expansion. Federal monies for the G. I. Bill of 1944 and the Housing Acts of 1946 and 1949 likewise added fuel. The railroad industry reflected the broader national experience.[33]

What did the postwar future hold? The year 1946 was not reassuring. When President Harry Truman lifted price and wage controls, inflation soared. Coal miners put a crimp in the domestic economy by striking, as did rail labor. Truman responded by taking over the railroads in the name of the government. Train and engine crews walked off the job anyway on May 24 in a strike that lasted three days. Settlements on wage issues followed, but the strike of 1946 sent a signal that relations between labor and management in the rail industry would be tense during the postwar years. Moreover, nasty strikes in the meatpacking industry and again in the coal fields further troubled the domestic economy and roiled the political landscape.[34]

Fortunately, however, there were contraindicators. Housing starts nationwide in 1949 were 1,349,000, up sharply from 139,000 during the war year 1944. The result was heavy demand for construction material of all kinds. Lumber, mostly from the Pacific Northwest, and much of it in "roller cars looking for a home" (i.e., shipped from mills before sold) and "billed in transit," flowed to Missouri in an unremitting stream. Movement of grain continued at record levels after V-J Day, stimulated in part by programs designed to feed war-ravaged Europe. That, of course, was especially critical to Missouri and its railroads.[35]

In the public eye, the World War II experience reinforced the long-standing view that railroads represented the nation's transportation backbone. Automobiles, trucks, and airplanes certainly would compete with railroads in the postwar era, but railroads would, as before, provide America's basic method of overland transport.

FIGURE 3.16. Railroad prosperity depended on national prosperity as exemplified by activity on the Cotton Belt. Don L. Hofsommer Collection.

Of War and Peace   111

The nation's highway system at the end of the war in 1945 was much as it had been five years earlier, but the Federal Aid Act of 1944 established a national system of interstate highways, demanded that states select routes connecting principal metropolitan areas, and authorized $500 million annually for the first postwar years. And with peace the War Production Board lifted its ban on the manufacture of civilian motor vehicles. Americans predictably and enthusiastically renewed their love affair with motor vehicles. Every GI came home dreaming of a civilian job, a home, a family—and an automobile. The motoring public clamored for Ford's "All New Mercury," General Motor's Buick with "Dynaflow Drive," or the "New 1946 Nash." With tires and fuel now readily available and benefited by the new and better system of roadways, emboldened truckers bought more and larger rigs and took up a vigorous campaign to lengthen hauls with heavier payloads. The age of the true long-distance semi-tractor-trailer was dawning. At the same time, air traffic began to increase. Before the war, flying had been strictly for the few, the rich, and the somewhat daring. The war, however, transformed the technology of aircraft design and production. With lessons thus learned, builders such as Douglas and Lockheed unveiled planes like the DC-7 and the Super Constellation, which were more commodious, more reliable, and cheaper to operate per seat mile. Air travel began to lose its rakish image.[36]

The hard times of the 1930s left much of the railroad industry in financial tatters. Many companies sought the protection of the bankruptcy courts. Recovery took a jagged path. Perhaps Chicago & Alton offered the most complex story. In receivership during the Great Depression and controlled by Baltimore & Ohio, the Chicago & Alton was reorganized in 1947 and then acquired by Gulf, Mobile & Ohio. Among other roads serving Missouri, Chicago Great Western emerged from the courts in 1941; Wabash in 1943; Chicago, Milwaukee, St. Paul & Pacific and Illinois Terminal in 1945; and Chicago, Rock Island & Pacific in 1947. Missouri Pacific's reorganization efforts seemed more complex; success would come later.[37]

Impressive capital expenditures followed more generous cash flows. The new President Harry S. Truman Bridge at Kansas City, jointly owned and operated by Milwaukee Road and Rock Island, was dedicated on May 23, 1945, and in 1946 and 1947 the Burlington acquired ownership of the bridge over the Mississippi River between Alton, Illinois, and West Alton, Missouri; in the following year, it expanded Murray Yard at Kansas City; and in 1949 it established radio communication between switch engines and yard offices at Kansas City. Several roads embraced or expanded the use of centralized traffic control (CTC). Missouri–Kansas–Texas deferred decisions on CTC, investing heavily instead on block signals, but before the decade was out the Chicago &

FIGURE 3.17. Burlington, Rock Island, and Santa Fe were among the Missouri railroads that invested heavily in centralized traffic control. Don L. Hofsommer Collection.

Alton boasted 85 miles of CTC, Rock Island had 737 miles systemwide, and Santa Fe had 520 miles in operation with expansive plans beyond. Rock Island devoted huge resources to improvement of its Golden State Route, with line changes in Iowa and Missouri (between Mercer and Mill Grove) and massive bridging in Kansas. Chicago Great Western did not opt for CTC (its traffic density was too light), but management did allocate monies for upgraded track structure. No longer would the Chicago Great Western be called "Cinders, Grass & Weeds" or "Can't Get Worse."[38]

All "steam railroads" serving Missouri were, to one degree or another, devoted to conversion of operation to diesel-electric motive power. Strikes in the coal fields that produced shortages and then escalating coal prices hastened the process. Diesel locomotives had been around, of course, since the 1920s—mostly transfer engines and switchers—but during the next decade they made a splash as motive power for shiny streamliners such as Burlington's *Pioneer Zephyr* and General Motors' muscular FT locomotives designed for heavy freight duty. Steam builder American Locomotive Company joined with General Electric and Baldwin paired with Westinghouse to bring out their own lines of diesel locomotives. The Santa Fe put one of its broad-shouldered 2-10-4s to the test on Cardy Hill near Marceline, Missouri, and those tests showed the giant steamer to be a worthy addition to Santa Fe's motive power arsenal—but with all factors considered, the Texas-type steamer could not compare favorably with the new four-unit FT diesels. The long era of steam was doomed. Chicago Great Western, as an example, claimed at the end of 1949 that 100 percent of its passenger trains and 99 percent of its freight were headed by diesels. Other railroads did not lag behind in the conversion to diesel power.[39]

Even at this late date, there was a bit of intrigue on Missouri's strategic railroad landscape. Santa Fe had a historic interest in reaching the St. Louis gateway, had tried to get there during the late nineteenth century, and had failed, but its desire to connect tracks of its own to Missouri's largest metropolis did not disappear. During the immediate postwar years when Chicago & Alton went into play, as Baltimore & Ohio walked away from that property, and as it would be picked up by Gulf, Mobile & Ohio, two additional railroads, Burlington and Santa Fe, hatched a plan by which Burlington would acquire the Alton line across Missouri to Kansas City and use it to its own advantage but also allow Santa Fe operating rights. Other carriers—Missouri Pacific, Rock Island, Frisco, and Cotton Belt—objected, and the Interstate Commerce Commission nixed the idea. That hardly ended Santa Fe's desire to expand into St. Louis.[40]

Railroaders were, with very good reason, proud of their industry's wartime accomplishments. Despite that pride, managers remained nervous about the future, especially about their passenger business. The past offered curiously mixed signals. Railroads had witnessed tremendous shrinkage in passenger volume during the two decades between the wars, but the glut of business in 1940–45 restored passenger service to profitability. That glut, however, had been involuntary. Would passengers continue to ride passenger trains when alternative means of transportation were again available? Members of the influential American Association of Railroad Superintendents took a dry-eyed look at the future. There was no turning back the power of the automobile, they decided: "It is a personal transportation that none of the other agencies can match." Moreover, said the superintendents, "regardless of cost or other disadvantages, the motor car is enjoyed by many for the sheer pleasure of driving." On the other hand, they concluded that the intercity motor bus had little appeal apart from the low-cost transportation it provided. Air travel, however, remained an active question. In the past, passenger transportation by air had been more of a curiosity than a serious commercial threat. Significant advances in aeronautical engineering, the result of World War II, changed that calculus. Now the Air Transport

Association of America estimated that 1,200 planes with 40,000 seats would take to the skies by the end of 1947 and offer a clear threat to long-distance rail service. Consequently, while railroad operating managers anticipated potential profit in high-volume, low-fare coach travel, they were less optimistic about the parlor car and sleeper business. In any event, superintendents concluded, potential success depended on the carriers' clear devotion to several considerations: dependability, high speed, safety, comfort, cleanliness, courtesy, and competitive rates.[41]

Many of these variables hinged on equipment. Before being extinguished by exigencies of war, the movement to stainless-steel streamliners had resulted in 108 such trains in service. That trend continued, as did dieselization, after the war when railroad executives committed to a determined run at passenger business. Costs promised to be enormous in rolling stock alone. More than half of the industry's 28,403 units of passenger-carrying equipment were more than twenty-five years old and mostly exhausted due to the press of age and heavy use during the war. Replacement would be necessarily slow as basic American industry retooled to meet domestic demand and as that demand mushroomed. Early in 1946, American railroads had on order 1,657 passenger cars (743 coaches and 676 parlor, club, lounge, and sleeper) and 194 head-end cars (baggage, mail, and express).[42]

National trends, as always, were mirrored across Missouri. Extensive changes marked the traditional advent of daylight saving on April 28, 1946. Traditional service, like Pennsylvania's from St. Louis to vacation spots in northern Michigan, was restored, as were higher-speed schedules such as for the New York Central's *Southwestern Limited* and the *Knickerbocker*. New equipment was ordered (257 cars by Pennsylvania alone) as well as entire new trains—Wabash's *City of Kansas City* and Missouri Pacific's *Texas Eagle*, for example. The improvement process accelerated. Illinois Central bought additional equipment and refurbished old cars for its new *City of New Orleans*, Frisco announced diesel power and streamlined cars for the *Meteor* and joined with Katy to advertise similar plans for their joint *Texas Special*, and Pennsylvania in 1949 unveiled its all-Pullman *Spirit of St. Louis*. Burlington continued to expand its fleet of *Zephyrs*, three of which—*Mark Twain*, *General Pershing*, and *Zephyr-Rocket*—already served Missouri. Even the nearby electrified Illinois Terminal, which tapped the St. Louis market, joined the parade of railroads that unveiled new postwar streamlined trains. Several roads teamed up to offer the convenience of through sleeping cars between East Coast cities and destinations in Texas and Oklahoma without the need to change trains in St. Louis. Baltimore & Ohio combined with Frisco and Katy in one pattern and with Missouri Pacific in another; New York Central joined Missouri Pacific as well as with Frisco and

Katy. Missouri Pacific also allied with Pennsylvania to run the flagship *Sunshine Special* cooperatively—at least for a while—as a complete train between New York and Texas through St. Louis. The two railroads additionally implemented a joint car-washing operation at St. Louis.[43]

Terminal Railroad Association participated in the industry's overall postwar modernization program. Business was so great during the war and for several months thereafter that steam locomotives drew switching chores at St. Louis Union Station. But the Terminal Railroad continued to add diesels—up to a total of forty-eight in 1945 and seventy-two five years later—with steam power declining accordingly. Meanwhile, municipal authorities and others proposed construction of two elevated runways and a downtown air terminal adjacent to Union Station. In fact, however, this was a comprehensive plan for several modes of transport—air, rail, and bus, all of which, supporters noted, would be connected to nearby parking lots, truck and rail terminals, and warehouses for perishable commodities. Nothing came of the bold plan.[44]

Advocates of the downtown air terminal warned that it was time for St. Louis to decide if it was going to be a "whistle stop on transcontinental and international air routes or a major United States air terminal." Lambert Field was totally inadequate, they charged. Public demand for air service had clearly increased. American, by late 1947, sold tickets at the fashionable Jefferson Hotel for its Chicago–St. Louis–Mexico City run; Chicago & Southern's ticket office was at the equally fashionable Statler, where passage could be booked for Memphis, Little Rock, or Houston; Eastern boasted service to sunny Florida; Mid-Continent provided Douglas DC-3 airliners to Des Moines and Minneapolis; and Trans-World included a St. Louis stop on its transcontinental route between New York and Los Angeles and San Francisco. As it developed, Lambert Field was expanded—reflecting a routine of publicly funded support for aviation around the country. Railroaders' worst fears were realized during the late 1940s and 1950s. During the height of its operation in the 1920s, Pullman had served one hundred thousand guests nightly, and the company was referred to as "the World's Greatest Hotel." But in 1947, even as Pullman's transportation dominance eroded, the federal government concluded antitrust action against Pullman by which car-building was separated from ownership and operation. Participating railroads acquired the cars and leased them back to Pullman for operation. In 1950, Pullman and domestic airlines each carried thirteen million passengers.[45]

As the nation's second-largest railroad terminal, St. Louis was bound to be a barometer for national traffic trends. Train travel at Union Station declined by a whopping 30 percent during the three months following September 1, 1946. Four of sixteen ticket windows were shuttered, and 70 of 170 ticket clerks were released. At Tower One (Perry), only

262 of 304 levers were necessary to operate the station's track maze. Nationwide, passenger business was down in 1946 by nearly one-third compared to 1945; but it was still more than a third higher than during the former peacetime peak of 1920. This curious pattern was mirrored on the one hand by Missouri Pacific, which routinely ran three sections of its fine *Sunshine Special*, and on the other by Rock Island, Chicago & Eastern Illinois, Cotton Belt, Nickel Plate, and Southern, each of which was down to one daily train each way at Union Station. For that matter, both the Chicago & Eastern Illinois and Southern would exit the St. Louis passenger trade in the late 1940s, and Rock Island would join them early in 1950. In contrast, Gulf, Mobile & Ohio (successor to Mobile & Ohio) returned to Union Station in 1945 and two years later, following its acquisition of Alton (formerly Chicago & Alton), became one of the busiest proprietors of Union Station with twenty-two daily trains. At the close of the 1940s, Union Station hosted 143 trains, with Missouri Pacific; Gulf, Mobile & Ohio; Wabash; and Pennsylvania being the most active participants.[46]

The circumstance across the state to the west was very much the same, where Kansas City Union Station remained a vibrant place even though the number of train travelers had declined from wartime peaks. Late in 1947 Santa Fe advertised twenty-two major passenger trains daily

FIGURE 3.18. Steam and diesel locomotives often appeared together on the railroad landscape of St. Louis and Missouri during the late 1940s and early 1950s. Nickel Plate and Cotton Belt had both reduced service to one train each day in and out of St. Louis Union Station, as seen here in March 1947. The superiority of diesel over steam was indisputable. Carrier after carrier rushed to complete its conversion. Harold K. Vollrath photograph, Don L. Hofsommer Collection.

Of War and Peace 117

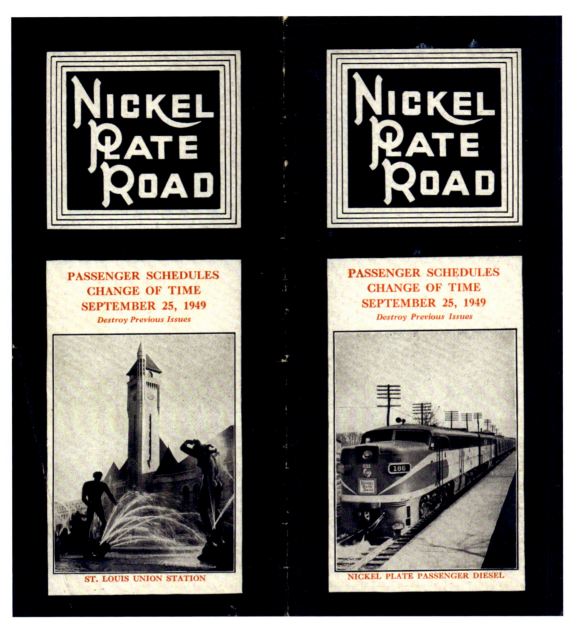

FIGURE 3.19. Nickel Plate's 1949 timetable cover featured St. Louis Union Station. The New York, Chicago & St. Louis Railroad, or "Nickel Plate Road," was a minor player among the two dozen railroads that utilized St. Louis Union Station. It was essentially a Midwestern carrier that linked the Missouri metropolis with Cleveland and Buffalo as well as cities and villages along the way. Schwantes-Greever-Nolan Collection.

to or through Kansas City with service to or from Chicago, Southern California, Tulsa, and Galveston, plus "motor trains" running between Fort Madison, Iowa, and Kansas City and Chanute, Kansas. Missouri Pacific was not far behind with six daily runs in St. Louis–Kansas City service plus trains to or from Omaha, Lincoln, Wichita, Joplin, Fort

FIGURE 3.20.
In 1950, Pullman and domestic airlines each carried thirteen million passengers. Baltimore & Ohio's elegant *National Limited* featured several sleepers, many in interline service to and from points southwest of St. Louis. Here it is leaving St. Louis Union Station. Don L. Hofsommer Collection.

Smith, and Little Rock. The Burlington placed three passenger trains on its St. Louis–Kansas City and Kansas City–Omaha/Lincoln lines, with other offerings to Denver. Wabash also shared the St. Louis–Kansas City corridor with a trio of runs, and Rock Island, too, offered a single entry in that crowded chute. The Rock Island also featured trains to Colorado Springs and Texas points (Dallas, Fort Worth, and Houston), not to mention candidates on its busy Minneapolis/St. Paul–Des Moines–Kansas City route and, of course, its Golden State Route from Chicago southwestward. Chicago Great Western challenged on the vertical axis from Minnesota, and the Milwaukee Road also participated in the Chicago–Kansas City competition. Union Pacific dominated passenger connections to Denver and Cheyenne, Kansas City Southern enjoyed a lock on travel to New Orleans and Port Arthur, and while St. Louis–San Francisco jousted with Santa Fe for Tulsa boardings, Katy tilted with

Of War and Peace   119

FIGURE 3.21.
"First with Newest," Gulf, Mobile & Ohio became one of the busiest proprietors of St. Louis Union Station. Schwantes-Greever-Nolan Collection.

Rock Island for Houston patronage. Missouri–Kansas–Texas trains had the advantage to San Antonio, and St. Louis–San Francisco to Memphis and Birmingham.[47]

Every carrier featured a named train—some more noteworthy than others, but all of them impressive. Among the famous trains using Kansas City Union Station were Santa Fe's *Chief*, Burlington's *General Pershing Zephyr*, Chicago Great Western's *Mill Cities Limited*, Milwaukee Road's *Southwest Limited*, Rock Island's *Twin Star Rocket*, Kansas City Southern's *Southern Belle*, Katy's *Bluebonnet*, Missouri Pacific's *Colorado Eagle*, Frisco's *Kansas City–Florida Special*, Union Pacific's *Pony Express*, and Wabash's *City of Kansas City*.[48]

Increasingly threatened by other modes of transportation, railroad companies serving Missouri looked for innovative ways to retain at least the long-distance passenger trade. General Motors joined the fray with its sleek and graceful *Train of Tomorrow*—diesel powered with streamlined Astra Dome cars, air-conditioned throughout, and equipped for radio reception and telephonic opportunities. "Better trains follow better locomotives," General Motors boasted as it pointed with obvious and understandable pride to its own two-thousand-horsepower unit heading the train on a nationwide tour. Burlington on its own had developed a "panoramic coach," the first of the famous Vista-Dome cars. Another way to impress passengers was simply to offer more convenient service. To that end eastern roads (the Pennsylvania, New York Central, and

Baltimore & Ohio) teamed with western partners (Missouri Pacific, Katy, and Frisco) to establish through coach and sleeping car assignments so that customers did need to change trains in St. Louis. "Through Service With No Change of Trains En Route on the Sunshine Special Between Texas and New York," shouted an enthusiastic Missouri Pacific. New York Central joined with Frisco on through operation to Oklahoma City, Baltimore & Ohio worked with Frisco and Katy for Washington–San Antonio, and Pennsylvania linked with Frisco for New York–Tulsa. And competitors Katy and Frisco for many years collectively sponsored their jointly operated and wonderfully appointed *Texas Special*—an arrangement that pleased owners and patrons alike. And, as if to remind on the matter of convenience, Missouri Pacific noted that there were "no stairs to climb" at St. Louis Union Station and "new escalators for the convenience of travelers in Kansas City's Union Station."[49]

Surely the most recognizable rail passenger in 1948 was Missouri's own Harry S. Truman, who as president of the United States and as the Democratic nominee for the election that year found that a "whistle stop" campaign over thirty-one thousand miles of rail was the sure path

FIGURE 3.22.
Frisco's *Meteor* was one of the numerous named trains that served Missourians and linked their state to distant destinations. Schwantes-Greever-Nolan Collection.

Of War and Peace

FIGURE 3.23.
Surely the most recognizable rail passenger in 1948 was Missouri's own Harry S. Truman, president of the United States. Don L. Hofsommer Collection.

back to the White House. As vice-presidential candidate with Franklin D. Roosevelt in 1944, Truman had volunteered to fly from place to place in the campaign. Roosevelt, however, responded by saying, "Don't fly; ride the train." Truman was happy to do so—then and often in the future. Baltimore & Ohio and Missouri Pacific took President Truman and former British prime minister Winston Churchill to Missouri in March 1946, where Churchill delivered his famous "Iron Curtain" speech at Westminster College in Fulton. In 1948 Truman crisscrossed the nation from Boston to Los Angeles and Seattle to San Antonio and Baltimore. In mid-September Rock Island delivered him to Dexter, Iowa, where he delivered one of his legendary "give 'em hell" speeches to a crowd of just under one hundred thousand at the National Plowing Match. Rock Island then took Truman to Kansas City, where it handed the campaign train to one of Union Pacific's handsome steam engines for a romp west to Denver. Truman spent election day at Independence and voted in his home precinct.

Prognosticators had given Truman little chance of victory over Republican Thomas E. Dewey, but when Missouri Pacific's polished diesels roared eastward from Independence on the morning of November 4, a smiling, victorious Truman lounged in the resplendent Ferdinand Magellan bringing up the rear. When the train backed into St. Louis Union Station, awaiting crowds surged to greet the newly elected president, who delighted his admirers by holding aloft the previous day's early edition of *Chicago Tribune* with banner headline reading, "DEWEY DEFEATS TRUMAN."[50]

Passenger operation was the glamorous part of the industry, but brawny freight brought the most gross revenue. Among Baltimore & Ohio's fleet of premier freight trains was St. Louis 97, charged with whisking priority lading from the eastern seaboard to the St. Louis gateway. Nickel Plate earned customer satisfaction by providing reliable high-speed service in a region of the country thick with alternative rail routings. (Nickel Plate derived three-quarters of its business from connecting lines.) Rock Island urged shippers to "Ship via Rocket Freight" and proclaimed itself as "America's Most Modern Freight Service." Frisco established a *T-C Train* (transcontinental) or *California Flash*. Missouri Pacific hustled fresh fruits and vegetables, cattle, and baled cotton out of the Rio Grande Valley and Gulf Coast region of Texas. Atchison, Topeka & Santa Fe hosted a steady stream of *GFX* (green fruit) trains eastward out of California. In addition, Santa Fe carded what it labeled the "Spud Special," bearing refrigerated cars loaded with 160 hundred-pound bags of potatoes billed typically from the Bakersfield area and destined for eastern markets. Santa Fe likewise was a major player in the movement of wheat from trackside elevators in Kansas and beyond. To accommodate this freight and all other commodities, Santa Fe added to its sprawling Argentine Yard in Kansas City, Kansas.[51]

During the immediate postwar period, labor relations were, in a word, contentious. The Fireman's National Diesel Agreement, signed by the carriers and the Brotherhood of Locomotive Fireman and Engineers in 1937, stipulated that a fireman should be employed on diesel locomotives pulling main-line or streamline trains and on all such locomotives having ninety thousand pounds of weight or more on the drivers. But as more diesel locomotives went into service, the Brotherhood of Locomotive Engineers insisted that an "assistant engineer" was needed on such locomotives; the Brotherhood of Locomotive Fireman and Engineers then demanded a second fireman. Both groups wanted the weight-on-drivers classification used to set graduated rates of pay for crews on steam locomotives extended to include diesels. In 1943, a presidential board approved the weight-on-driver request and urged that two men at all times should be in the cab of multiple-unit diesels in high-speed passenger service. Both brotherhoods agreed, but the matter flared up again in 1948. Negotiations followed, and in the end the principle was established that a fireman, only one, was needed on multiple-unit locomotives in ordinary road service. That was hardly

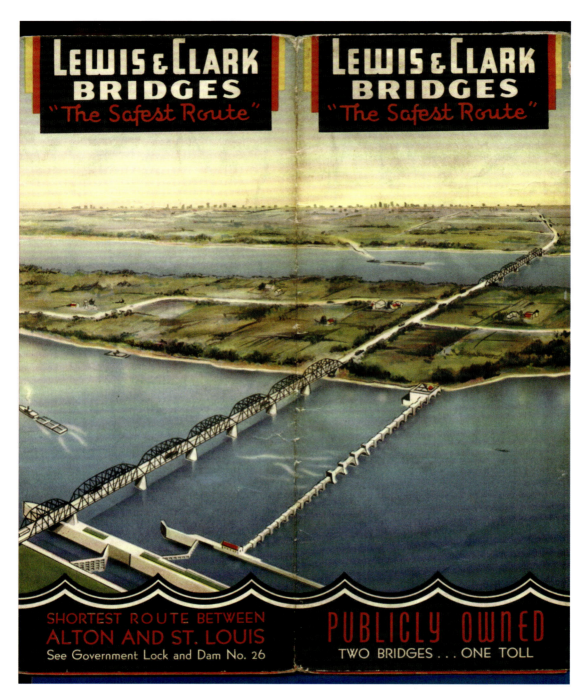

FIGURE 3.24. Advertising for the Lewis and Clark Bridge seemed to mimic the commercial art that had long been featured in rail travel publications, but unlike Missouri's investor-owned railroads, many of them struggling to make ends meet, the bridge across the Mississippi River was a publicly owned enterprise. Schwantes-Greever-Nolan Collection.

Impact of War: American Railroads

	1940	1944
Revenue ton miles (thousands)	333,767,510	738,642,302
Revenue passenger miles (thousands)	23,135,375	92,683,414
Gross earnings (thousands)	$4,083,596	$9,236,567
Net operating income (thousands)	$618,100	$1,283,527
Locomotives in use	30,104	37,439
Freight cars in use	1,515,870	1,976,210

the last of the matter. Labor's greatest overall interest, however, was in gaining wage increases beyond those obtained during the hectic war years. Brotherhoods demanded better pay coupled with changes in work rules. The carriers resisted, and strikes followed. President Truman appointed emergency boards, brotherhoods resisted, emergency boards were convened, and each side glared at the other. Nevertheless, before the 1940s ended, brotherhoods had gained much in terms of wages, benefits, and work rules that left railroad companies saddled with huge increases in the cost of labor as well as onerous work rules that quickly proved a heavy liability against modal competition that grew increasingly robust. In the highly competitive world of transportation, railroad managers would have to find some way of squaring labor output with labor costs if their companies were to survive.[52]

The brand-new Wabash Streamliner, "City of Kansas City," offers you luxurious service between St. Louis and Kansas City. This up-to-the-moment Wabash train is the first Streamliner to operate wholly within the boundaries of the great State of Missouri.

—*The Locomotive on This Train Is a Diesel*, a brochure issued circa 1950s by the Electro-Motive Division of General Motors

4

A Fluid State

Given its central geographic location and bracketed as it was by gateway cities on its eastern and western flanks, it was hardly a surprise that Missouri in the 1950s would host some of the nation's finest passenger trains. To St. Louis each day flowed a steady stream from New York City—dispatched by Baltimore & Ohio, New York Central, and Pennsylvania. Others arrived from Cleveland (Nickel Plate), Louisville (Southern), Nashville (Louisville & Nashville), and Dallas (St. Louis Southwestern). Down the crowded Chicago–St. Louis corridor came trains from Gulf, Mobile & Chicago, Illinois Central, and Wabash. Chicago, Burlington & Quincy put forward its offerings from Burlington and Savannah; Missouri–Kansas–Texas from San Antonio; Gulf, Mobile & Ohio sent entries from Mobile and Jackson; Illinois Central offered connections from Carbondale and cities in the Deep South; Missouri Pacific featured a selection from Omaha, Pueblo, Laredo, and Wichita; and St. Louis–San Francisco brought passengers from Memphis and Oklahoma City. Illinois Terminal added flavor with its frequent interurban service from East Peoria and Springfield. And back they went, these many trains, back to their respective origins or to their several connections.[1]

Across the state at Kansas City, much the same pattern of train arrivals and departures prevailed. Santa Fe, Milwaukee Road, Burlington, and Rock Island, all competed for passengers along the vital Chicago–Kansas City corridor. Customers in the St. Louis–Kansas City chute likewise had multiple choices—Missouri Pacific and Wabash. The same was true between Kansas City and Tulsa (Santa Fe and Frisco), Minneapolis and Kansas City (Chicago Great Western and Rock Island), Kansas City and Houston (Katy and Rock Island), and Kansas City and Omaha (Burlington and Missouri Pacific). In addition, Frisco sent trains to Birmingham, Joplin, and Springfield (via Clinton); Rock Island to Denver, Fort Worth, and Los Angeles (with Southern Pacific); Missouri

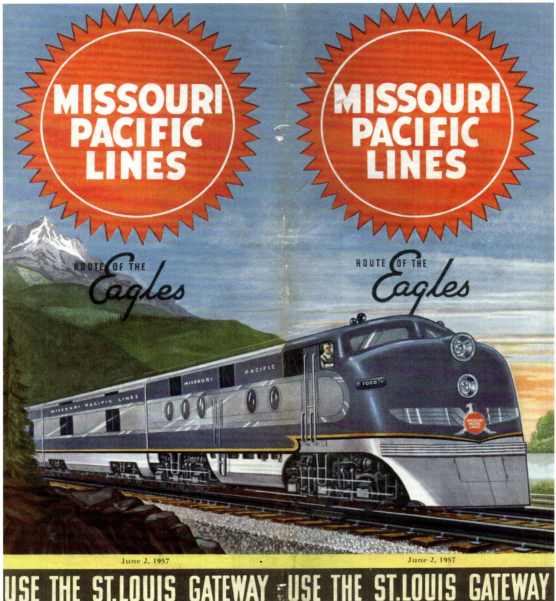

FIGURE 4.1.
Missouri Pacific 1957 timetable cover. Missouri Pacific was proud of its post–World War II fleet of streamlined trains, their colorful exteriors made possible by the replacement of steam with cleaner-burning diesel motive power. Schwantes-Greever-Nolan Collection.

Pacific to Joplin and Little Rock; Kansas City Southern to Shreveport and New Orleans; and Union Pacific to Salina, Denver, Cheyenne, and beyond. Not to be forgotten were the many trains carded by Santa Fe to Southern California and the Texas Gulf Coast. The vast majority of these numerous offerings were named trains that sought long-haul customers, but there were others providing unceremonious local service—Rock Island's "motor" (gas-electric) Belle–Kansas City, Union Pacific's "motor" Kansas City–Topeka–Grand Island, Frisco's "motor" Kansas City–Joplin, Santa Fe's "motor" Fort Madison–Kansas City,

Milwaukee Road's "motor" Davenport–Kansas City, and Gulf, Mobile & Ohio's Roodhouse–Kansas City rattler.[2]

Several trains running to Missouri or within the state were particularly noteworthy—among them Baltimore & Ohio's *National Limited* (diesel-electric all the way and with a stewardess-nurse, St. Louis to Washington), New York Central's *Knickerbocker* (with a lounge sleeping car, St. Louis to New York), and Pennsylvania's *Spirit of St. Louis* (with no coaches). Louisville & Nashville's *Dixie Limited* handled a through sleeper to Atlanta and Montgomery; Katy continued to team with Frisco

FIGURE 4.2. After the end of World War II, the electrified Illinois Terminal added a streamliner to its St. Louis–Peoria, Illinois, service. This image comes from the cover of a 1953 timetable. Schwantes-Greever-Nolan Collection.

A Fluid State   129

FIGURE 4.3.
Unexpected elegance: the Burlington briefly assigned this historic equipment to its St. Joseph–Brookfield connection for the *Kansas City Zephyr*. Chillicothe offered significant boardings at 12:59 p.m. for the eastbound run, seen here in May 1953. Don L. Hofsommer photograph.

to host the *Texas Special* to San Antonio from St. Louis; Burlington promoted its *Mark Twain Zephyr* from St. Louis north to Burlington, Iowa; Gulf, Mobile & Ohio advertised its *Alton Limited* in Chicago–St. Louis service, but Illinois Central countered with its *Green Diamond* in that same competitive corridor; Wabash and Union Pacific sponsored the *City of St. Louis* with through sleepers from St. Louis through Kansas City to Los Angeles, San Francisco, and Seattle; and Missouri Pacific worked with Denver & Rio Grande Western to put its *Colorado Eagle* on an arrangement that served the St. Louis–Kansas City–Pueblo–Denver market ("Planetarium-dome Coaches between St. Louis and Denver daily"). Kansas City Southern's *Southern Belle* was as refined as its very name. Missouri–Kansas–Texas declared that "Famous! Table d'Hote Meals" were a feature of "Katy Dining Car Service!" Santa Fe proclaimed its *Super Chief* to be the "Train of the Stars," and, in fact, the Hollywood smart set typically chose Atchison, Topeka & Santa Fe between Chicago and Los Angeles.[3]

In 1952, the nation's railroads ordered 666 cars of one kind or another for passenger service; since 1945 they had spent nearly $622 million for capital improvements, mostly for rolling stock. The St. Louis Cardinals traveled by train; railroads such as Illinois Central employed city passenger agents; and, sleek, brightly painted, efficient diesel locomotives hauled more and more of the country's passenger trains. Modernization continued. Nickel Plate took delivery of streamlined sleepers for its St. Louis train; Missouri Pacific, which had acquired "planetarium-dome

FIGURE 4.4.
Katy Meals advertisement. Dinner in the diner was a prized feature of long-distance travel by train. Schwantes-Greever-Nolan Collection train.

cars" for its *Colorado Eagle* in 1948, added such equipment to its *Missouri River Eagle* and *Texas Eagle* in 1952; and, in 1950, Wabash added the *Blue Bird*, a sparkling domeliner in the Chicago trade, and then purchased additional dome cars for the *City of Kansas City*. Baltimore & Ohio aggressively advertised through sleeper service to the Southwest from eastern points aboard its *Diplomat* and connections at St. Louis with the Frisco-Katy *Texas Special* and Frisco's *Meteor*. Baltimore & Ohio also admonished, "Ride the National whenever you can," referring, of course, to its *National Limited*, which featured a splendid "Sun Room Observation Lounge" for "chatting, reading, and fascinating views" and

FIGURE 4.5.
Atchison, Topeka & Santa Fe was the railroad most favored by Hollywood stars—in this case, Alan Ladd and his family aboard the Santa Fe's exquisite *Super Chief*. Don L. Hofsommer Collection.

a diner "where good meals are the rule, and courtesy a pleasant plus." Santa Fe was equally chic, rolling out in 1948 a splendid *Texas Chief* and in 1956 outfitting its *El Capitan* as a luxury coach train with "Hi-level" cars (two levels without vestibules offering greater carrying capacity) as a firm statement of confidence in the passenger trade. Santa Fe likewise added to its famous stable of high-quality trains with inauguration of the *San Francisco Chief*, a premier flyer to the Bay Area, on June 6, 1954.[4]

Not all passenger trains were assigned Railway Mail Service responsibilities, but most handled Railway Post Office (RPO) cars as well as assorted storage cars for mail and express. St. Louis remained a primary end point and head-out center for the Railway Mail Service. Railway Post Office runs *from* all points of the compass focused on St. Louis, where, as for passengers and express, connections were made *to* all points of the compass. In 1950, the Pennsylvania and New York Central continued to deliver most of the volume from New York City, while Baltimore & Ohio trains hauled most of it west from Washington, DC. Of the routes to and from Chicago, Gulf, Mobile & Ohio's Chicago & St. Louis RPO dominated. Missouri Pacific's St. Louis & Kansas City RPO

and St. Louis & Little Rock RPO prevailed to the west and southwest, as did Illinois Central's St. Louis, Carbondale & Memphis RPO and Louisville & Nashville's Nashville & St. Louis RPO to the southeast. In general, these routes complemented one another to perfect an intricate web with heavily loaded night trains connecting with heavy-capacity day trains and vice versa. An example was the Pennsylvania's Pittsburgh–St. Louis RPO, which reached St. Louis at 7:30 a.m. to connect with one of Missouri Pacific's St. Louis & Kansas City RPOs; that train, upon its arrival in Kansas City at 2:10 p.m., handed off to other RPO routes leading to Omaha, Denver, Los Angeles, and other destinations. Another

FIGURE 4.6.
Kansas City Southern 1953 timetable cover. During the early 1950s, when many railroads still saw a future in passenger train travel, timetable covers grew especially attractive. Schwantes-Greever-Nolan Collection.

A Fluid State   133

FIGURE 4.7. This 1957 advertisement emphasized through service via St. Louis. During much of the decade, Pennsylvania's *Penn-Texas* conveyed a colorfully attired collection of sleeping cars between East Coast cities and St. Louis. From there Frisco, Katy, and Missouri Pacific streamliners forwarded them to cities in Oklahoma and Texas. Schwantes-Greever-Nolan Collection.

example was Illinois Central's number sixteen, the St. Louis, Carbondale & Memphis, whose clerks in the sixty-foot RPO car assigned that run made connecting pouches for fifteen of the twenty-two other RPO runs diverging from St. Louis.[5]

It was much the same across the state at Kansas City—another hub where RPO routes converged and diverged. Rock Island dominated in the Minneapolis–St. Paul/Kansas City corridor and shared responsibility for Texas points with several others; Union Pacific dominated mail service to the West, Burlington to and from Council Bluffs–Omaha, and Kansas City Southern to New Orleans. But Santa Fe dominated—not just between Kansas City and Chicago but all the way to Los Angeles. Its train number seven was assigned three RPOs from Chicago to Kansas City, two beyond, trailing a dozen or more storage cars. Head-end traffic, including revenue from carrying first-class mail, express, storage mail, and other business, earned the country's railroads $221,000,000 in 1946, despite the fact that the Post Office Department had not raised mail pay rates for nearly twenty years. By 1960 these revenues would rise to $431,000,000.[6]

The express business was nearly as old as the railroad industry itself, and the two were linked inextricably. That reality was mirrored at St. Louis in the very nature and operation of Union Station with large and impressive express facilities lined up along the station's flanks. Those operations had been consolidated temporarily under the United States Railroad Administration, and, on March 1, 1929, most of the nation's trunk carriers joined to purchase the

Mail by Rail

Early in the nation's railroad era, mail moved aboard cars in closed pouches, but en route sorting aboard specially designed Railway Post Office (RPO) cars began early in the 1860s. Railway Post Office routes soon proliferated, converging on or diverging from principal cities like St. Louis, Kansas City, Chicago, Council Bluffs, and St. Paul. In most cases RPO cars were included in the consists of regularly scheduled passenger trains, but solid mail trains did move along primary rail arteries—Chicago–Kansas City–Los Angeles over the Santa Fe, for example. These routes were designed to complement one another so as to form an intricate national web as night trains connected with day trains and vice versa in a mail system intended to serve every nook and cranny of the United States.*

Virtually every RPO line had a nickname and internally was referred to in that style. Colorful examples included the following:

> Cincinnati & St. Louis = "Sin & St."
> Kansas City & Memphis = "The Leaky Roof"
> St. Louis & Parsons = "The Preacher"
> St. Louis & Memphis = "The Scissorbill"
> Kansas City & Pueblo = "The Doghouse"†

FIGURE 4.1.1. Efficient post office workers sorted mail en route. For more than a century, Railway Mail Service provided an intricate web connecting tiny towns with bustling cities across the nation. En route sorting of mail aboard the railway post office between Minneapolis and Kansas City ended on October 27, 1967, and this Kansas City–based crew took their labors elsewhere. Don L. Hofsommer Collection.

---

* William J. Dennis, *The Traveling Post Office: History and Incidents of the Railway Mail Service* (Des Moines: privately published by the author, 1916), 5–32; James E. White, *A Life Span of Reminisces of the Railway Mail Service* (Philadelphia: Deemer & Jaishon, 1910), 7–14; Clark E. Carr, *The Railway Mail Service: Its Origins and Development* (Chicago: A. G. McClung, 1909), 1–32.
† Byron Alden Long and William Jefferson Dennis, *Mail by Rail: The Story of the Postal Transportation Service* (New York: Simmons-Boardman, 1951), 181–84.

---

assets of what once had been independent companies and finally merged them as the Railway Express Agency. A few months earlier, Terminal Railroad had announced plans to increase capacity of Union Station, particularly for handling express, baggage, and mail, which, after all, comprised fully 35 percent of all cars entering or leaving the facility. Ten tracks would be added on the west, necessitating destruction of

FIGURE 4.8.
This photograph of the Frisco's *Oklahoman* as it hauls a lengthy consist of head-end cars loaded with mail, express, and baggage through the complex trackage of St. Louis Union Station suggests a bright future for the investor-owned railroad industry in the passenger-carrying trade, but such optimism was misplaced. Patrick D. Hiatte photograph.

five express houses and relocation of that activity to an immense single structure on the east. Fully equipped and linked to station platforms by way of ramps, subway corridors, and elevators, the new facility even featured a dormitory to accommodate express messengers laying over between runs.[7]

Express billings could be exotic, or they could be mundane. For example, a baby hippopotamus in transit to Des Moines required personnel at St. Louis to administer frequent baths to keep the animal's hide from cracking. Railway Express also transported jewelry, money, live birds, fish, nursery stock, baby chicks, cut flowers, ice cream, and baked goods. In some cases, items were billed to residential customers—musical instruments for members of River City's Boys Band, as popularized in Meredith Willson's *Music Man*. More likely to be found in the delivery truck, however, were packages and parcels moving from manufacturers and wholesalers to local retail outlets. That traditional revenue base was under attack, though, as Americans turned to direct mail concerns such as Sears, Roebuck and, after 1912, to package delivery by parcel post.[8]

Union Station in St. Louis remained the city's premier icon. Fred Harvey operated its two finest restaurants—one on the main level, the fanciest, and the other close to the gates, essentially a coffee shop. The

136   Missouri Railroads

FIGURE 4.9. Cotton Belt's Florida Street freight station in St. Louis was a hive of activity—cars being loaded and unloaded in a frenzy. Much of this business was on behalf of freight forwarders (consolidators who handled less-than-carload traffic). Terminal Railroad shuttled cars between the Cotton Belt's St. Louis freight house and its yard in East St. Louis. Don L. Hofsommer Collection.

FIGURE 4.10. Terminal Railroad Association of St. Louis was a major player on both sides of the Mississippi River. The hostler at Granite City, Illinois, is about to put the Terminal Railroad's muscular 0-8-0 to its assigned crew on September 5, 1953. Don L. Hofsommer photograph.

Harvey House on the main level attracted not only rail patrons waiting for trains but also locals who were particularly drawn to Sunday dinners. Near the station itself, at the corner of Twentieth and Eugenia Streets, west of the train shed, stood a large brick structure housing the "Railroad Y," which provided a home away from home to railroad workers, RPO clerks, and express messengers. Inexpensive lodging at the YMCA occasionally included educational programs and even luncheons.[9]

If passenger operation was the glamour side of the railroad industry, it was the gritty freight business that paid most of the bills. Across the Mississippi River from St. Louis was a bewildering maze of yards, team tracks, freight houses, engine facilities, icing docks, interchange tracks, yard offices, and industrial spurs—many of them owned by major carriers using the St. Louis gateway from the northeast, east, southeast, south, and even southwest. These same carriers accommodated the metropolitan area's many shippers. Frenzied freight-related activity on the St. Louis side of the Mississippi River was not as intense, but located there were additional yards and other facilities owned and operated by individual companies—Burlington, Wabash, and Missouri Pacific among them. Freight houses of Katy, Wabash, Burlington, Frisco, Rock Island, and Cotton Belt with others hugged the shoreline between Merchants and Eads Bridges.

Not surprisingly, the Terminal Railroad Association of St. Louis was a prominent and vital player in connecting everything together—not just at Union Station but in serving nearly four hundred miles of track to make connections with virtually all railroads as well as Federal Barge Lines, Mississippi Valley Barge Line, and innumerable shippers including

St. Louis National Stock Yards. In a similar way, Alton & Southern (A&S)—an operation featuring about 150 miles of track—connected directly with all major carriers on the Illinois side and with most roads on the Missouri side by way of trackage rights over the city-owned MacArthur Bridge. The Alton & Southern served some forty trackside industries, but its revenues derived principally from switching charges and divisions from trunk-line hauls.[10]

FIGURE 4.11. Movement of livestock remained an important part of the freight traffic mix for many railroads. In Missouri much of it focused on packers in Kansas City. Don L. Hofsommer Collection.

A Fluid State 139

Strawberries in Season

During the 1920s and continuing well into the next decade, the annual strawberry season was for the Frisco as short as it was important. Both the Merchants' Refrigerator Dispatch and American Railway Express Company sent cars to St. Louis in late April and early May and handed them to the Frisco for inspection, repairs if needed, and cleaning. Then the refrigerator cars were off to Frisco stations in the Ozarks, southwestern Missouri, and northwestern Arkansas—especially Monett and Sarcoxie in Missouri.*

The routine was impressive. At Monett, for example, berries began to arrive early in the afternoon for inspection by prospective buyers and were then loaded—420 crates per freight car, 448 per express car. Iced and ready to roll, cars were then assembled into "strawberry specials," thirty to forty cars per train, moving mostly north to Kansas City or east to St. Louis at sunup. The cars required approximately ten and a half hours to reach Kansas City and fourteen hours to reach St. Louis, with re-icing required at each of the locations. At Kansas City, after re-icing, cars were taken to Union Station, where they were delivered to connecting carriers. On May 29, 1928, as a representative example, the first cars were interchanged to Wabash at 5:30 p.m., the last cars to Santa Fe at 6:50 p.m. In 1928, Frisco billed 2,460 carloads of strawberries, a record, sending them to several states and even Canada.†

Missouri Pacific was similarly engaged. Most of Missouri Pacific's shipment derived from Arkansas stations, but it also gained strawberry revenue from the Carthage, Missouri, area. In 1934, Missouri Pacific handled nearly 1,800 carloads, virtually all routed via St. Louis.‡

---

* "Moving Strawberries on Time," *Railway Age*, October 13, 1928, 698–700.
† *Railway Age*, June 30, 1928, 1533.
‡ *Railway Age*, April 14, 1934, 558.

The story was very much the same in Kansas City, where Kansas City Terminal handled chores at Union Station but also offered interline connecting service for all "steam railroads" as well as providing a general freight switching business. Burlington, Wabash, Kansas City Southern, Missouri Pacific, Frisco, and Katy all operated major yards on the Missouri side, as did Rock Island, Union Pacific, and Santa Fe across the state line in Kansas. As was the case at St. Louis, considerable freight traffic simply moved through, interchanged from one road to another, but also like St. Louis, the Kansas City metropolitan area received and generated appreciable volumes of business—grain elevators, mills, stockyard, packing houses, manufacturing plants, wholesale houses, lumber yards, food processors, and others using team tracks.[11]

Of course, not all freight business in Missouri came from or went to the state's two major cities. Other urban centers—St. Joseph, Cape Girardeau, Springfield, and Joplin among them—likewise boasted a wealth of important customers. Railroads counted 226 customers at St. Joseph—everything from scrap metal and bakery goods to serum products and beer. Much smaller Savannah produced freight revenue from shippers or receivers of animal feed, farm implements, automobiles, poles, phosphate, seed, newsprint, hardware, scrap iron, and petroleum products that included liquefied petroleum gas. Even smaller communities like Dearborn could be counted on to produce billings of grain, tobacco, hogs, and cattle. At other locations around Missouri could be found producers of lime, lead, zinc, coal, and chemicals of various types. Automobile assembly plants in and about St. Louis and Kansas City received parts and dispatched set-up automobiles and trucks. Burlington serviced Continental Can Company's plant at St. Joseph, International Paper's facility at St. Louis, Farmers Association's grain elevator at Kansas City, a meatpacking plant at Macon, and a coal-fired electrical generating plant at Machens, a village up the Mississippi River from St. Louis. Coal arriving via the Frisco fed a similar electrical generating plant at Kansas City.[12]

One bright spot for freight traffic was the increased number of automobiles and small trucks that moved to dealers by rail. In an earlier era, motor vehicles had moved in boxcars, but truckers subsequently gained almost all of that business. Railroads ultimately responded with bilevel and then trilevel cars and gradually won back an appreciable portion of those billings. Missouri rail lines that served assembly plants—such as Burlington, Frisco, and Wabash—were particularly aggressive in the pursuit of this freight.[13]

Piggyback, trailers-on-flat-cars (TOFC), provided another area of growth, although there was ongoing debate whether cargo in trailers was cargo coming out of boxcars and whether or not the business was compensatory. Chicago Great Western was a piggyback pioneer, but the industry in general was slow to warm to the concept. Eventually, however, some carriers and then more of them sought to gain or regain high-rated commodities—pointing to TOFC from freight forwarders, common carrier truckers, the Post Office Department, and manufacturers of auto parts and even set-up automobiles. The Santa Fe and Burlington were particularly dogged in the pursuit of this business.[14]

Arguably the best-known freight train in the area was Cotton Belt's *Blue Streak Merchandise*, which celebrated its twenty-fifth birthday in October 1956. South Texas and California less-than-carload lading had long since become part of its tonnage, and, indeed, it had evolved to serve both transcontinental and regional patrons from St. Louis. During

FIGURE 4.12. Railroads recaptured much of the set-up automobile traffic by employing bilevel and then trilevel cars. Norfolk & Western moved that business in regularly scheduled expedited trains, one of which pauses in St. Louis in September 1966. Norfolk Southern photograph.

the 1960s the *Blue Streak Merchandise* frequently held title as the world's fastest freight train. There were other contenders, among them Frisco's QLA, an expedited train linking St. Louis with Los Angeles, running on Frisco rails to Quanah, Texas; Quanah, Acme & Pacific to Floydada, Texas; and Santa Fe beyond. Wabash, with an eye to solidifying a powerful relationship with Ford Motor Company in 1962, instituted its Cannon Ball Freight Service from Detroit to St. Louis and beyond—trains handling both set-up automobiles and parts.[15]

There was another important wrinkle in freight movement—a rising volume of long-haul business expedited by run-through trains. An important example of this was an agreement between Cotton Belt and New York Central to run connecting trains, with power and cabooses, through East St. Louis from Pine Bluff, Arkansas, to Indianapolis, Indiana. Service began on September 7, 1966. Four months later Pennsylvania Railroad joined in a similar operation between Pine Bluff and its Enola Yard near Harrisburg, Pennsylvania.[16]

* * *

A number of short-line railroads were sprinkled about in Missouri. True to its corporate identification, Missouri–Illinois Railroad had 172 miles of operation in Illinois and in Missouri south of St. Louis and above Cape Girardeau. Union Terminal, St. Joseph Belt, and St. Joseph Terminal all handled switching duties at St. Joseph, as did Kansas & Missouri Railway & Terminal on both sides of the river at Kansas City. Hannibal Connecting linked local customers at that Mississippi River community with Chicago, Burlington & Quincy, and Bevier & Southern transported coal from a mine near Bevier to an interchange with the Burlington. Manufacturers Railway at St. Louis, a satellite of brewery giant Anheuser-Busch, made connections with all railroads at East St. Louis and St. Louis through the Alton & Southern, Terminal Railroad, and Missouri Pacific—operating on its own nearly forty-three miles of track and dispatching a steady stream of beer from the gigantic brewery and receiving in turn numerous carloads of barley malt and other commodities.[17]

Companies continued to improve plant by easing curves, reducing grades, and adding centralized traffic control. Burlington took great pride in opening its Centennial Cut-Off—accomplished by rehabilitating

FIGURE 4.13. Frisco proudly advocated its QLA, an expedited train that linked St. Louis with Los Angeles: Frisco west to Quanah, Texas; satellite Quanah, Acme & Pacific to Floydade, Texas; and Atchison. Topeka & Santa Fe beyond. Don L. Hofsommer Collection.

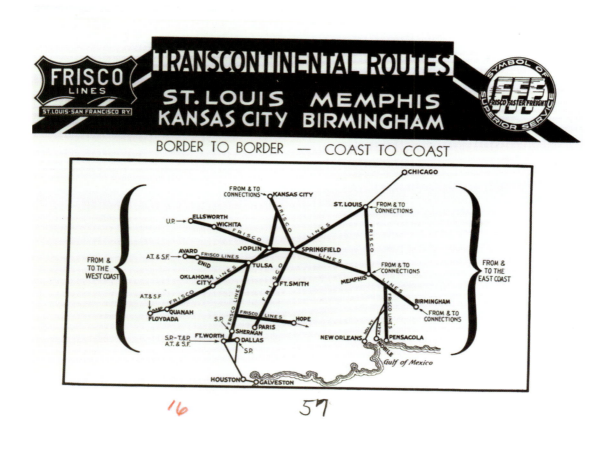

A Fluid State   143

its Carrollton Branch and building nearly fifty miles of new line. The aggregate cost was more than $16 million, but the improvement facilitated a noteworthy reduction in transit times for freight and passenger trains alike. Frisco, too, made headlines by announcing a thirty-three-mile new line that extended from its Salem Branch to nearby lead deposits and served the needs of smelters and mills in southeast Missouri. Frisco expected all excavation and bridge work to be completed by the summer of 1967.[18]

* * *

Rail carriers large and small hurried to complete dieselization of operations. Capitalization requirements for conversion were stupendous, but as one official put it, "the investment was worth every cent." Steam required much more time for servicing, repairing, and inspecting than diesels. Mass-produced interchangeable parts favored diesels; and diesels had a much more favorable availability ratio. In addition, diesels made better over-the-road time, with frequent stops for coal and water eliminated. Moreover, steam required massive service facilities—roundhouses, back shops, blacksmith shops, and mills, as well as coal and water stations—and a huge attending labor force that diesels did not. Chicago Great Western and Gulf, Mobile & Ohio reported that they were fully dieselized in 1949. Cotton Belt followed in 1953. In the process many roads dieselized certain segments of line, concentrating steam at specific locations. Nickel Plate, for example, did this before "officially" dropping the fires on its magnificent fleet of steam locomotives in August 1960. At the end of 1949, Burlington rostered 739 steam locomotives along with 393 diesels of various types. By 1963 the railroad owned a mere 7 steam locomotives along with 654 diesels.[19]

The superiority of diesel over steam was indisputable. Yet not even the flintiest-eyed accountant nor the most hardened industrial engineer would argue that there was a substitute for the sight, sound, and fury of awesome steel giants powered by steam. The whine of their turbo generators; the pulsating beat of air compressors; the panting urgency of an iron steed ready for labor; the mixed smells of steam, coal smoke, and valve oil; the wail of a steam whistle distinctive to the artistry of the engineer—all of these sounds, smells, and sights spoke to something deep in the human soul. Of all splendid inventions, perhaps the steam locomotive was the most humanized—its moods singularly apparent, its breathing acute and purposeful as that of any life form, its very being boasting of brawny self-assurance. The diesel's superiority was unquestioned, to be sure, but an important and tangible quality of railroading passed when fires were extinguished for the final time on the nation's dwindling fleet of steam locomotives.[20]

The passenger-carrying trade presented an increasingly mixed picture. The Korean Conflict added a distinct war flavor to operations from mid-1950 into 1953. Troop trains again pounded along the tracks, and Union Station in St. Louis, for example, thronged with recruits lined up to board Frisco trains to Fort Leonard Wood. Partially because of military business, total industry volume stabilized in 1951 and 1952. Discretionary travel was encouraged. For its part, Pennsylvania Railroad reminded St. Louisans of the vacation-season *Northern Arrow,* a through train to Michigan's northern resort country. Illinois Central's *City of Miami* served the needs of vacationers headed to Florida, and hundreds rode its special trains to New Orleans for the annual Mardi Gras hilarity.

FIGURE 4.14.
Steam motive power required considerable time and expense for servicing, repairing, and inspecting. Missouri Pacific was quick to replace steam with diesels on its passenger assignment, but on this day in 1950 its handsome 5321 roars into Tower Grove with first number 15, maid-of-all-work on the St. Louis–Kansas City circuit. Don L. Hofsommer Collection.

A Fluid State 145

FIGURE 4.15.
Military special trains reappeared on Missouri rails during the Korean conflict. Don L. Hofsommer Collection.

Illinois Central also catered to University of Illinois football fans with *Pigskin Specials* from St. Louis to Champaign. Four special trains hauled three thousand fans to the Army-Illinois game in 1959. And on May 13, 1958, after a game against the Chicago Cubs in which Stan Musial scored his three thousandth hit, a special Illinois Central train returned the Cardinals to St. Louis, making several stops en route for cheering baseball enthusiasts to salute "Stan the Man." There were other bright spots. The Pennsylvania and New York Central agreed to honor each other's tickets at competitive points such as St. Louis; Wabash announced "Silver Dollar Dinners" on its diners; Baltimore & Ohio, Nickel Plate, and other railroads promoted group economy rates; Missouri Pacific offered two roomettes for the price of one double bedroom; Missouri Pacific and Baltimore & Ohio established through Slumbercoach cars to the Southwest on the *National Limited* and *Texas Eagle*; and Pennsylvania joined Hertz to promote a rail-auto plan. Baltimore & Ohio counseled, "Avoid the Highway Strain—Go By Train."[21]

Long a feature of the industry were overnight sleeping-car lines, which, during the early 1950s, still included innumerable options from St. Louis, for example. In the important Chicago corridor, Illinois Central's *Night Diamond*; Gulf, Mobile & Ohio's *Midnight Special*; and Wabash's *Midnight* collectively wheeled ten sleeping cars nightly.

Wabash and Missouri Pacific sent other cars to Kansas City and Omaha, Baltimore & Ohio and Louisville & Nashville tapped Louisville, Wabash and New York Central served Detroit, Baltimore & Ohio and Pennsylvania wrestled for traffic to Washington, Frisco and Missouri Pacific vied for travelers to San Antonio and Fort Worth, Nickel Plate and New York Central bid for business to Cleveland, Illinois Central and

FIGURE 4.16. Railroads encouraged discretionary travel as a way to keep ticket agents busy. Don L. Hofsommer Collection.

A Fluid State 147

FIGURE 4.17.
In this view the Pullman porter on Rock Island's *Golden State* takes a brief break at Kansas City Union Station in June 1967. Don L. Hofsommer photograph.

Frisco carried passengers to Memphis, Baltimore & Ohio and New York Central rushed sleepers to Cincinnati, and ancient rivals Pennsylvania and New York Central dueled for advantage at Indianapolis and on extended night runs to New York. Additional nightly cars were dispatched by the Burlington (with Rock Island) to St. Paul–Minneapolis; Wabash to Des Moines and Toledo; Pennsylvania to Pittsburgh; Katy to Bartlesville; Gulf, Mobile & Ohio to Montgomery; Illinois Central to New Orleans; Frisco to Dallas, Joplin, Springfield, Oklahoma City, and Fort Smith; Louisville & Nashville to Nashville and Atlanta; Missouri Pacific to Denver, Wichita, Galveston, Hot Springs, Lake Charles, El Dorado, and Shreveport; and Cotton Belt to Pine Bluff.[22]

Yet all was not well. The best passenger trains earned high marks, but Americans nevertheless turned increasingly to other modes of passenger transport. Revenues for passenger service nationwide in February 1953 were 9 percent under the same month in 1952. The drop was most alarming in the first-class trade, with eighty-two Pullman lines in the United States and Canada terminated in 1953. In 1945, 891,128,000 patrons had boarded trains to roll up an impressive 91,717,226,000 passenger miles; in 1953, only 456,817,000 persons used rail transport, aggregating 31,655,134,000 passenger miles. Domestic airlines hauled twice as many passengers as Pullman—twenty-six million to thirteen million (they had been tied at thirteen million in 1950). In 1954, American Airlines handled more passengers than any single railroad. Braniff International employed DC-3s, as did Mid-Continent. "No cinders, no mud, no detours," boasted Mid-Continent. "You owe it to yourself to try it." Ozark, a St. Louis–based air carrier, also entered service across Missouri and nearby states. And the new competition did not diminish the love affair Americans had with their automobiles. Automobile manufacturers could barely keep up with demand. Bus companies added insult to injury. "Greyhound can take you anywhere," jeered that company.[23]

148　　　　Missouri Railroads

FIGURE 4.18.
Folk-song enthusiasts will easily recall "City of New Orleans" as sung by Arlo Guthrie and others. For many years the Illinois Central's daylight speedster burnished the rails between Chicago and New Orleans. Schwantes-Greever-Nolan Collection.

Meanwhile, the Railway Express Agency staggered into an uncertain future. The company handled 100,833,505 shipments during the first six months of 1945 and a total of 114,292,704 billings during the same period for 1946. It used twelve thousand rail cars daily in 1949 and acquired more capacity by converting former troop sleepers into express refrigerator cars in 1950. That dominance eroded quickly, however, as parcel post claimed greater volumes, as the trucking industry successfully lobbied to restrict Railway Express's over-the-road rights, and as the United Parcel Service gained new momentum. Systemwide, Railway Express shipments fell to eighty million in 1951. The company scrambled throughout the decade, looking for ways to stay alive. One way was to divert express shipments to highway trailers loaded on flatcars—piggyback. Such shipments commenced in 1959 from St. Louis to Chicago aboard Wabash freights. Unfortunately, diversions such as this further reduced income attributable to passenger operations.[24]

* * *

Appearances could be deceiving. Indeed, it was impossible to tell from casual observation of trackside platforms of Union Stations at Kansas City or St. Louis during the holiday season that Railway Express and America's passenger trains were in trouble. On those platforms stood row after row of four-wheel express trucks loaded high with boxes of clothing from New York's garment district, all mixed with various and sundry shipments, and carton after carton of citrus fruit from Florida's Indian River district, the Rio Grande Valley of Texas, and California's Coachella Valley. Those same platforms also groaned under long rows of trucks heavily laden with locked pouches of letter mail and number-three

A Fluid State   149

sacks stuffed with newspapers, magazines, and parcel post. Planning for the annual rush of mail began after Labor Day when the Railway Mail Service convened a joint conference between railroad and postal officials. Determinations were made as to destinations requiring "special cars" of both first-class and parcel post; as to adequate manpower, trucks, and tractors at the station; as to an appropriate number of storage cars for all runs; and as to precise times that RPO cars would be set in the station before clerks reported for duty. The Railway Mail Service insisted that RPO cars be placed in the first section of any multiple-section trains and demanded adequate protection for all mail on the cars or anywhere else on railroad property. Baltimore & Ohio contracted for a daily special mail and express train for most of December from Jersey City to St. Louis and return, New York Central promised two sections of two trains—one passenger and one mail and express—between Cleveland and St. Louis, and Missouri Pacific similarly scheduled second sections for mail and express between St. Louis and Texarkana and between St. Louis and Kansas City.[25]

Despite the efficiency of the Railway Mail Service, its existence was tenuous. "The Railway Post Office," said a senior postal official in 1954,

FIGURE 4.19. On platforms at Union Stations in Kansas City and St. Louis could be seen row after row of four-wheel carts piled high with clothing from New York's garment district mixed with various and sundry shipments. Don L. Hofsommer Collection.

"is one of the most ingenious of all transportation devices" and, he predicted, would be with us for a long time, though on fewer routes. Railroads, he observed, were partially responsible for this decline since they often chose to be relieved of branch-line and local service, which the Post Office Department was forced to replace with Highway Post Offices or with Star Routes (trucks). Beyond that, however, the Post Office engaged in an experiment to fly "3-cent surface mail," which, the same postal officer said ominously, was "meeting all expectations."[26]

Indeed, air was already skimming priority mail from the rails. To hold what business they had, rail carriers would have to become more efficient in the movement of mail. One way to do that involved "containerization" of mail—a policy embraced by the Santa Fe between Chicago and Kansas City aboard its *San Francisco Chief*.[27]

* * *

In 1960, Santa Fe served Missouri stations on its Chicago–Kansas City leg with seven elegant passenger trains in each direction. "Luxury is the rule," and train travel approaches perfection "aboard the *Golden State*," said Rock Island—"the comfortable, low-altitude way between Chicago and Kansas City to El Paso, Tucson, Phoenix, Palm Springs, and Los Angeles." And Rock Island offered complimentary morning and afternoon coffee for sleeping car and parlor car passengers aboard its splendid *Twin Star Rocket* on the Minneapolis–Kansas City–Houston circuit. In the same year, seventy-two trains served St. Louis Union Station—Missouri Pacific leading with nineteen, Wabash following with thirteen. High quality was still the definition for service on Baltimore & Ohio's *National Limited*; Frisco's *Meteor*; Gulf, Mobile & Ohio's *Abraham Lincoln*; Missouri Pacific's *Texas Eagle*; Pennsylvania's *Spirit of St. Louis*; and Wabash's *Blue Bird*. The *Texas Eagle* routinely operated as two separate sections. Illinois Central added a sleeper to its *City of Miami* connection and actively solicited group movements between Florida and St. Louis.[28]

FIGURE 4.20. Santa Fe maintained its traditional standard of excellence, typified by this genial attendant on its *Texas Chief*. Don L. Hofsommer photograph.

A Fluid State

St. Louis, Malden, Paragould, Jonesboro, Stuttgart, Pine Bluff

(Read Down)

Miles from St. Louis		TABLE No. 1	No. 7 Daily
0	Lv	ST. LOUIS, Mo.	11.00 PM
4	Lv	Valley Junction, Ill.	11.15 PM
66	Lv	Chester	12.39 AM
85	Lv	Gorham	1.07 AM
125	Lv	Thebes, Ill.	1.58 AM
128	Lv	Illmo, Mo.	2.05 AM
135	Lv	Rockview	....
141	Lv	Delta	....
146	Lv	Randles	....
155	Lv	Bell City	2.40 AM
163	Lv	Avert	....
169	Lv	Idalia	....
176	Lv	Dexter	3.08 AM
184	Lv	Bernie	....
193	Lv	MALDEN	3.38 AM
200	Lv	Campbell, Mo.	3.48 AM
210	Lv	Piggott, Ark.	4.01 AM
214	Lv	Greenway	....
220	Lv	Rector	4.15 AM
228	Lv	Marmaduke	c 4.21 AM
238	Lv	PARAGOULD	4.43 AM
250	Lv	Brookland	....
260	Ar	JONESBORO	5.05 AM
260	Lv	JONESBORO	5.15 AM
268	Lv	Gibson	....
272	Lv	Otwell	....
280	Lv	Weiner	5.40 AM
284	Lv	Waldenburg	....
290	Lv	Fisher	....
296	Lv	Hickory Ridge	f 5.55 AM
302	Lv	Tilton	....
307	Lv	Fair Oaks	f 6.06 AM
322	Lv	Hunter	....
327	Lv	Zent	....
329	Lv	Fargo	....
334	Lv	Brinkley	6.38 AM
349	Lv	Clarendon	6.56 AM
355	Lv	Roe	....
368	Lv	STUTTGART	7.20 AM
379	Lv	Humphrey	....
386	Lv	Wabbaseka	....
390	Lv	Altheimer	c 7.40 AM
402	Ar	PINE BLUFF, Ark.	8.00 AM

PASSENGER TRAIN EQUIPMENT
Trains 7 and 8

10-Section, 2-Compartment, Drawing-Room, Pullman

Available Tri-Weekly Between St. Louis and Pine Bluff:

Car 1, Southbound Train 7, Operates from St. Louis Sunday, Tuesday and Thursday.

Car 2, Northbound Train 8, Operates from Pine Bluff, Monday, Wednesday and Friday.

Chair Cars Daily Between St. Louis and Pine Bluff.

Pine Bluff, Stuttgart, Jonesboro, Paragould, Malden, St. Louis

(Read Down)

Miles from Pine Bluff		TABLE No. 2	No. 8 Daily
0	Lv	PINE BLUFF, Ark.	10.30 PM
12	Lv	Altheimer	c10.50 PM
16	Lv	Wabbaseka	....
23	Lv	Humphrey	....
34	Lv	STUTTGART	11.17 PM
47	Lv	Roe	....
53	Lv	Clarendon	11.39 PM
68	Lv	Brinkley	12.03 AM
73	Lv	Fargo	....
75	Lv	Zent	....
80	Lv	Hunter	....
95	Lv	Fair Oaks	f12.28 AM
100	Lv	Tilton	....
106	Lv	Hickory Ridge	f12.39 AM
112	Lv	Fisher	....
118	Lv	Waldenburg	....
122	Lv	Weiner	12.54 AM
130	Lv	Otwell	....
134	Lv	Gibson	....
142	Ar	JONESBORO	1.20 AM
142	Lv	JONESBORO	1.30 AM
152	Lv	Brookland	....
164	Lv	PARAGOULD	2.07 AM
174	Lv	Marmaduke	c 2.17 AM
182	Lv	Rector	2.27 AM
188	Lv	Greenway	....
192	Lv	Piggott, Ark.	2.40 AM
202	Lv	Campbell, Mo.	2.53 AM
209	Lv	MALDEN	3.12 AM
218	Lv	Bernie	....
226	Lv	Dexter	3.33 AM
233	Lv	Idalia	....
239	Lv	Avert	....
247	Lv	Bell City	4.01 AM
256	Lv	Randles	....
261	Lv	Delta	....
267	Lv	Rockview	....
274	Lv	Illmo, Mo.	4.35 AM
277	Lv	Thebes, Ill.	....
317	Lv	Gorham	5.28 AM
336	Lv	Chester	5.57 AM
398	Lv	Valley Junction, Ill.	7.28 AM
402	Ar	ST. LOUIS, Mo.	7.45 AM

Heavy figures indicate PM—Light figures indicate AM

c—Stops on signal to receive or discharge revenue passengers to or from St. Louis or Pine Bluff.

f—Stops on signal to receive or discharge revenue passengers.

W. G. DEGELOW
General Traffic Manager
St. Louis 2, Mo.

R. A. PENDERGRASS
General Freight and Passenger Agent
Tyler, Texas

But the bloom was off. An internal study at Baltimore & Ohio as early as September 1952 revealed that its passenger service was operating in the red and that on the St. Louis run out-of-pocket costs exceeded revenues for the *Metropolitan* and the *Diplomat,* while the luxurious *National Limited* eked out only a tiny net profit. Pro-passenger Illinois Central identified the passenger deficit as "Railroad Enemy No. 1." Caught between declining revenues and escalating costs, railroads often felt they had no recourse but to discontinue passenger trains. Decreased patronage usually led to decreased service; one fed the other. By 1960, the Burlington and Louisville & Nashville were down to a single train each in St. Louis service, and New York Central was down to one passenger and one mail train. Gone from Union Station was Katy, which withdrew in early 1959; Cotton Belt left Union Station in 1958 for its East St. Louis terminal as a prelude to stopping all service in 1959; and Nickel Plate also exited in 1959. Gone also was Wabash service to Des Moines, and gone were the Illinois Central *Daylight* and *Night Diamond*, among other name trains. Louisville & Nashville along with Pennsylvania and New York Central closed their downtown St. Louis ticket offices.[29]

What explained this precipitous decline in rail passenger patronage? Modal competition. The automobile, improved highways, and inexpensive fuel combined to provide Americans with delightfully personal transportation unmet by any other mode. In 1950–55, twelve million additional automobiles were registered across the country, an increase of 29 percent, and during the same years about a hundred thousand miles of rural highways were paved for heavy-duty use. That did not end the story. High-speed, limited-access, multiple-lane interstate highways were on the drawing boards and after 1956 became a reality across the United States. During those same years, aeronautical engineers were designing and manufacturers would then produce a massive wave of jet aircraft sure to make air transport even more inviting for the long-distance traveler.[30]

More discontinuance notices were posted. Gulf, Mobile & Ohio ended its celebrated motorcar train between Bloomington (Illinois) and Kansas City on April 10, 1960. Chicago Great Western wrapped up its passenger service in Missouri with last runs between Minneapolis and Kansas City on April 27, 1962. The Pennsylvania and Missouri Pacific decided to terminate their through New York–San Antonio sleeping-car service in 1961; Baltimore & Ohio and Missouri Pacific made a similar decision on their Baltimore–San Antonio service in 1964. Finally, Baltimore & Ohio in 1965 did the unthinkable and trimmed its *National Limited* back to Cincinnati, which left St. Louis bereft of that premier service.[31]

Opportunities remained for the rail industry to strut its stuff or to demonstrate the elegance of rail travel. In September 1955 Katy moved the Ringling Brothers and Barnum & Bailey circus to Joplin, and in 1971 Louisville & Nashville hauled the same spectacle from Louisville to East St. Louis, where the Terminal Railroad forwarded it to Missouri Pacific, which continued the circus train to Kansas City, and the Frisco did likewise to Memphis. The Burlington was especially aggressive in creating passenger volume through excursions and tours. President Harry C. Murphy even held two Burlington steam locomotives off scrap lines to pull "educational steam excursions for youngsters." Here was an opportunity to "study railroad transportation and the passing of the steam locomotive," urged Burlington publicists. "Ride behind the Iron Horse . . . Enjoy class companionship . . . Bring your camera." Children

FACING, FIGURE 4.21. There is something very sad about the Cotton Belt timetable issued in 1958 because it was typical of the downward trend in passenger travel on many American railroads. No longer did Cotton Belt passenger trains link St. Louis with Texas destinations, and soon it discontinued even this remnant to Arkansas. Schwantes-Greever-Nolan Collection.

FIGURE 4.22.
Its workday over, Burlington's 5632 lopes off to the engine terminal in Kansas City on October 9, 1960. Don L. Hofsommer photograph.

of all ages flocked to see steam locomotives roar across the Midwestern landscape. Murphy reported that 35,198 elementary students rode behind steam power in 1962. A year later a total of 182,761 passengers took advantage of the road's expansive range of excursions and tours. Special movements on several roads added flavor. Entertainer Jackie Gleason in August 1968 departed Los Angeles on a private car added to the rear of Santa Fe's *Super Chief*. At Kansas City it was handed over to Missouri Pacific's *Missouri River Eagle* and at St. Louis to Illinois Central's *Seminole*. Via other connections the Gleason car gained its Miami destination. Somber but dignified would describe the train that moved the body of President Dwight D. Eisenhower from Washington, DC, to his burial site at Abilene, Kansas. Eisenhower died on March 28, 1969, but plans for the train had been long in place. Over the days of March 31 and April 2, the ten-car Eisenhower special train trundled along the rails of Chesapeake & Ohio/Baltimore & Ohio to St. Louis, Norfolk & Western to Kansas City, and Union Pacific beyond.[32]

* * *

The hammer dropped in 1967 when the Post Office Department announced that it would soon end en route sorting of mail aboard its

FIGURE 4.23.
Ticket agents working for investor-owned roads soon would become a remnant of the past. Don L. Hofsommer Collection.

mobile rail cars and that storage mail would otherwise be diverted from trains. Over the previous century, the Railway Mail Service branch of the Post Office had developed an extremely intricate system of routes that depended on the integrity of interconnected rail routes in a national system. Railway Post Office routes on the Baltimore & Ohio from the East relied on the Missouri Pacific, Frisco, and other rail carriers to forward mail to destinations in the West and Southwest. One route fed

A Fluid State 155

another, day trains fed night trains, and so forth. Absent such connections the mail delivery system would flounder. The case of the *Zephyr-Rocket* illustrates the point. Its overnight northward journey from St. Louis via Burlington and Rock Island rails fed westbound and other daylight departures of Northern Pacific and Great Northern at St. Paul. Conversely, southbound trains to St. Louis brought mails to daylight runs of Missouri Pacific, Frisco, Louisville & Nashville, and others for forwarding to postal patrons in the East, South, and Southwest. When Burlington and Rock Island terminated their joint operation on April 7, 1967, a vital link, a crucial connection, was broken. It was merely a harbinger of terminations to come. Primary RPO routes serving St. Louis and Kansas City—St. Louis & Kansas City, Minneapolis & Kansas City, and even the Santa Fe's vaunted trains 7 and 8 along with all other RPO routes on Santa Fe—were eliminated by year's end. Surviving only temporarily were Chicago & St. Louis (one overnight post office car on the Gulf, Mobile & Ohio); Cincinnati & St. Louis, a similar operation on the Baltimore & Ohio; and one car in either direction on Pennsylvania's Pittsburgh & St. Louis route.[33]

With the loss of mail revenue, the regular trickle of train-off applications became a veritable torrent. "With passenger train losses mounting," said Burlington in 1967, "it was necessary to discontinue trains which served no public convenience or necessity and which were operating at substantial out-of-pocket losses." Burlington quickly plucked one set of trains out of the Kansas City–Omaha circuit and trimmed back its *Kansas City Zephyr* to Chicago–Quincy. Illinois Central in 1968 ended passenger service between St. Louis and Chicago by limiting its train to Illinois service between Chicago and Springfield only. That same year, the Illinois Central terminated one set of St. Louis–Carbondale trains, and two years later it sacked that connection entirely. Rock Island axed its *Golden State* to end Chicago–Kansas City–Los Angeles service on February 21, 1968. Missouri Pacific ended sleeping-car service on all trains, and Frisco and Katy simply exited the passenger-carrying trade. Operations at St. Louis Union Station reflected as much. In 1969 only thirty-two trains per day called at the place (down from sixty-four as recently as 1966). The president of giant Southern Pacific said bluntly, "The long-haul passenger train has outlived its usefulness."[34]

The "passenger problem" was hardly the only difficulty facing the railroad industry in the 1950s and 1960s. Long overregulated, larded with excess capacity, burdened by antiquated work rules and high labor costs, shackled by a self-imposed "this is the way we have always done it" mentality, and saddled with competition aided variously by tax dollars, the entire industry, some observers thought, was quite likely headed for the dustbin of history.[35]

FIGURE 4.24. St. Louis–San Francisco train #102, the Southland, upbound from Birmingham to Kansas City, paused at Springfield, Missouri, on March 24, 1967. Frisco would soon be "freight only." Don L. Hofsommer photograph.

Indeed, much of the industry's distress was historic, the war years and immediate postwar boom confusing patterns long in place. From the turn of the century through 1920, freight tonnage and collective revenues had advanced more rapidly than the country's general business activity. Thereafter, however, rail tonnage and revenue continued to rise in absolute numbers but declined compared to industrial production. For example, the Federal Reserve Board index of industrial production rose from ninety in 1925 to two hundred in 1950, but tonnage originated on Class I railroads increased during those same years by slightly less than 9 percent. One bright spot for the rail industry was rapid dieselization, which markedly increased operating efficiency between 1945 and 1952, when gross tons per freight train hour increased by one-third. Yet wage rates more than doubled between 1939 and 1949. The same was true of the increased dollars required for fuel, supplies, and taxes. And in 1949 nonoperating employees shifted from a six-day workweek of forty-eight hours to a five-day, forty-hour workweek with no loss of pay. Rate increases authorized by regulators, as always, lagged behind escalated costs, and now, more than ever, rate increases risked loss of business to other modes of transport. Operating costs absorbed more

A Fluid State 157

and more of gross revenue; net earnings declined accordingly. "Dim future depresses rail stocks," intoned *Business Week* late in 1953. Indeed, several Wall Street analysts and other observers were pessimistic about the rail industry. In 1952, railroads' share of intercity freight volume had dropped to 54.9 percent, with truckers, pipelines, and inland waterways splitting the remainder in almost equal chunks.[36]

Railroad owners and managers frowned at disappointing statistics showing manufacturers earning from 10 to 20 percent on their investments in 1949 while railroads earned a paltry 2.75 percent. Railroad interests complained that they were caught between dramatically rising costs of labor and material on the one hand and a strangulating inability to raise rates to cover those increases on the other. For most railroaders and owners, the problem came down to one issue: stultifying government regulation or—as they preferred to say—overregulation. "We are not opposed to regulation," said Pennsylvania's Chairman M. W. Clement, "but it should be by law and not by emotion." Clement's view, embraced by most rail managers at the time, was that regulation at state and federal levels had become a "super management" that enforced "its business judgment—or political judgment—upon railroad rates and practices, gradually undermining the capacity of railroads to provide the quality of transportation under just and reasonable rates that managerial initiative, unhampered, can provide." An independent report from the Brookings Institution echoed Clement, arguing that the Interstate Commerce Commission had become, in effect, the board of directors for the railroads, at least with respect to general pricing practices—substituting its business judgment for that of rail managers. Moreover, reminded Pennsylvania's Clement, railroads were obliged by public policy to perform certain obligations at a loss while profitable services were made to subsidize the competition. Clement cited, as an example, public support for airlines—which, he argued, "enjoy tax-built, tax-free airports, tax-maintained airways, and a big mail subsidy"—while Pennsylvania and all other railroads handled mail at a loss: "Railroads, in other words, subsidize the government and the government subsidizes our competition."[37]

The growth and expanding strength of pipelines, waterways, and especially motor trucking (private as well as intercity common carrier and contract) were of even greater concern. Trucks admittedly often provided faster and more flexible service at lower rates—particularly in short-haul and medium-distance competition. Although the issue was sharply debated, truckers benefited greatly from publicly owned and maintained roadways for which they paid only marginal portions. While regulated under the federal Motor Carrier Act of 1935, restrictions on truckers were never as onerous as for railroads. Regulated intercity truckers tripled vehicle miles and more than doubled tonnage carried

FIGURE 4.25. Operating costs absorbed more and more of gross revenue; net earnings declined accordingly. How could this be sustainable? A Cotton Belt track gang at work. Don L. Hofsommer Collection.

during the brief period 1945 through 1953, handling 6.5 percent of all intercity ton miles in 1945 but climbing to a healthy 17 percent by 1953.[38]

The railroad industry was in trouble. In 1953, American railroads handled 53 percent of ton miles, down from 63 percent in 1939. Freight revenues in 1954 were $7.8 billion, about equal to what they had been in 1948; however, net income was $683 million, essentially that of 1946. This, managers and investors complained in unison, was after railroad companies had spent lavishly to modernize plant, motive power, and rolling stock. In 1953, return on investment for the industry was a mere 4.19 percent; in 1954, it dropped to 3.00 percent. Indeed, 1954 offered a glimpse into an unpromising future. Railroads in that year suffered greater declines in the level of operations and earnings than most other basic industries; ton miles were off nearly 10 percent, operating revenues dropped by more than 12 percent, and net income plummeted by more than 25 percent. Furthermore, the decline in net would have been greater had not much scheduled maintenance been deferred. And as one railroad president famously said, "Fictitious earnings derived through deferred maintenance are in reality not net income but unreported liquidation of capital."[39]

A Fluid State

One Wall Street firm gloomily concluded that the industry appeared to "be in a struggle for survival," and *Business Week* called railroad securities "one of the stock market's lame ducks." *Forbes* was no less pessimistic: "In a year [1956] when the rest of the economy was exuberantly setting new records, the $34 billion railroad industry remained inconsolably stalled," it groaned. Matters only worsened. Net income for the country's largest, or Class I railroads, in 1957 was 14 percent below 1956; they handled 2,344,661 fewer cars, down 6.2 percent in one year alone. Several roads failed to earn adequately to meet fixed interest and rental charges. The New York, Ontario & Western simply expired and removed 541 miles from the map of American railroads.[40]

Rail carriers in the northeastern United States were of particular concern. At New York, New Haven & Hartford, the president in August 1958 angrily denied that his road soon would be bankrupt, but that grim prospect quickly became reality. And Anthony P. Arpaia, former chairman of the Interstate Commerce Commission and later a senior manager at Railway Express, said simply, "Railroads in the East are in serious trouble." Erie, for example, had held its own during the 1950s until spiraling operating expenses and the national recession of 1958–59 dramatically curtailed its net income. Erie was not alone.[41]

A few federal policymakers took note. Senator George Smathers (D-Florida) even admitted, "Available statistics indicate that the American railroads are heading for serious trouble." Matters rocked along an uncertain course. Congress passed the Transportation Act of 1958, and President Dwight Eisenhower signed it into law. Among other things the new federal law required the Interstate Commerce Commission to be a bit more liberal in granting railroad requests and authorized the ICC to overrule state regulatory agencies on rail petitions to abandon lines or eliminate money-losing services.[42]

Winds of change swirled across the nation during the 1960s. It was a time of President John F. Kennedy's New Frontiers, then President Lyndon B. Johnson's Great Society. It was a time of war, social revolution, rebelliousness, nonconformity, and turmoil. One historian argued that it was an era "full of conflict, protest, and idealism. A time when society began to confront unresolved ills and embraced reform." For the country's railroads, the decade of the 1960s—particularly the latter half of it—could only be described as grim. But, yes, tentative steps by some politicians and some managers sought to address and maybe even redress the rail industry's collective malaise.[43]

"The past year, from the point of view of net earnings, was far from satisfactory," President Jervis Langdon informed Rock Island shareholders early in 1965. Net income in 1964 had been less than in any year since 1948, when the company was reorganized. "Even more disturbing is the outlook for 1965," Langdon continued. "There is a distinct possibility

FIGURE 4.26. Rock Island in 1966 reported a mere $1.9 million net income, which resulted from sales of land and tax refunds. This westbound train, passing Kansas City's Sheffield Tower on October 30, 1966, offers the illusion of prosperity. Steve Patterson photograph.

... that the company can do no better than to break even." Langdon proved to be overly optimistic. Rock Island actually registered a deficit of $1.5 million, ending the payment of all dividends after the first quarter. During 1966, Rock Island recorded an annual net income of merely $1.9 million, but that was only the result of sales of land and tax refunds.[44]

Rock Island was hardly alone in its pain. In 1961, the country's Class I railroads collectively reported a net income of only $384 million and only $574 million in the following year—the increase in 1962 partly the consequence of new federal tax policy that included investment credits plus accelerated depreciation. These changes were beneficial for all rail carriers, although they tended to aid the more prosperous roads—Santa Fe and Union Pacific as examples—with less advantage for Rock Island and others that were struggling. Chicago Great Western handled 252,087 carloads in 1959, only 207,554 in 1967. Its net income in 1959 had been $2,728,000, but it dropped to a measly $362,884 in 1967. The Milwaukee Road generated more ton miles in 1967 than in 1960, and it posted higher net operating income, but considered in terms of inflation its performance was hardly impressive. The same was true at Illinois Central, where freight revenue in 1956 had been $248.9 million, rising only to $256.7 million in 1967; net income in 1956 had been $23.8 million, up very modestly to $25.3 million in 1967. Even the vaunted Burlington Route shuddered, its working capital of $9.7 million on January 1, 1968, dropping to $2.7 million by year's end. The

A Fluid State

TABLE 4.1. Systemwide operating ratios (ratio of operating expenses to operating revenues)

	Passenger		Freight		Total	
	1960	1966	1960	1966	1960	1966
Santa Fe	130.24	123.61	70.41	70.10	78.51	76.94
Burlington	128.41	129.01	71.79	70.30	81.21	78.59
Chicago Great Western	142.60	—	70.43	75.68	73.51	75.68
Milwaukee Road	139.04	131.60	72.83	73.53	81.58	79.43
Rock Island	136.86	146.72	70.23	75.40	80.17	82.52
Illinois Central	125.18	138.51	74.19	70.60	81.14	78.19
Union Pacific	147.52	139.51	62.86	65.29	72.79	72.14

newly impoverished Burlington was forced to defer maintenance on its historically well-groomed infrastructure.[45]

Capital and labor intensive as always, railroads sought to reduce expenses by cutting jobs and by negotiating more productive work rules with the various union organizations. A White House Commission told President John F. Kennedy that the industry was unreasonably saddled with thousands of "featherbedders"—employees who served no useful purpose. The industry heartily agreed, but operating unions took serious exception to this claim. Some work rules were, to be sure, ridiculously wasteful of company resources. Yet organize labor perceived the term "featherbedding" to be an indictment of all contract workers. The result was an acrimonious and in terms of morale a counterproductive conflict. In the end, arbitration awards and compromise agreements allowed carriers to reduce numbers in specified crafts.[46]

Particularly at issue was the matter of firemen on diesel locomotives. Illinois Central's Wayne A. Johnson called the firemen's shovel an "expensive antique" since diesel firemen had no coal to scoop. The issue ended in arbitration and then the courts, which ruled that firemen (except on passenger trains) were not required. Employees with low seniority could be dismissed; others would be offered alternative employment within individual companies. Ultimately, 90 percent of locomotive firemen would be eliminated.[47]

There were other contentious labor issues. For instance, for operating crafts a full day's pay was based on a distance of one hundred miles, a relic of the steam era. Thus, it was possible for the crew of a diesel-powered passenger train to collect a full day's wages in just two or three hours, and a freight crew a little more depending on how long it took to cover the hundred miles. On the Santa Fe, for example, that distance equaled runs between Fort Madison, Iowa, and Marceline, Missouri; and between Marceline and Kansas City. Moreover, freight crews throughout the land by union agreement and/or state law comprised a conductor, an engineer, a fireman, and two brakemen—no matter how long the train or whether switching was to be done en route. Another issue had to do with agents and telegraphers. Was it necessary for railroads to have open stations every few miles—each one manned by telegraph operators—in an age of telephone, teletype, and radio communication that made the telegraph redundant at best and obsolete at worst, and when the sale of tickets to passengers, the handling of less-than-carload freight, and the billing of carload lots were greatly reduced or simply had disappeared? This matter was loaded with emotion, maybe even more than passenger train discontinuance, because the local depot for decades had been the focal point of any community—a source of pride and importance. Any attempt to trim or end agency service was bound to excite fierce opposition with anger directed at the rail carriers. Yet the days of dependence on railroad transportation had vanished and with it the centrality of the depot and its function as a community's portal to the world. Railroad companies would make that case to public authorities in one of many campaigns to get control of costs in a changed and rapidly changing competitive climate.[48]

Despite significant headwinds, railroad managers convinced boards of directors to make important capital investments. Illinois Central joined with Chicago, Burlington & Quincy to acquire a barge loading dock on the Mississippi River at East St. Louis. Burlington on its own account constructed a "one-spot" freight-car repair center at East St. Louis and made improvements at North Kansas City. Rock Island added a new facility at St. Louis for handling piggyback business and enlarged three tunnels on its St. Louis–Kansas City line to accommodate passage of triple-deck automobile cars. The Santa Fe authorized $12 million for expansion and computerized operation of Argentine Yard in Kansas City, Kansas, and in 1965 alone ordered 111 new 2,500-horsepower diesel locomotives. Chicago Great Western took delivery of seventeen new diesel locomotives along with a fleet of state-of-the-art boxcars. Katy

FIGURE 4.27. The *Texas Special* was an innovative joint operation by Frisco and Katy to take advantage of a combination of tracks that provided the shortest route between St. Louis and Texas. Schwantes-Greever-Nolan Collection.

A Fluid State 163

ordered twelve new locomotives as well as rolling stock in the form of hoppers, covered hoppers, gondolas, bulkhead flat cars, and boxcars.[49]

The year 1967 proved especially difficult for the country's railroads. Chicago Great Western's load count was down by twenty thousand cars from 1966, a slide of nearly 10 percent and representative of the rail industry at large. Reduced billings reflected a slump in the national economy but also served to point up the need for public policy that finally recognized inequitable governmental posture toward various modes of transportation. President John F. Kennedy had been sympathetic to change, but his successor, Lyndon B. Johnson, was rather more focused on his Great Society programs and became fully ensnared by the woes created by the Vietnam War. Still, at least some politicians recognized that railroads needed a fairer shake.[50]

*   *   *

Merger was one area that railroad managers and public policymakers grudgingly conceded as appropriate medicine, but the process nearly always proved slow and painful. The merger movement—as much a part of the railroad mosaic as locomotives and cars, rail and ties—gained momentum during the 1960s, though the path forward was uneven. Illinois Central sought control of the Chicago & Eastern Illinois and failed; Frisco and Southern studied each other to no avail, as did Chicago Great Western and Soo Line. Southern Pacific's Cotton Belt missed a golden opportunity to gain the Chicago gateway by acquiring the Chicago & Eastern Illinois only to see rival Missouri Pacific join with Louisville & Nashville to acquire that carrier and then divide its operations and plant between them. With the passage of time, the merger movement gained additional momentum. In 1960, Erie combined with Delaware, Lackawanna & Western to form Erie Lackawanna. During the following year, Canadian Pacific placed three of its American corporate flags under the Soo Line banner, while in 1963 Chesapeake & Ohio gained control of Baltimore & Ohio. Norfolk & Western moved boldly in 1964 to merge Nickel Plate, lease Wabash and Pittsburgh & West Virginia, and gain control over Akron, Canton & Youngstown. Seaboard Coast Line resulted from the merger of Atlantic Coast Line and Seaboard Air Line in 1967, and a year later, closer at hand, Chicago & North Western gathered in midsized Chicago Great Western. But the big news in 1968 was the combination in the East of the archrivals New York Central and Pennsylvania to form Penn Central, which, in turn, expanded that same year with the addition of the New York, New Haven & Hartford. No decision, however, was immediately forthcoming on the combination of Burlington with Great Northern, Northern Pacific, and others to form

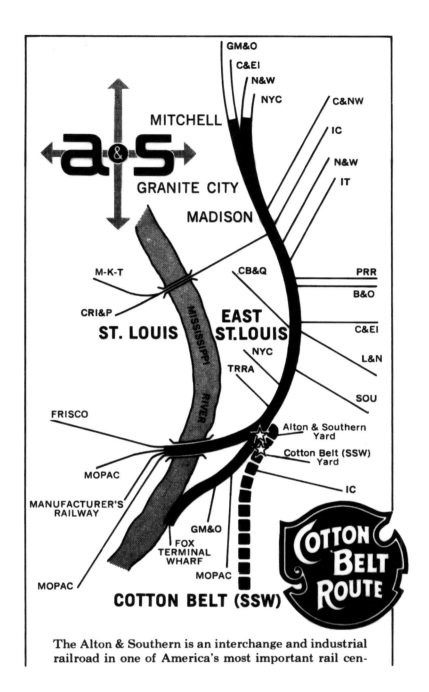

FIGURE 4.28. Cotton Belt was delighted to take an ownership stake in Alton & Southern. Don L. Hofsommer Collection.

what became Burlington Northern. The matter still rattled through the federal bureaucratic labyrinth and sluggish courts.[51]

Although it did not resonate greatly on the national scene, a rough-and-tumble contest to acquire the Alton & Southern captivated attention in the St. Louis area. This local carrier handled about 35 percent of all traffic passing through the city and even looked to increase that

A Fluid State   165

FIGURE 4.29.
Missouri Pacific's Redball "hotshot" number 76 featured four diesel units towing no fewer than 160 cars at Jedburgh, Missouri, on August 14, 1963. Acquisition of Missouri's oldest railroad by Union Pacific in 1997 dramatically altered the state's rail landscape. Steve Patterson photograph.

volume with the inauguration of its new electronic St. Louis Gateway Yard lying adjacent to Cotton Belt's tiny Valley Junction facility. When St. Louis Southwestern offered to buy the Alton & Southern late in 1965, it excited active opposition from Terminal Railroad of St. Louis and a counteroffer from Missouri Pacific as well as interest from both Illinois Central and Chicago & North Western. Out of a curious set of circumstances, ownership of Alton & Southern passed to Missouri Pacific and Chicago & North Western, but then the Chicago road lost interest and Cotton Belt purchased its one-half interest. The deal would not be effective until August 1, 1973.[52]

Authority for all of this resided with the Interstate Commerce Commission, which had shown in the Alton & Southern matter no particular talent. But compared with its handling of the campaign of Southern Pacific and Union Pacific to acquire Rock Island, the Interstate Commerce Commission in the Alton & Southern case looked brilliant. Southern Pacific's interest dated from 1962, and eventually it and the Union Pacific agreed that if permitted, they would essentially divide the financially ailing Rock Island, with Southern Pacific slicing off the railroad's southern portion (including the Kansas City gateway) and Union Pacific the northern (including both the Chicago and St. Louis

FIGURE 4.30. Firemen assigned to diesel locomotives seemed "an expensive antique." Missouri Pacific's daily local drifts into the siding at Delta, Missouri, to clear Cotton Belt's St. Louis raceway on July 3, 1963. Steve Patterson photograph.

gateways). Papers were filed with the Interstate Commerce Commission in September 1964. Regulators dawdled; the Rock Island atrophied; regulators dawdled; the Rock Island atrophied. The 1960s would be exhausted with no decision forthcoming from the ossified federal regulatory agency.[53]

What was the future of the American railroad industry? Did it have a future? Only the most sanguine observer could be optimistic. Investors increasingly threw up their hands in despair and concluded that railroads would never again be profitable buys. Small wonder that rail shareholders supported moves to diversify with the creation of holding companies. Illinois Central Industries served as an example, its articles of incorporation stating it was incorporated "as a corporate vehicle for diversification. It is contemplated that this company will become the parent of Illinois Central Railroad and will acquire other enterprises in an effort to provide a broader earnings base and to develop additional sources of income"—adding that "we continue to believe in the future of the railroad business, and particularly in the future of the Illinois Central." But that claim sounded more than defensive. Diversification at Illinois Central Industries accelerated dramatically. That company's annual report for 1968 contained enthusiastic recitations regarding its collective holdings—Abex, Fluid Control, Industrial Hydraulics, Friction Control, Wear Control Products, Waukesha Foundry, Chandeysson Electric, and—oh, yes—Illinois Central Railroad, last in line, as if a footnote. Santa Fe, Union Pacific, Katy, and Chicago & North Western hastened to join the holding company ranks. In 1968 Northwest Industries extolled its diverse collection of entries—Michigan Chemical, Velsicol Chemicals, Acme Boot, Fruit of the Loom, Union Underwear, Lone Star Steel, and Universal Manufacturing, with the Chicago & North Western railroad dead last in the listings. "The establishment of Northwest Industries, Incorporated, as a major company in today's economy is unmistakable," enthused its president, and, as if to underscore that point, he proposed a three-for-one stock split. Shareholders were delighted.[54]

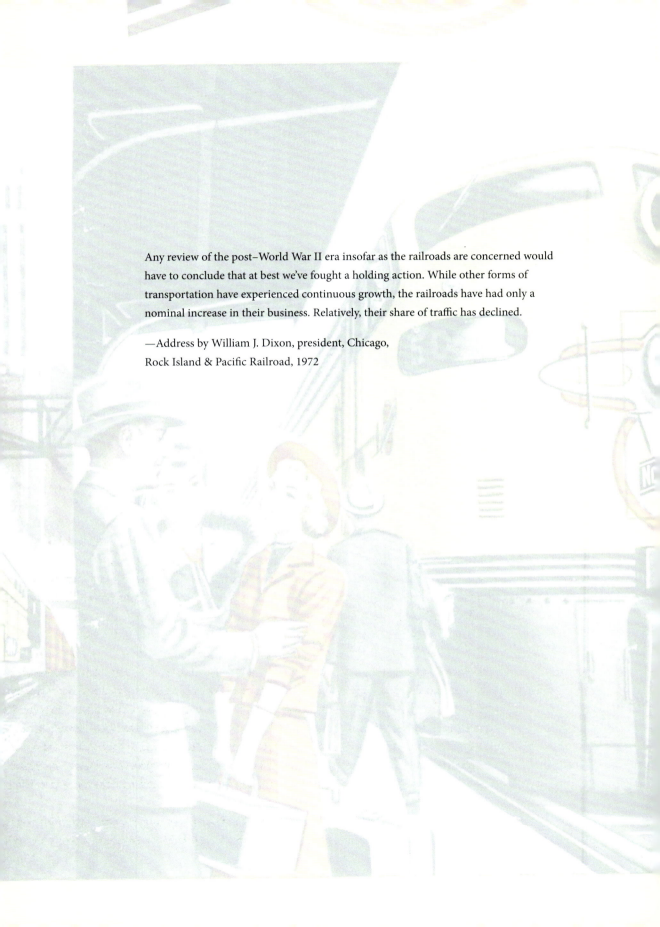

Any review of the post–World War II era insofar as the railroads are concerned would have to conclude that at best we've fought a holding action. While other forms of transportation have experienced continuous growth, the railroads have had only a nominal increase in their business. Relatively, their share of traffic has declined.

—Address by William J. Dixon, president, Chicago,
Rock Island & Pacific Railroad, 1972

5

Debilitated and Downsized

Railroad watchers, securities analysts, and investors were patently nervous as the 1970s dawned. Several landmark events wholly unthinkable just a few years earlier gave them reason to feel apprehensive about the state of American railroads.

Chicago & North Western recorded a dramatic earnings turnaround from a pretax loss of nearly $15 million in 1969 to pretax earnings of over $2 million a year later, but owners nevertheless determined to shed themselves of rail assets and focus Northwest Industries on various other holdings. In a transaction completed in 1972, North Western managers created an employee-owned company to acquire the rail properties. The Milwaukee Road in 1970 experienced the highest level of operating revenue in its history and tallied more revenue ton miles than in any year since 1945, but rail operations produced a depressing net loss of $8.9 million. Illinois Central, too, rolled up record operating revenues, yet its net operating income before taxes was a disheartening half-million dollars less than in 1969.[1]

Several major roads across the United States, including some of the largest rail carriers in the Midwest, struggled with problems of liquidity. A major crisis occurred during the summer of 1970 when Penn Central—barely two years old—went bankrupt. The railroad's unthinkable downfall ranked as the biggest business failure in American history to that time. Small wonder that its collapse sent a violent shudder through the entire industry and beyond. "Even though we are many different companies," explained Southern Pacific's chief executive, "we are also an integrated rail system. The failure or disability of any part of this system affects the health of the whole."[2]

Southern Pacific hoped to protect its own health and advance vitality of the industry by taking a stake in the Chicago, Rock Island & Pacific

FIGURE 5.1. Chicago & North Western 1957 timetable cover. For the most part, the tracks of the Chicago & North Western managed to avoid Missouri until it acquired Chicago Great Western, but its fate was inexorably tied to the state's rail carriers, and together they endured the stomach-churning financial roller-coaster ride that began in the late 1950s. Schwantes-Greever-Nolan Collection.

and hoped, with Union Pacific, to acquire and divide the venerable property. Time was of the essence, but regulators at the Interstate Commerce Commission only continued to dawdle, even as Rock Island's infrastructure and operations visibly deteriorated.

Rock Island had ranked twenty-seventh (in annual revenues) among all American transportation companies as recently as 1968. The railroad anticipated 156,000 more carloads of business in 1969 than in 1968, yet it sustained net losses of $9.3 million in 1969 and nearly twice that amount, or $16.7 million, in 1970. Rock Island was bleeding to death. "Only massive infusions of cash which Union Pacific stands committed to advance—once the merger is approved—will save Rock Island and enable it to become a viable unit in a strong transportation system," groaned the road's Jervis Langdon. Union Pacific was, indeed, ready to spend at least $200 million to modernize portions of Rock Island (essentially everything east of Omaha and northeast of Kansas City). In July 1970, an Interstate Commerce Commission examiner made a preliminary recommendation that Rock Island be acquired by Union Pacific and that southern and southwestern segments of the road be conveyed to Southern Pacific, but several competing roads screamed "foul," and the feckless Interstate Commerce Commission retreated into its protective bureaucratic shell.[3]

Another merger proposal, also long in the works, finally matured to reality on March 2, 1970, with birth of the Burlington Northern, the nation's largest railway, with 24,398 route miles and a service area that stretched from Chicago to Puget Sound and from Montana to Texas.

FIGURE 5.2.
With the widespread discontinuance of passenger trains, St. Louis Union Station became a sleepy place. Don L. Hofsommer Collection.

Debilitated and Downsized

Who Shot Missouri's Passenger Trains?

In 1959, David P. Morgan, the esteemed editor of *Trains*, devoted the magazine's April issue to answering the question, "Who Shot the Passenger Train?" For more than a century, America's extensive network of railroad passenger trains had been a wonder to behold, but by 1959 thousands of formerly well-patronized trains appeared to be in terminal decline.*

FIGURE 5.1.1.
A Pennsylvania advertisement from the 1930s emphasized its trains offering convenient connections between Missouri and destinations farther east, a convenience that disappeared when Amtrak quit running its *National Limited*. Schwantes-Greever-Nolan Collection.

True, many plug locals had been dumpy and slow, featuring weatherbeaten hand-me-down coaches, but they did provide reliable daily connections to the outside world for thousands of rural communities across the United States that today have no commercial transportation of any type. As for the posh and speedy "limiteds" and "expresses" with lengthy consists that included Pullman sleepers with comfortable beds for overnight travel, dinner in the diner, and clean and modern coaches, these were trains that inspired considerable pride both in their railroad owners and in the cities they served. What could be finer than travel aboard the *Super Chief* of the Atchison, Topeka & Santa Fe as it glided across the landscape of northern Missouri on its daily journey between Chicago and Los Angeles or the Missouri Pacific's *Colorado Eagle* with its daily sprint between the Mississippi River at St. Louis and the Rocky Mountains at Denver?

Today, if a resident of the St. Louis area wishes to travel to Indianapolis, for example, one option is to drive Interstate 70, which inevitably entails running the

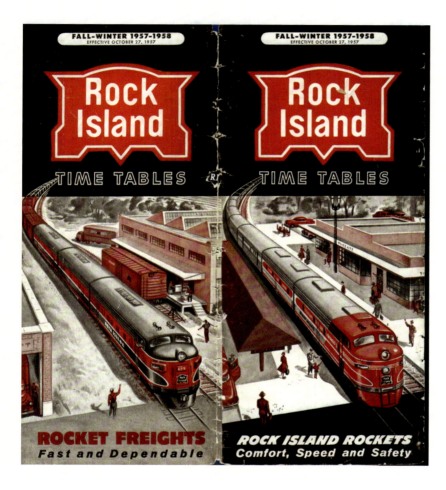

FIGURE 5.1.2. Rock Island 1957 timetable cover. Judging from the impressive artwork featured on a timetable the railroad issued in 1957, the Rock Island was still a mighty fine line. Schwantes-Greever-Nolan Collection.

gauntlet created by an annoying sequence of construction zones and their attendant bottlenecks and slow going. Another all-too-frequent annoyance is encountering wall-to-wall semitrucks, blockades that regularly occur when one eighteen-wheeler pulls out to pass another one traveling only slightly slower, and together they plug both lanes and slow Interstate 70 traffic for miles. The other main travel option is to fly, but Southwest flights require passengers to head west from St. Louis to Kansas City, where they connect to flights that head east to Indianapolis. The odd arrangement no doubt makes sense to the airline, but it is a time-wasting discombobulation for travelers.†

FIGURE 5.1.3.
How far is an hour? This advertisement appeared in the late 1940s and suggested the spatial challenge that America's passenger railroads sought to overcome during the late 1950s and 1960s. The largest railroads continued to advertise for passengers, but an increasing number of former rail passengers favored air travel to reach their destinations. Schwantes-Greever-Nolan Collection.

How FAR is an hour?

How civilized it was in earlier days to board one of the streamlined trains operated by the New York Central System or Pennsylvania Railroad, competitors between St. Louis and Indianapolis, and enjoy the onboard amenities while rumbling over the Mississippi River and then whizzing across the rural landscape of Illinois and Indiana. The creation of Amtrak in 1971 preserved a skeletal network of passenger trains, including the *National Limited,* which for a few years continued to link St. Louis and Indianapolis on its daily dawdle between New York and Kansas City, but some stretches of track had deteriorated to the point of danger, and Amtrak quit running the road-weary train in 1979.

Into Burlington Northern went Great Northern and Northern Pacific along with nearly wholly owned Spokane, Portland & Seattle and Chicago, Burlington & Quincy. During its first year, 1970, Burlington Northern moved more grain than the combined total of its antecedent roads in any previous year, and coal volumes rose by over 50 percent compared to 1969. Some of these coal billings reflected low-sulfur fuel from awakening fields in Wyoming and Montana.[4]

Burlington Northern reported success in "fitting together the managerial, operational, and financial components of the constituent companies

So, who or what shot Missouri's passenger trains? The state's largest railroads spent millions of dollars to upgrade passenger equipment and service during the late 1940s and into the early 1950s, and so the Chicago, Rock Island & Pacific, Missouri Pacific, and like-minded carriers were originally very optimistic about the future of long-distance rail travel. What dashed their expectations?

First, air travel grew much more popular after the end of World War II in 1945, and the number of travelers by air would surpass those by long-distance trains during the mid-1950s and continue to climb. At the same time, President Dwight D. Eisenhower signed federal legislation that in 1956 launched the construction of the Interstate Highway System, which in coming years would crisscross the United States and offer an alternative to travel by train. Commercial users of America's limited-access superhighway system, notably intercity truck and bus operators, gained the advantage of speed and convenience, but the greatest gainers were the ever-growing legions of private motorists, who eschewed intercity public transportation and took to the open road in their own Fords, Dodges, and Cadillacs. On August 2, 1956, less than six weeks after President Eisenhower signed the Federal-Aid Highway Act into law, Missouri was the first in the United States to award contracts for construction, one of which funded the initial miles of the Mark Twain Expressway, Interstate 70, in St. Charles County outside St. Louis.‡

All but a handful of the nation's finest passenger trains seemed to be sliding downhill toward oblivion during the 1960s, and with the removal of the US mail from the railroads in 1967, the pace of abandonment quickened, because without the mail subsidy the number of trains that bled red ink increased dramatically. Railroads raced to end the money-losers just as soon as regulators allowed. Trimming and pruning continued until the coming of Amtrak in May 1971.§

---

* *Trains*, April 1959, 14–47 passim.

† For more information on this topic, see Carlos Arnaldo Schwantes, *Going Places: Transportation Redefines the Twentieth-Century West* (Bloomington: Indiana University Press, 2003).

‡ Phil Patton, *Open Road: A Celebration of the American Highway* (New York: Simon & Schuster, 1986); Earl Swift, *The Big Roads: The Untold Story of the Engineers, Visionaries, and Trailblazers Who Created the American Superhighways* (Boston: Houghton Mifflin Harcourt, 2011).

§ Geoffrey H. Doughty, Jeffrey T. Darbee, and Eugene E. Harmon, *Amtrak, America's Railroad: Transportation's Orphan and Its Struggle for Survival* (Bloomington: Indiana University Press, 2021).

---

into a smooth functioning entity." That was in stark contrast to the Penn Central debacle in the East, and Burlington Northern's relatively healthy balance sheet stood in sharp contrast to those of the Rock Island and several other railroads large and small. Burlington Northern notwithstanding, the industry needed help, and it needed to help itself. Rivalries and egos were put aside, and in 1969, the board of directors of the Association of American Railroads created a study group called "America's Sound Transportation Review Organization" (ASTRO), which urged a new approach to rail passenger service. That recommendation resulted in congressional passage of the Rail Passenger Act of 1970, a measure signed into law by President Richard M. Nixon on October 30, 1970. The legislation called for a National Railroad Passenger Corporation, a quasi-governmental agency initially called Railpax and later known as Amtrak, to provide essential intercity rail passenger service starting May 1, 1971.[5]

*   *   *

By early 1971 only ghostly remnants of the American passenger train's belle epoque remained. Gone in the East was the famous *Twentieth Century Limited*; gone in the West was the equally famous *California Zephyr*. But a few stars remained, among them Santa Fe's *Super Chief* ("Super: now there's a prefix for you," exclaimed *Train's* editor David P. Morgan), which still sped across northern Missouri. Indeed, Santa Fe carded eight trains daily through Marceline—*Super Chief/El Capitan, San Francisco Chief, Texas Chief*, and *Grand Canyon*—each one spiffy in Santa Fe's admirable tradition. Missouri Pacific was down to twin turns on the St. Louis–Kansas City circuit and one turn from St. Louis to Texarkana (coaches and grill car only). Union Pacific scheduled two trains west from Kansas City to Denver and beyond, and Santa Fe sent one train daily southwest to Tulsa. Gulf, Mobile & Ohio boasted three daily trains between Chicago and St. Louis (*Abraham Lincoln, Limited*, and *Midnight*—sans sleeper); Louisville & Nashville was down to a coaches-only train to serve St. Louis entry, as was Baltimore & Ohio. Penn Central ran an unnamed rattler to Pittsburgh and a train named the *Spirit of St. Louis* between St. Louis and New York City, though it was a one dirty coach remnant of the luxurious all-Pullman train of the early 1950s. Norfolk & Western continued the *Wabash Cannonball* tradition in St. Louis service, while Burlington Northern ran a Kansas City–Omaha turn, the sole survivor of the many splendid passenger trains formerly operated by Chicago, Burlington & Quincy and St. Louis–San Francisco.[6]

Amtrak as agreed to by the Nixon administration was meant not only to save a remnant of America's intercity passenger train service but also, and perhaps more importantly, to save the bankrupt Penn Central by lifting its unmanageable burden of passenger service. Penn Central and other participating railroads were required to pay Amtrak, over a three-year period, a total amount equal to the lesser of (1) 50 percent of a railroad's fully distributed passenger deficit for 1969 or (2) 100 percent of the avoidable loss, as determined by Interstate Commerce Commission regulators, of a passenger railroad in 1969 or (3) 200 percent of the avoidable loss for 1969 over routes within the basic Amtrak system. Railroads could pay cash, or they could transfer their rail passenger

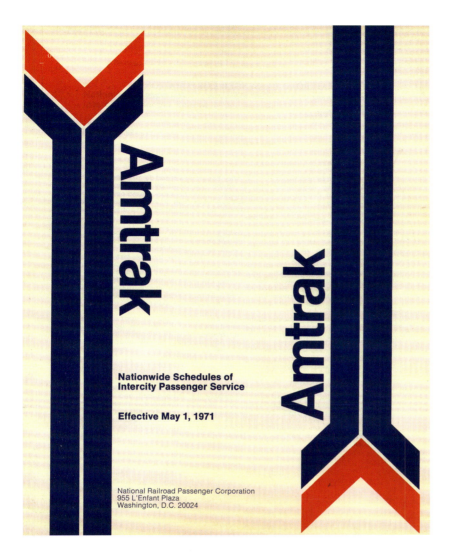

FIGURE 5.3.
Amtrak's first nationwide timetable cover dates from May 1, 1971, the day it began operating a remnant of the once-extensive network of passenger trains that crisscrossed the United States. The slim document, which required only a few pages to list all long-distance trains that continued to operate across the nation, provided a poignant contrast to the fat monthly volumes of the *Official Guide of the Railways* that in the late 1920s required more than a thousand pages to do the same. Schwantes-Greever-Nolan Collection.

equipment to Amtrak. Its planners cobbled together a national network that for Missouri included only a smattering of routes: for Santa Fe, Chicago–Los Angeles and Chicago–Houston, one train set each; for Gulf, Mobile & Ohio, Chicago–St. Louis, two round trips daily; and for Penn Central–Missouri Pacific, New York/Washington–St. Louis–Kansas City, one daily. The end came for all others on April 30, 1971. Some long-distance trains did not reach terminals until May 1 or May 2, but on May 1 Amtrak was responsible for starts over its highly abbreviated national system, which some doomsayers believed was the last gasp of America's intercity passenger trains and which, they further predicted, would follow the stagecoach into the dustbin of history.[7]

The creation of Amtrak hardly ended railroad problems, sad to say. Not surprisingly, then, diversification under broad authority given holding companies gained momentum—urged on by investors and analysts who saw little if any positive future for rails. In 1970, Union

Pacific Corporation significantly expanded its existing oil, natural gas, and pipeline operations by acquiring Champlin Petroleum Company, which held refineries as well as 1,250 Champlin-brand service stations in fifteen states throughout mid-America. Union Pacific Corporation's aggressive move in acquiring Champlin came despite the fact that, on a comparative basis, its railroad was doing well—with the longest average hauls of any American railroad, with an operating ratio that hovered around 75.0, and with income from operations that had risen nicely during the 1960s and continued to do so into the following decade. Elsewhere, revenue ton miles at the Milwaukee Road in 1972 posted a heartening gain of 7 percent over the year earlier, but the railroad in 1972 became a subsidiary of Chicago Milwaukee Corporation, which predictably announced plans for diversification. The mood at Burlington Northern was mixed. The net operating income from Burlington Northern's nontransportation businesses represented nearly 50 percent, and chief operating officer Robert W. Downing expressed disappointment "over the lack of growth in net transportation operating income," which, he noted, had "remained static over the past three years."[8]

The startling collapse of Penn Central and the rapidly failing rail network in the Northeast riveted public attention. Penn Central's track conditions deteriorated, service levels fell, and labor unrest in 1973 led to a strike. Investors talked openly of liquidation, and politicians discussed nationalization. Penn Central would not survive. But Penn Central's service area was characterized by several densely populated regions and numerous significant pockets of heavy industry requiring reliable rail service. And, of course, Penn Central and the other bankrupt roads in the Northeast represented a cancer that might, if left unchecked, eventually bring down the railroads of Missouri, if not the entire American rail industry. A reluctant Congress finally moved, ordering the Department of Transportation to study problems in the Northeast and to recommend plans for restructuring the industry there. The result was the Regional Rail Restructuring Act of 1973 (3R Act), which established the United States Railway Association to plan and launch a Consolidated Rail Corporation (Conrail). The United States Railway Association would do more than decide the fate of Penn Central, however. In the end, it added all bankrupt railroads in the East (except Ann Arbor and Boston & Maine) to Conrail—itself a monumental federally sponsored rail carrier that when born on April 1, 1976, united public and private interests. Before that, however, planners boldly proclaimed that Conrail was not to serve as a catch-all for every line of its predecessor companies. Rather, Conrail would be a much slimmer model—shorn of many unremunerative branches and even a few main routes. It would, to be sure, result in dislocation and pain for some customers, and it would very clearly restructure rail operations across a broad expanse of the United States from New York, Boston, and Washington west to Detroit, Chicago, and St. Louis.[9]

Back in the Heartland, Rock Island focused on movement of export grain from "landlocked" northwest Iowa, initiating fifty-four-car rates on corn and soybeans conveyed in "jumbo" covered hopper cars destined for Gulf tidewater at Houston—using Rock Island tracks all the way. "Unit train" movements expedited lading, greatly increased car utilization, and proved profitable for the rail carrier and its customers alike. The new Rock Island arrangement required economy of scale for trackside elevators, demanded concentration of shipping at specific locations, put at risk small independent and cooperative operators, and subjected Rock Island's weary track structure to considerable pounding by strings of hopper cars heavily laden with tons of corn and soybeans. Nonetheless, the concept proved popular and quickly grew in size. In 1972 Rock Island moved slightly more than one hundred unit trains across Missouri to the Gulf Coast and approximately two hundred trains in 1973. *Modern Railroads* was so impressed by Rock Island's energetic marketing campaign that in 1972 the trade journal awarded the railroad second place in its "Golden Freight Car" competition.[10]

Other roads took note. Motivated in part by export demand from the Soviet Union in 1972, North Western, Norfolk & Western, Illinois Central, and Burlington Northern joined the unit train movement. North Western, with limited long-haul opportunity, nevertheless opened fifty-car rates to the Gulf for shippers in 1972. Norfolk & Western moved 282 hundred-car grain trains in 1973, up by nearly 70 percent over the year earlier. Norfolk & Western also authorized rates to the Gulf in fifty-car lots via its connections at St. Louis. Illinois Central Gulf (created by the merger of Illinois Central and Gulf, Mobile & Ohio in 1972) eventually sponsored several options. Its "Rent-a-Train" concept allowed a shipper sole use of a 115-car train to haul agricultural commodities, "Mini-Train" was designed to compete with trucks by hauling grain short distances, and "Country Grain Train" provided trainload movement from a single assembly point to a single destination. Burlington Northern, with line haul outlets to the Gulf as well as Puget Sound on the Pacific Ocean, nevertheless was slow in this regard—in part because the railroad was preoccupied with development of its coal business from mines in Montana and Wyoming and in building up its main coal-hauling routes.[11]

Burlington Northern was indeed engaged in a vast and very expensive campaign to upgrade segments of its huge system for the purpose of handling a growing demand for low-sulfur coal—a campaign viewed with considerable skepticism by those who argued that the railroad industry had seen its best days. But Burlington Northern management and its board of directors persisted, and by 1979 the company had invested $2.4 billion in new rail equipment and upgraded roadway since its merger in 1970. Management was dry-eyed, saying, "We view the future with optimism but not without a degree of uncertainty." The franchise was sound, offering shippers, for example, single-line service from the Pacific Northwest all the way to its Chicago, Kansas City, and St. Louis gateways. Plus, there was the promise of increased revenue from coal billings. In 1970, Burlington Northern handled three million tons of coal and operated an average of one unit train weekly. By the end of 1975, it dispatched an average of eleven unit trains daily—many of them destined for customers in Missouri or passing through the state on

FIGURE 5.4. Missouri Pacific early saluted the growing popularity of intermodal traffic. Schwantes-Greever-Nolan Collection.

their way to more distant destinations. By 1977 coal traffic accounted for nearly one-quarter of Burlington Northern's total gross freight revenue.[12]

There were additional bright spots in the traffic mix of Missouri railroads. Frisco received auto parts for the Chrysler plant at Valley Park, near St. Louis, and hauled setup automobiles to Irving, Texas, near Dallas, and to Floydada on its subsidiary Quanah, Acme & Pacific in West Texas. Vigorous solicitation resulted in Frisco also receiving billings from General Motors, American Motors, and International Harvester. Burlington Northern added capacity at Kansas City to accommodate a growing volume of motor vehicle imports from Asia and delivered to the West Coast cities of Portland and Seattle, which provided the company with long hauls and handsome revenue. Frisco took pleasure in announcing that St. Joe Minerals Corporation would open a mine and a mill on its line at Brushy Creek, that Conagra would locate a large pet-food-processing mill at Rolla, and that new electrical generating plants would go online at Springfield and at Rush Island. Rock Island noted that its piggyback business in 1972 had increased by 10 percent over the previous year, and Santa Fe in 1973 recorded nearly 14 percent growth of its trailer-on-flatcar traffic over 1972. Burlington Northern was happy, too, with the 1970s growth of its trailer-on-flatcar and container-on-flatcar business. Union Pacific installed a piggyback ramp at St. Joseph, and Norfolk & Western added them at Columbia, Moberly, Kansas City, and St. Louis.[13]

*   *   *

There were, of course, changes in patterns of traditional traffic for Missouri railroads. Over the years they had hauled a seemingly endless number of cattle, hogs, and sheep to Chicago, where Nelson Morris, Philip D. Armour, Gustavus F. Swift, A. A. Libby, and John Cudahy emerged as titans of meatpacking. Other livestock headed for the slaughterhouses of Kansas City. Before World War I, a negligible volume of livestock had traveled by truck, but by 1930 they hauled approximately 30 percent. Just prior to World War II, trucks hauled 63 percent, and immediately following the war that figure increased to nearly 70 percent. The decline in shipment of fresh and cured meat, tallow, and hides from Armour, Cudahy, Swift, Wilson, and other area Kansas City packers was not as rapid or as dramatic as for Chicago, but change came to the meat industry as a result of gradual decentralization. One by one the big Chicago packers shut down during the 1950s and into the next decade. The same was true at Sioux City, Omaha, Fort Worth, and Kansas City, where stockyards and giant packing houses fell silent, and that meant the loss of significant business for Missouri railroads.[14]

FIGURE 5.5.
The movement of cattle by rail, long a staple traffic from trackside pens to packers at Kansas City, St. Joseph, St. Louis, and East St. Louis, disappeared as great packing companies decentralized and packing plants such as those at Kansas City closed. Don L. Hofsommer Collection.

The grain business likewise underwent great change. Part of this reflected a pronounced shift from feeding cattle in the Corn Belt to locations in the Southwest. The result was the need to move corn in large billings and often by unit trains to giant feedlots such as those in Hereford, Texas. Another significant shift was the increased tonnage of Midwestern grain headed to Texas Gulf ports for export, which favored Missouri railroads with tracks running south or southwest. Chicago & North Western, serving as it did much of corn-rich Iowa, delivered a steady stream of corn to the Santa Fe, Frisco, Katy, and Kansas City Southern. In this instance, Rock Island had the advantage of single-line haulage all the way from Iowa to Gulf Coast ports. Still another change involved wheat and flour milling. St. Louis and later Kansas City were important grain markets and milling centers benefiting especially Santa Fe, Missouri Pacific, Union Pacific, and Rock Island—all of which had important lines extending into the great Kansas wheat belt. Not surprisingly, much of Kansas production found its way eastward for value adding at Missouri mills—Kansas Flour Mills Company of Kansas City and Aunt Jemima Mills of St. Joseph, for example. But the business of grain milling, like meatpacking, was decentralized, with the shuttering of great processing facilities and much Midwest wheat headed for export.[15]

* * *

American Refrigerator Transit

American Refrigerator Transit was born in 1881, a Jay Gould enterprise intended to meet the needs of shippers served by his Missouri Pacific and Wabash lines. Beer, meat, butter, and eggs billed from Wabash stations moved to Texas destinations, for example, and the St. Louis Produce Company routinely dispatched "roller cars" (billed in transit) to customers on Wabash lines. Later on, Colorado peaches shipped from Grand Junction and potatoes from the San Luis Valley moved by Denver & Rio Grande Western to Pueblo and then over Missouri Pacific tracks to destinations farther east, fresh vegetables of all sorts traveled to market from fields in the Rio Grande Valley of Texas via Missouri Pacific, and peaches and strawberries from Missouri Pacific stations in Arkansas sought customers in St. Louis and other markets. American Refrigerator Transit likewise met the needs of the smaller meatpackers (Royal Packing, St. Louis; Seitz Packing, St. Joseph; Central Packing, Kansas City) as well as Goodwin Poultry & Eggs at Jackson, Missouri. The company had cold-storage facilities at Kansas City and St. Louis and en-route icing facilities at various locations, and in the 1930s it erected a car shop at St. Louis to service the needs of its 12,200-car fleet. Offices were located in the Missouri Pacific Building in St. Louis.*

---

* Stuart T. Maher, G. J. Michels Jr., and Gene Semon, *American Refrigerator Transit* (Berkeley: Signature, 2017); John H. White, *The Great Yellow Fleet: A History of American Railroad Refrigerator Cars* (San Marino: Golden West Books, 1986.

FIGURE 5.2.1. Prior to mechanical refrigeration, men needed to add ice to cars along the way to their destinations. Don L. Hofsommer Collection.

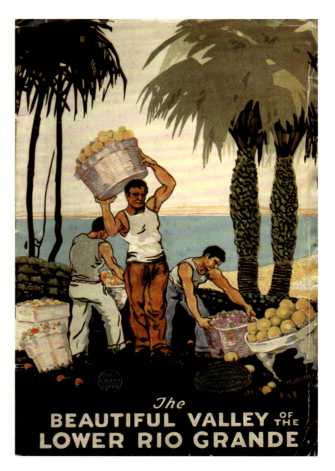

FIGURE 5.2.2. Gulf Coast Lines, a Texas component of the Missouri Pacific empire, issued this brochure to salute its role in transporting food grown in the Rio Grande Valley to the dinner tables of America. Schwantes-Greever-Nolan Collection.

FIGURE 5.6.
Shipment of grain in boxcars came to an end when consignees demand receipt of covered hopper cars only. Don L. Hofsommer Collection.

Freight trains rarely garner headlines, but Santa Fe in 1968 boldly defied that tradition with introduction of its *Super C* handling containers and trailers only on a 34.5-hour sprint from Chicago to Los Angeles. The speedy train with its premium rates did not attract the traffic volume Santa Fe expected, but it certainly showcased the railroad's marvelous steel highway and its devotion to intermodal business. Santa Fe also joined with Frisco and Seaboard Coast Line to inaugurate daily expedited transcontinental freight service between Richmond, Virginia, and Richmond, California, with four-day transit times. On August 1, 1973, Santa Fe and Frisco announced they would reconfigure their run-through arrangement to hand off trains at Avard, Oklahoma, instead of Floydada, Texas—"improving service," they insisted, "between Southeast and California points." For its part, Burlington Northern began new through service between Minneapolis–St. Paul and Kansas City and from St. Louis to the Pacific Northwest. Norfolk & Western joined with Santa Fe to institute *Supercharger* freight service between Detroit and Kansas City, where lading could be switched to Santa Fe trains for various West Coast or Texas destinations. Frisco put forward an important new wrinkle by agreeing with operating crafts to make interdivisional runs from Springfield, Missouri, to Tulsa, which saved the need to change train crews at an intermediate terminal.[16]

Capital, as always, was expensive, and managers had to make exacting cases that skittish boards of directors might or might not accept. Santa Fe found funds adequate to further modernize its already impressive Kansas City yard at Argentine, as did Frisco for its yard facility at Springfield. Additionally, Frisco invested in a sophisticated microwave system with towers such as that at Valley Park and plowed money into centralized traffic control (1,377 miles systemwide by 1978). Burlington Northern in 1977 took delivery of 650 additional covered hoppers, 500 open-top hoppers, and 123 "high-horsepower" locomotives and expanded its intermodal facility at Kansas City.[17]

* * *

Just as it was essential to invest in property for the purpose of maintaining stability or gaining competitive advantage, so, too, was it essential to cut costs when justified or even to eliminate traditional operations. Steely-eyed accountants saw that dollars could be saved by closing the many "open agency" stations strung out along railroads throughout Missouri. Absent passenger trains, with the decline and then demise of the express service and less-than-carload freight business, with increased use of radio for communication, and in some cases with implementation of centralized traffic control for the movement of trains, open stations manned by agents and/or telegraph operators served little purpose. Every carrier moved to close stations and reap the savings. Frisco, with 1,278 route miles in Missouri, sought to ease the pain of this historic transition by implementing what it labeled a Central Agency Plan whereby one employee in van served several communities. Other roads implemented similar plans. Another way to reduce the operating ratio was simply to take out track and thus reduce maintenance and all related expenses—in other words, to abandon line segments. The intricate web of branches and feeders that Chicago, Burlington & Quincy had spiked into place across southern Iowa and northern Missouri, and which had benefited the railroad during the decades of near monopoly, had become a distinct liability during the new age of all-weather roads and fierce highway competition. The intricate web of lightly used tracks mostly vanished bit by bit over the years. Burlington itself initiated the pruning by lifting twenty-seven miles of track between Cameron Junction and Kearney, Missouri, in 1962. This was hardly an isolated instance. Katy shed its twenty-four-mile branch to Moberly in 1975, and Frisco dropped thirty-eight miles of its East Lynne–Bolivar route and four miles from Brooks Junction to the southeastern Missouri community of Vanduser in 1977. Track abandonment across the state soon followed.[18]

Doctoring a Sick Railroad

Katy was ill. William Neal Deramus III, recently of the Chicago Great Western, was summoned to medicate an ailing Missouri–Kansas–Texas in 1957. His prescription: "Cut all personnel to the lowest possible number that will still permit daily conduct of business." Employee numbers dropped from 8,000 in 1956 to 2,817 in 1960. Further medication called for minimum facilities, longer freight trains, and no frills of any type. As Deramus slashed what he regarded as unnecessary expense, employee morale sagged, track deteriorated, locomotives failed, newspapers in on-line communities voiced complaints, passengers and shippers revolted, and the St. Louis Chamber of Commerce expelled Missouri–Kansas–Texas from membership. After spending three years doctoring Katy, Deramus decamped for Kansas City Southern, where he again administered his favorite elixirs. His successor, Claude T. Williams, continued the Deramus treatment at Missouri–Kansas–Texas, but the company woes persisted.*

A new "doctor of railroads" was summoned. John W. Barriger III, who joined Katy in early 1965, said of Deramus and his brutal treatment of the railroad's ills, "He did not know the difference between hacking and pruning." The St. Louis–raised Barriger insisted that "you can't starve a railroad into success." Upon becoming Katy's newest physician, Barriger launched a paint-up, clean-up, fix-up campaign along with running additional freight trains, buying new locomotives and rolling stock, and a making diligent effort to reattract business. But he was unemotional as to Katy's passenger trains, which continued to bleed red ink until the railroad ended all of them shortly after its new leader arrived. "The green light is ON at Katy," Barriger enthused. But the green light was not on everywhere across the system, and, in fact, significant line abandonments resulted in a much-slimmed-down Missouri–Kansas–Texas that proudly maintained its independent status for many years after Barriger retired in 1970.†

---

* Don L. Hofsommer, *Katy Northwest: The Story of a Branch Line Railroad* (Boulder: Pruett, 1976), 151–53.

† John W. Barriger to Don L. Hofsommer, August 19, 1973; *Milwaukee Journal*, October 24, 1965; "The Green Light Is ON at Katy," advertising brochure; H. Roger Grant, *John W. Barriger III: Railroad Legend* (Bloomington: Indiana University Press, 2018), 152–70.

FACING, FIGURE 5.3.1. Missouri–Kansas–Texas struggled valiantly to survive as an independent, but it was not to be. Union Pacific acquired Katy in 1988. Don L. Hofsommer Collection.

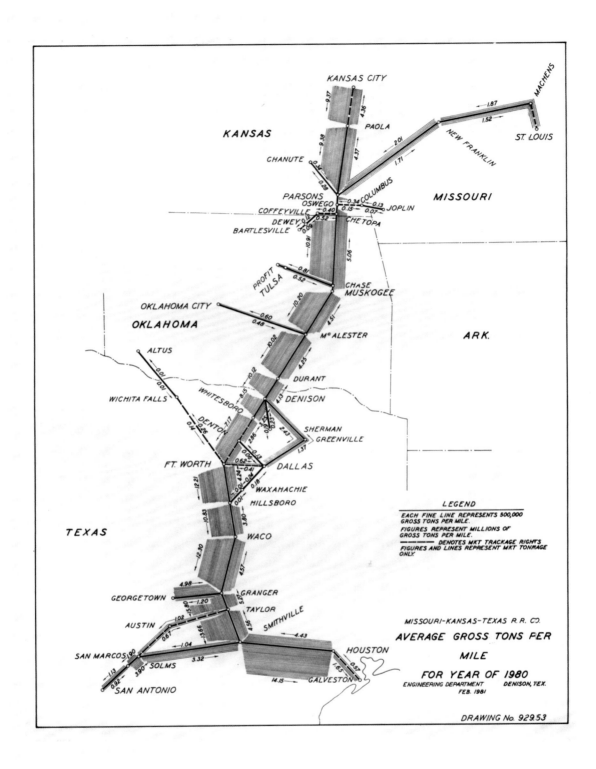

Owners and managers of some railroads—Santa Fe, Burlington Northern, and Union Pacific—were more optimistic about the industry's future than others. Illinois Central Gulf was among the pessimists. Its leaders complained that their company continued to mirror adverse conditions afflicting the entire railroad industry, which, it said, was "highly leveraged" and saddled with "high fixed costs, rapidly escalating labor and material costs"—but at the same time faced with "reduced carloadings during a recession" and unable to adjust rates rapidly enough to meet higher costs or eliminate unprofitable services.[19]

The gloomy assessment by Illinois Central Gulf managers was no doubt informed at least partially by the intransigence, or incompetence, of the Interstate Commerce Commission regulators who seemed frozen in place by the joint attempt of Southern Pacific and Union Pacific to acquire and then split the Rock Island. That case had been before the Interstate Commerce Commission since the mid-1960s and even a decade later was yet to be resolved. Finally, the ICC's administrative law judge recommended granting the Southern Pacific–Union Pacific applications but attached major conditions that included a "grand design" for restructuring the nation's rail system west of the Mississippi River. Thus, when the federal regulatory body finally on December 4, 1974, approved the merger of Rock Island into Union Pacific and concurrent purchase by the Southern Pacific of Rock Island lines south of Kansas City, the two applicants equivocated. Company officers undertook another hurried inspection of the Rock Island's infrastructure and equipment to determine the cost of rehabilitation, but the results of their assessment proved depressing: the cost in 1974 dollars for a five-year upgrade program would likely total nearly $2 billion. That sobering amount of money did not include acquisition costs, interest payments, and the like. This financial albatross caused managers of both Southern Pacific and Union Pacific to throw in the towel and end their fight to acquire the Chicago, Rock Island & Pacific.[20]

Back during the Progressive Era of the early twentieth century, President Theodore Roosevelt had advocated continuous, informed, and expert regulation of the nation's railroads that only the federal government could supposedly provide. Nonsense, argued historian Albro Martin: "An administrative body that innovates is a contradiction in terms." Martin's equally caustic but accurate assessment was that the Interstate Commerce Commission stupidly denied carriers rate increases even as Congress passed legislation restricting managerial prerogatives. The cumulative effect was capital malnourishment and a stultifying atmosphere that drove the spirit of enterprise from the railroad sector. Regulation, Martin concluded, simply failed. Why? Because the "philosophies of archaic Progressivism were applicable to problems and conditions which no longer existed . . . [and] . . . because the Commission simply did not constitute the fearless, impartial, and wise body which regulation presupposed. It was a boy on a man's errand." Alas, federal regulators remained entrapped in the mindset that rail carriers enjoyed monopoly control of American transportation. That was hardly the case.[21]

*   *   *

The year 1974 proved vexing in the extreme—national political turmoil occasioned by scandals in the Nixon administration that finally drove the president from office and an economy that skidded into crisis. Inflation topped 10 percent, auto sales dropped by 20 percent, housing starts plummeted by 40 percent, and unemployment soared above 7 percent by year's end. In sum, the United States found itself entrapped by a nettlesome combination of recession and inflation. Illinois Central Gulf, for example, experienced a whopping 92 percent escalation in fuel costs despite a nearly 10 percent decrease in fuel consumption. Consumer confidence slumped, which meant accompanying drops in industrial production and declines in new orders. The slack economy was mirrored in the nation's rail yards. Milwaukee Road reported a decline of 31 percent in operating income with freight volume down in all key commodity areas, "including major revenue-producing groups such as farm products." Milwaukee also admitted that "bond interest matters are of considerable concern to us."[22]

The collective impact of the negative variables was absolutely devastating to the Chicago, Rock Island & Pacific, which experienced substantial physical and financial deterioration during the nearly decade-long dithering by the Interstate Commerce Commission. Deferred maintenance was epidemic, derailments were routine, delays to lading were typical, equipment always was in short supply, and the railroad company was utterly without resources to do anything other than patch and repair. It hemorrhaged $43,878,967 in net losses over the four-year period 1970–1973. The railroad lacked good options. "Turning Rock Island around won't be done overnight," admitted John W. Ingram, Rock Island's latest president. But, he added, "the route structure has very good potential," and, Ingram went on, "we want to fix rather than patch." Rock Island was in desperate shape nevertheless, having lost $23,097,000 in 1974 alone. Increased rates promised a widened revenue stream, but crushing inflation more than extinguished that benefit. Expenses, particularly fuel costs, rose dramatically, and carloadings plunged by 20 percent early in 1975 to reflect the national recession. On February 14, 1975, employees were told bluntly, "The sheriff is breathing down our neck. It's time to rally round the Rock if we want it to be here next year. The barrel is empty." It was, indeed. On March 17, Rock Island had no choice but to seek reorganization and redemption under the terms of the Federal Bankruptcy Act. Judge Frank J. McGarr immediately approved its petition, appointed William M. Gibbons as trustee, and ordered continued rail operations to continue.[23]

The Rock Island was hardly alone among the struggling rail carriers that served Missouri. With a ten-thousand-mile route structure that stretched from the Ohio River through Chicago and continued west all the way to Puget Sound, the Milwaukee Road's problem was too few tons spread over too many route miles. Like Rock Island, the Milwaukee Road had once ranked among the bluest of blue-chip investments, but no more. It had courted and been courted by neighboring Chicago & North Western, had often talked marriage with others but to no avail, and had lost a bid to join giant Burlington Northern. Members of the Interstate Commerce Commission in permitting the creation of Burlington Northern in 1970 had given Milwaukee access to numerous western markets and gateways with the hope of creating competitive parity in common service areas. That possibility quickly evaporated, however, and the Milwaukee Road again sought inclusion in the Burlington Northern network. Officers of both roads quietly toured Milwaukee's primary routes, but Burlington Northern managers were appalled at the level of deferred maintenance and worried that federal regulators would drag their heels in permitting abandonment of Milwaukee lines made redundant by the merger of the two transcontinental railroads. Finally, Milwaukee's board of directors sought $50 million more than Burlington Northern was willing to pay. Talks ended. On December 19, 1977, the Chicago, Milwaukee, St. Paul & Pacific filed a voluntary petition for reorganization under the Federal Bankruptcy Act. In terms of bankrupt mileage, it now ranked with Rock Island as one of America's two most woebegone railroads.

Measured by Interstate Commerce Commission accounting standards, the Milwaukee Road bled $12.1 million in 1976 and another $36.2 million in 1977. Stanley E. G. Hillman, the court-appointed trustee, was directed to operate the company's property and, if possible, to develop a plan of financial reorganization. "I do not presently subscribe to the view, as expressed by some," insisted Hillman, "that rationalization of Midwest railroads means that those presently in reorganization must necessarily die or be dismembered and sold off." Neither did he ignore the possibility.[24]

All this malaise occurred against the backdrop of a roller-coaster national economy. When Gerald Ford succeeded Richard Nixon as president in 1974, the country was running headlong into its most severe recession since the 1930s, oddly characterized by double-digit inflation and high unemployment along with soaring energy costs. Pressure eased in 1976, but the economy thereafter grew slowly, and the years of President Jimmy Carter's administration (1977–1981) were consumed by a recurrence of rampant inflation, high unemployment, and escalating fuel costs.[25]

For the court-appointed overseers of Milwaukee Road and Rock Island fortunes (or lack thereof), there was no opportunity to bet on the future or build for a boom. Circumstances forced William Gibbons, Rock Island's court-appointed trustee, to become a compulsive traveler as he visited with shippers, community leaders, public policymakers, and the company's own employees. The railroad exhibited a measure of vitality in 1976, earned a Harriman award for safe practice in 1977, and picked up a *Modem Railroads* prize in 1978 for innovative employment of mini-trains on branch lines. But the balky grain market of 1977 again spilled red ink across company books. And there was more bad news. The largest holder of Rock Island first mortgage bonds now pressed vigorously for liquidation—to get out of business and sell off all assets. Contract agreements with the company's labor unions were up for renewal or alteration—negotiations that could prove dangerous and even fatal since Rock Island was in no condition to add dollars to its operation. In all, Gibbons's task was hardly enviable, but he soldiered on nevertheless, doing what he could with very meager resources. Newly leased locomotives were gussied up with a new paint scheme and named for friends of the company, and so forth. Primary energies were devoted to what Gibbons called Rock Island's spine, its Chicago-to-the-Gulf line. Gibbons was delighted when the Milwaukee Road agreed to

FIGURE 5.7. When it extended a line of tracks across the northwest quadrant of Missouri to link Chicago with Kansas City, the railroad was known as the Chicago, Milwaukee & St. Paul, and it was nicknamed the "St. Paul" and not "Milwaukee Road." The "Pacific" portion of its name dates from the mid-1920s and the railroad's emergence from the humiliations of bankruptcy. As this brochure cover suggests, much of its advertising saluted its electrified route west from Chicago and Minneapolis to Seattle and the North Pacific Coast. Its line to Kansas City was of secondary importance. Schwantes-Greever-Nolan Collection.

Debilitated and Downsized 193

route through trains between Milwaukee, Chicago, and Kansas City on Rock Island tracks between Muscatine, Iowa, and Polo, Missouri, a distance of 243 miles. (The Rock Island and Milwaukee Road already had joint agreements between Davenport and Muscatine and between Polo and Kansas City.) The joint arrangement enabled the Milwaukee Road to downgrade and possibly abandon its parallel route across part of Missouri, bring welcome revenue to Rock Island, and perhaps win nods of approval from government bureaucrats who favored such voluntary coordination. Other Rock Island arteries were not as viable.[26]

Milwaukee Road trustee Stanley E. G. Hillman, early in 1978, thought "that most of the system can profitably be operated by a reorganized Milwaukee Road and that a reorganization will provide the greatest benefits to all of the interests in this proceeding." The gods, celestial and federal alike, frowned. Three months later Hillman commissioned independent consultants to determine "the basis for identifying Milwaukee Road's valuable routes, and determining whether they constitute a viable system." Continuation of Milwaukee's sprawling ten-thousand-mile system was out of the question, however. Indeed, a company spokesman in July said the Milwaukee Road wanted to concentrate its "efforts in Wisconsin and Minnesota, where we are the dominant carrier, and give up parts of Iowa where we are weak." Mother Nature took a hand. The winter of 1978–79 was dreadful, burying the Midwest in snowdrifts, plugging rail lines, disrupting traffic, depriving carriers of essential sustenance, and costing fortunes to maintain open lines. By March 1979, the Milwaukee Road trustee faced the very real prospect of terminating all rail service. A month later he cautiously concluded that Milwaukee "might become economically viable within a few years" if it could concentrate its existing resources on approximately 2,400 miles of its present 9,800 miles of route. That was for openers. "Available cash," he warned, would "be exhausted in early May. . . . I am compelled to take prompt and drastic action." That entailed an embargo effective May 8, 1979, on all freight except within the Milwaukee Road's 2,400-mile viable core, furloughing employees except those absolutely necessary to run trains on the core mileage, and an Interstate Commerce Commission order directing service by other railroads over "essential portions of embargoed lines."[27]

The vise tightened. Judge Frank McGarr, overseeing Rock Island's proceedings, in September 1978 granted Trustee Gibbons a seventh six-month extension on reorganization but hinted that this one might be the last. McGarr was under tremendous pressure from creditors and even the federal Department of Justice, which argued that the railroad was incapable of reorganization and should be liquidated.[28]

Matters only worsened, if that were possible. Two unions—the United Transportation Union and the Brotherhood of Railway & Airline Clerks—agreed to all issues but one, digging in their heels on the matter of retroactive pay. The Rock Island response was that it simply could not and would not shoulder any added financial burdens. Trustee Gibbon earlier had declared that "Rock Island's future, more than ever, is based almost entirely on the will of Rock Island people to survive. If Rock Island's managers, workers, and union leaders have the will, we shall prevail." But, he warned, "if they insist on business as usual, Rock Island won't survive . . . . Rock Island people will have to save themselves if we are to be successfully reorganized."

The Brotherhood of Railway & Airline Clerks called a strike on August 28, 1979, and the United Transportation Union followed suit the next day. A UTU spokesperson contended that Rock Island's management simply wanted to dump the railroad "and turn it into junk and maybe sell some of the property to other railroads. I don't think it's a railroad that wants to stay in business." He was badly informed, confusing William Gibbons and Rock Island managers with the road's major creditors, its major bondholder, the federal government, and competing railroads, which gleefully hoped for Rock Island's demise.[29]

Public pressure mounted as operations on the strike-bound Rock Island ground to a halt. President Carter finally issued a back-to-work order and instructed the Interstate Commerce Commission to request "directed service" of Rock Island lines by another carrier or carriers. On September 26, Kansas City Terminal, owned by twelve trunk roads, was designated to accomplish this task. The federal government promised to cover Kansas City Terminal operating losses and pay it a 6 percent operating profit—a great curiosity, critics thought, given federal parsimony toward Rock Island itself. Operation with Rock Island equipment and employees began on October 5, 1979, but the restart was halting at best. A week later trains were running on about three-quarters of Rock Island lines, but at less than 20 percent of service levels prior to the strike on August 28. There seemed no glimmer of hope for either Rock Island or Milwaukee Road.[30]

For that matter, what of the entire railroad industry? At one point during these dark days, nearly 25 percent of all rail mileage in the United States was in the hands of federal bankruptcy courts. Disaster seemed on the doorstep. Nationalization—a federal takeover of the failing roads—was a matter of serious consideration by both academic analysts and several influential politicians.[31]

*　*　*

Small wonder that many observers regarded Union Station facilities at Kansas City and St. Louis as huge mausoleums entombing a categorically obsolete past and absolutely devoid of future utility—metaphors for the entire railroad industry. Only two Union Station tracks at St. Louis

FIGURE 5.8. Small wonder that many regarded St. Louis Union Station as a huge mausoleum entombing a categorically obsolete past and possessing no future utility. Only two tracks were needed by Amtrak. Pictured here is the westbound *National Limited* on July 17, 1978. Don L. Hofsommer Photo.

were required for Amtrak's needs, Harvey's fine restaurant was closed, the Western Union office stood vacant, and employees outnumbered customers within the sleepy and deteriorating edifice. As it developed, Amtrak chose to relocate from the massive building to a modest prefabricated structure—quickly dubbed "Amshack" or "St. Louis Union Trailer"—to the east on Sixteenth Street. A final Amtrak train rumbled out of Union Station on October 31, 1978. The circumstance at Kansas City was much the same, although Amtrak remained a tenant within the decaying structure. Amtrak service in Missouri was modified in 1974 when passenger trains returned to Missouri Pacific tracks that ran south from St. Louis through Arkansas to Texas. In 1979 New York–Washington–St. Louis–Kansas City service ended, but double daily passenger trains were maintained between St. Louis and Kansas City. In 1979 the former *Texas Chief* (now *Lone Star*) ran its last miles, a move that left only a handful of trains to serve Kansas City—those via Missouri between Chicago and Los Angeles and the twin cross-state connections with St. Louis.[32]

Northbound and southbound, KATY hustles the goods. In a bright red fleet of all types of cars that includes 4000 brand-new and 6000 newly repaired and rebuilt cars—with 1800 more new ones on the way or on order. Big diesels (26 of them new) get shipments there on time.

—*KATY, Fast Freight—Dependable Schedules*, a circa-1970 brochure issued by the Missouri–Kansas–Texas Railroad Company

6

Winds of Change

The unstable economy of the 1970s, which included rampant inflation, harsh competition from Japan and western European nations, and substantial federal budget deficits coupled with energy crises and political scandal, sapped American vitality and national self-assurance. The Gerald Ford administration attacked inflation by slowing the economy with tight money, but that led to the worst economic downturn since the Great Depression, with unemployment rising to 9 percent in 1975.

Several traditional mass-production industries with comparatively inefficient methods of production, relatively lax quality control, and high payroll costs stumbled badly during the competitive race with determined foreign firms. Other American multinational corporations relocated their manufacturing overseas simply to stay in business by taking advantage of lower costs and less-expensive labor. Democratic candidate Jimmy Carter assailed the Republican Ford, pointing to high inflation and high unemployment, and when elected president in 1976 he promised to fix these problems and balance the federal budget. But succeed Carter did not. By 1979, the "misery index" (the combined total of inflation and unemployment rates) had climbed to twenty-one (up from fourteen in 1976), and during the 1980 election Republican Ronald Reagan flogged the hapless Carter accordingly.[1]

A handsome man of amiable disposition, Reagan had no master plan to repair the economy or restore national confidence, but he held tightly to a simple view that the United States had been let down by a succession of national leaders overly concerned with nagging dilemmas rather than determined to promote national optimism and thereby tap into an abundance of new possibilities. Reagan's great desire was to remove the shackles of government bureaucracy and to restore the American spirit of individualism, competition, and personal pride. He emphasized market

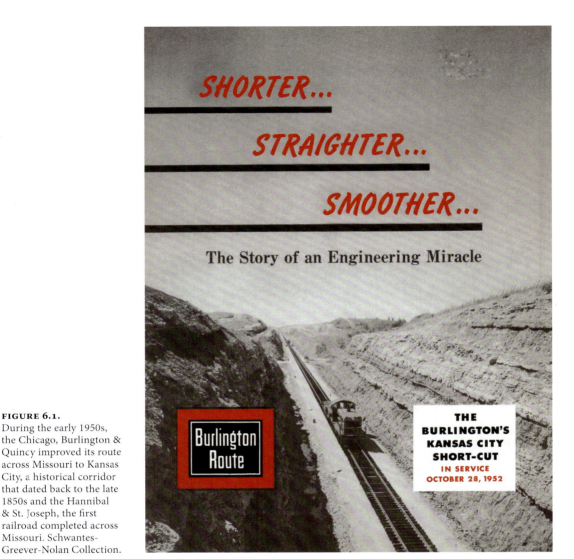

FIGURE 6.1.
During the early 1950s, the Chicago, Burlington & Quincy improved its route across Missouri to Kansas City, a historical corridor that dated back to the late 1850s and the Hannibal & St. Joseph, the first railroad completed across Missouri. Schwantes-Greever-Nolan Collection.

solutions to America's economic problems and issues. Congress passed and in 1981 Reagan signed legislation that collectively represented the largest tax reduction in the nation's history. Yet his panacea initially misfired. Inflation dropped to under 6 percent by 1983, but unemployment mushroomed to nearly 11 percent while real income continued to fall. Interest rates remained high and resulted in a strong dollar, but that resulted in a decline in exports, a flood of cheap imports, and the demise of some major American industries. Then came noticeable improvement. Unemployment in 1984 dropped to 7.5 percent, inflation moderated, the automobile industry regained its vitality, housing starts boomed, and consumer spending soared. The result was the most vibrant economy since the early 1960s—despite elevated interest rates, federal deficits that vaulted upward, escalating trade deficits, and a frightening stock market crash late in 1987.[2]

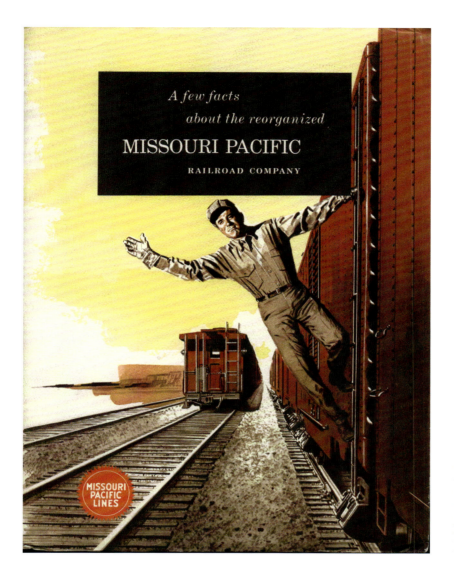

FIGURE 6.2.
Missouri Pacific issued a special brochure in 1956 to announce its emergence from a lengthy period of receivership. Schwantes-Greever-Nolan Collection.

It was in this changed and changing—often turbulent—environment that Missouri railroads sorted out their relationships with one other. Indeed, Missouri provided a microcosm of the altered national landscape. Across the upper Midwest, economic conditions had worsened, and as traditional smokestack industries declined, observers frequently referred to the region as the "Rust Belt." By contrast, businesses across the "Sun Belt" states of the South and Southwest thrived. The economic contradiction was reflected in one way or another by the rail companies serving Missouri.[3]

* * *

In 1980, Burlington Northern earned 5.63 percent return on investment, Santa Fe 7.84 percent, and Union Pacific 8.56 percent. St.

The Beer Railway

Manufacturers' Railway might plausibly have been nicknamed the "Beer Road" because it was the offspring of Anheuser-Busch and handled the rail transportation requirements of the St. Louis brewer. Founded in 1887, Manufacturers' Railway shipped Anheuser-Busch's outbound product—"Greatest of Malt Tonics"—as well as inbound grain, coal, filtration materials, paper products, and so on. The giant brewery was hardly the road's sole customer. Indeed, the surrounding area developed into a prime industrial area with a maze of team tracks and spurs leading off to serve lumberyards, packing plants, coal yards, cooperages, bakeries, distillers, basket and box companies, drug companies, and other breweries. By the 1930s, Manufacturers' offered common carrier service over nearly thirty-six miles of line, connecting in St. Louis primarily with the Missouri Pacific and Terminal Railroad, and, with access to the Municipal Bridge, it perfected connections with all roads that served East St. Louis, Illinois. In 1938, the company operated 604 freight cars under lease from the St. Louis Refrigerator Car Company.*

FIGURE 6.1.1.
A Manufacturers' Railway locomotive is busily switching refrigerated cars. James House photograph.

* Scott Muskopf, "The Beer Baron's Railway," in *The Manufacturers Railway Company* (St. Louis: Terminal Railroad Association of St. Louis Historical Society, 2019), 6–35; *Poor's Railroad Volume, 1938* (New York: Poor's, 1938), 567; *Official Guide*, May 1940, 1153.

Louis–based Missouri Pacific turned in an impressive 9.13 percent. In 1956 Missouri Pacific finally emerged from a complex receivership that had lasted twenty-three years, and shortly thereafter it imported an aggressive no-nonsense management team led by Downing Jenks. The railroad worked to clean up property and upgrade its infrastructure while at the same time providing shippers a better experience. With acquisition of the Chicago & Eastern Illinois's Chicago leg, Missouri Pacific possessed an attractive franchise that reached from Lake Michigan south to the Texas Gulf Coast and west to the foot of the Rocky Mountains at Pueblo, Colorado. Over the years Missouri Pacific fully absorbed satellites and clients (the venerable Texas & Pacific Railway among them) and otherwise simplified and perfected its ownership structure. In all, Missouri Pacific evolved into a very impressive enterprise.[4]

Run-through operations gained popularity because they reduced the transit time for freight, and it should be no surprise that Missouri Pacific, with multiple rail connections in St. Louis and Kansas City, became an early participant. Nor should it be surprising that Union Pacific, with multiple options to the West Coast from Kansas City, would function as a primary player in run-through operations. During the 1970s and into the next decade, Union Pacific engaged with Norfolk & Western, Frisco, Missouri–Kansas–Texas, Milwaukee Road, and Missouri Pacific to forge run-through agreements that expedited lading, made efficient use of motive power and rolling stock, and pleased customers and carriers alike.[5]

Absent from these important interline traffic arrangements was the Chicago, Rock Island & Pacific. Indeed, the road that Huddie "Lead Belly" Ledbetter immortalized in song during the 1920s as "a mighty fine line" was about to meet an unfittingly bitter end after more than a century of operations in Missouri. On August 28, 1979, the Brotherhood of Railway and Airline Clerks and the United Transportation Union struck Rock Island over the issue of retroactive pay. Shortly thereafter, the Interstate Commerce Commission, in a highly controversial decision, ruled that Rock Island was "cashless" and ordered service temporarily restored under the direction of Kansas City Terminal Railway. Meanwhile, Judge Frank J. McCarr ordered the Rock Island's trustee to develop a plan to demonstrate financial vitality for a highly abbreviated version of the railroad's formerly extensive network across the nation's midsection. The greatly shrunken carrier might viably operate its trains between Chicago and Council Bluffs, between Minneapolis and Kansas City, and along an assortment of Iowa branch lines, a network of approximately 2,200 miles. Failing that, McGarr demanded total liquidation. As unthinkable as that option was, it happened on January 25, 1980: "After 11:59 p.m. March 23, 1980, CRI&P will receive no traffic on line and will accept no traffic at interchange points" was the clipped message that said it all.

FIGURE 6.3. Older readers will readily recall music played from a record that spun at forty-five revolutions per minute. Usually that format allowed only one song to be recorded on each side of the platter, and it at first included no high fidelity or stereo. Rock Island and the Atchison, Topeka & Santa Fe were among a handful of American railroad companies celebrated in musical hits. Rock Island—the road that Huddie "Lead Belly" Ledbetter had immortalized as "a mighty fine line"—would meet an unfittingly bitter end after more than a century of impressive presence on the Missouri railroad landscape. Schwantes-Greever-Nolan Collection.

From Chicago the next day went out this brief notice: "The Kansas City Terminal Railway Co. as the directed rail carrier shall cease its operation of Chicago, Rock Island & Pacific RR on March 31, 1980. Due to this cessation of operation all craft positions unless previously notified . . . are hereby abolished effective 11:59 p.m. Monday March 31, 1980."[6]

Other carriers had begun sniffing at Rock Island's decaying body even while it yet breathed. "They resemble," thought Rock Island's John Ingram, "not sharks but an impoverished tribe on an island whose chief manner of earning a livelihood is to take in each others' laundry."

FIGURE 6.4.
Southern Pacific had a vested interest in the Golden State Route. Don L. Hofsommer Collection.

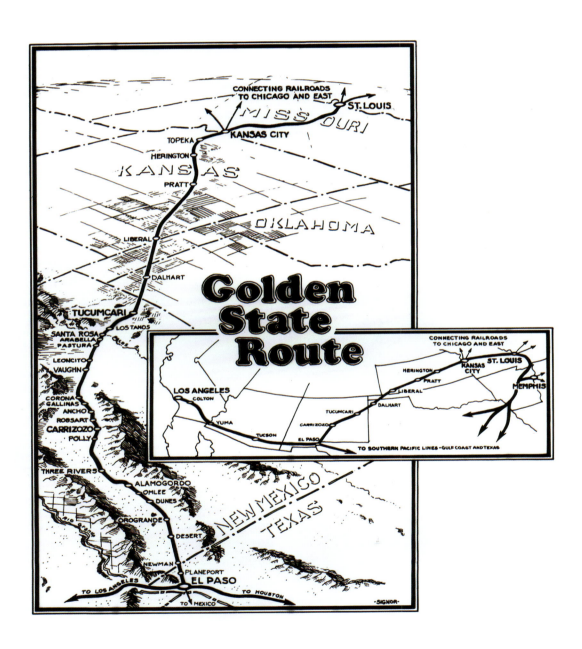

Winds of Change 205

Chicago & North Western was especially covetous of Rock Island's grain-gathering network across central and northwest Iowa, but this drew a howl from shippers, politicians, and the media. "We want a good financially viable carrier that runs to the Gulf of Mexico," insisted one grain merchant. "North Western [with a line only to Kansas City] simply doesn't qualify." Moreover, interjected other critics, with North Western aggressively abandoning its own lines across Iowa, what sense did it make for that railroad—itself hardly financially vibrant—to take on one additional weak line? Many public authorities and shipper groups put forth the candidacy of Kansas City Southern, which owned a line to the Gulf and connected with Rock Island at Kansas City. Kansas City Southern service in Iowa would form a logical and direct single-road channel to tidewater, but the railroad's chief executive William Deramus III chose not to aggressively pursue the acquisition. Much larger Burlington Northern, too, was a likely candidate, but it remained at best lukewarm to acquisition of Rock Island remnants and was otherwise focused on improving its coal lines that served mines in Wyoming and Montana.[7]

It fell to the Interstate Commerce Commission to assign directed service responsibilities while pieces of this puzzle were sorted out. It was not a pretty scene, foreshadowing, as it did, massive abandonment of track across the nation's midsection. Chicago & North Western received the ripest plums, including Rock Island's choice Minneapolis–Kansas City route and most of its Upper Midwest grain-producing lines. "This is not what many Iowa shippers and public officials want," complained an irritated *Des Moines Register*, which pointed out that the Chicago & North Western already owned a route to Kansas City (via its earlier acquisition of Chicago Great Western). But as it turned out, Chicago & North Western would have its way when in 1983 it gained virtually all Rock Island lines for which it had formerly provided directed service—including, of course, the vital Minneapolis–Kansas City chute.[8]

*   *   *

The story at Milwaukee Road was similarly disheartening but not as cataclysmic. The railroad, which lost $100 million during the three years before bankruptcy in 1977, sustained another loss of $82 million in 1978 and projected a deficit of $150 million for 1979, if the entire railroad remained in business. The Milwaukee Road's court-appointed trustee pointed out that it would require $1 billion to rehabilitate the entire 9,800-mile system, a financial impossibility. He therefore requested permission to embargo all but 2,400 miles of the carrier's route structure effective May 8, 1979. The court denied this proposition, and much legal wrangling followed. Three months later, on August 10, the road filed another request to reorganize as a much-slimmed-down

3,400-mile system—retaining, importantly, its line from Chicago to Kansas City but abandoning all operations west of Miles City, Montana, to the Pacific Coast.[9]

The Milwaukee question rumbled along a bumpy path to resolution. On November 4, 1979, President Jimmy Carter signed into law the Milwaukee Road Restructuring Act, which postponed once again the embargo but, crucially, transferred authority to permit abandonment, sale, or transfer of Milwaukee Road lines from the Interstate Commerce Commission to the reorganization court. On February 26, 1980, Judge Thomas McMillan dropped the hammer. The long-awaited embargo would take effect just days later at 12:01 a.m. on March 1.[10]

Milwaukee Road—now in highly abbreviated form—rocked along toward oblivion. Late in October 1981, Grand Trunk Corporation (a Canadian National property within the United States) announced its possible interest in acquiring the Milwaukee Road remnant. Seven months later Grand Trunk and Milwaukee Road signed a letter of intent, and the former quickly put traffic on primary Milwaukee routes—from Grand Trunk Western at Chicago and from Duluth, Winnipeg & Pacific at Duluth. The new arrangement was beneficial to both parties. Milwaukee needed the business, and for Grand Trunk, the Milwaukee Road made strategic sense because it connected two geographically separated Canadian National satellites, extended Grand Trunk's reach west to Kansas City and south to Louisville, and offered an end-to-end combination that would minimize loss of service and maintain maximum jobs. Milwaukee's trustee exclaimed that it would be "a marriage made in heaven." Milwaukee blossomed with traffic thrown to it by Grand Trunk, but that had the unintended consequence of attracting other suitors—Soo Line and Chicago & North Western. A bidding war erupted, Grand Trunk dropped out, and in the end Soo Line on February 19, 1985, took possession of Milwaukee properties, now confined to the Upper Midwest.[11]

*   *   *

Meanwhile, the sun was about to set for the final time on Huddie Ledbetter's "mighty fine" Rock Island line. On June 1, 1984, the Chicago, Rock Island & Pacific emerged from bankruptcy as the Chicago Pacific Corporation with about $210 million in cash plus real estate and mineral rights valued at $40 million and approximately $135 million in tax credits. Gone was the railroad itself—roughly 4,400 miles of the original route sold to other rail carriers and around 3,000 miles simply abandoned.[12]

When the Interstate Commerce Commission parceled out temporary service orders, Cotton Belt had become responsible for operating

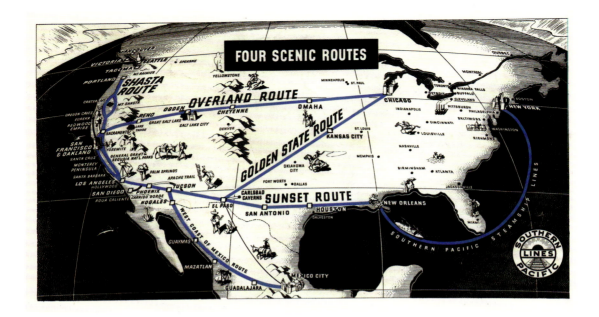

FIGURE 6.5.
The Golden State Route was one of several western corridors that Southern Pacific promoted. Schwantes-Greever-Nolan Collection.

the Santa Rosa–Tucumcari–Kansas City–St. Louis segment. Indeed, Southern Pacific—Cotton Belt's parent company—volunteered to maintain service on the Tucumcari–Kansas City portion of the Golden State Route. Southern Pacific, of course, had a vested interest. Through connections had existed since 1902, when Rock Island and two subsidiary companies completed tracks to Tucumcari and Santa Rosa. Joint solicitation of traffic had persisted even after Southern Pacific brought the Cotton Belt into its fold, and the Golden State Route remained the premier funnel for perishable traffic entering the Midwest from Southern California and Arizona. True, volume had fallen as trucks ran off with more and more of the perishable business and as Rock Island's infrastructure deteriorated, but loss of the Golden State Route would clearly disadvantage Southern Pacific against Santa Fe and, to a lesser extent, Union Pacific—especially in competing for time-sensitive cargo. To be sure, the Southern Pacific–Cotton Belt route between Los Angeles and St. Louis through Texas and Arkansas was still important, but that corridor was significantly longer (over four hundred miles) than those of competitors—a comparative liability for shippers in terms of delivery times and for the rail company in terms of maintenance, fuel, and labor costs.[13]

With those thoughts in mind, management and the trustee of the bankrupt Rock Island came to an agreement in April 1978 for the purchase of nearly a thousand miles of line, plus trackage rights, from Santa Rosa, New Mexico, to Kansas City and St. Louis along with the Bucklin–Dodge City Branch in Kansas. On December 29, 1978, Southern Pacific filed appropriate papers with the Interstate Commerce

FIGURE 6.6.
Down with the old, up with the new. Former Rock Island offices at Armourdale became offices of Southern Pacific's Cotton Belt ("Cotton Rock"). Don L. Hofsommer Collection.

Commission. If the federal regulators approved, title would be held by the Southern Pacific–controlled St. Louis Southwestern Railway. The price: $57 million.[14]

There was important support. On-line shippers and local governmental agencies rejoiced at the prospect of a healthy carrier taking over and extending the Golden State Route. Rock Island's management and the court-appointed trustee heartily applauded, and the railroad brotherhoods approved. Sale to the St. Louis Southwestern would, after all, preserve local service, restore competition on the historic transcontinental route, provide jobs, and generate tax revenues. Reactions among other railroads were mixed. Only Burlington Northern voiced support for the Southern Pacific/St. Louis Southwestern acquisition.

Winds of Change   209

Numerous other rail carriers, including Chicago & North Western, Missouri–Kansas–Texas, Norfolk & Western, and St. Louis–San Francisco opposed the big acquisition in one fashion or another, while Illinois Central Gulf, Milwaukee Road, Kansas City Terminal, and Western Pacific requested "conditions." Denver & Rio Grande Western sought to preserve the historic central or "Overland Route" via Ogden. Major complaints came from Atchison, Topeka & Santa Fe, which groused that it would lose nearly $57 million in gross revenues, and from Missouri Pacific, which not only opposed the purchase plan but itself sought to acquire Rock Island's Kansas City–St. Louis line—one that duplicated Missouri Pacific's own route that connected those two cities. Union Pacific, Southern Pacific's historic partner at their Ogden, Utah, junction, was thoroughly alarmed by the proposal. It feared that Southern Pacific would divert traffic from Ogden to Tucumcari, insisted on strict adherence to Central Pacific Conditions, and, apparently in retaliation, asked for rights over Southern Pacific lines to serve new customers in far-off Southern California. On the surface, the Tucumcari case seemed minor compared to the earlier and abortive Rock Island merger application, but in reality it fueled a massive transformation of the industry in the trans-Chicago West. The Interstate Commerce Commission concluded hearings on February 6, 1980, and promised a decision later that year. Federal regulators gave their approval on June 10, and Southern Pacific/ Cotton Belt soon launched their massive rehabilitation program of the Golden State Route.[15]

*   *   *

During the 1970s and 1980s, there was a constant swirl of rumors of rail mergers, internal studies of theoretical combinations at every company headquarters, and amalgamations in fact. Indiana's Monon gravitated to the Louisville & Nashville's orbit in 1971; Illinois Central combined with Gulf, Mobile & Ohio to form Illinois Central Gulf in 1972; Baltimore & Ohio, Chesapeake & Ohio, and Western Maryland became the Chessie System in 1973; Missouri–Illinois was folded into Missouri Pacific in 1978; and Grand Trunk Western gained Detroit, Toledo & Ironton in 1980. Norfolk & Western in 1981 picked up Illinois Terminal (the former interurban line once known as Illinois Traction and which had bridged the Mississippi River to gain entry to downtown St. Louis). Illinois Central Industries practically begged anybody to take its railroad. Southern Railway looked at Illinois Central Gulf in 1978, but talks went nowhere. Southern also eyed Missouri Pacific as a merger partner, while Missouri Pacific at one time or another pondered acquiring Illinois Central, Santa Fe, and Frisco.[16]

FIGURE 6.7.
A massive and very expensive program rehabilitated what had been Rock Island's Golden State Route. Don L. Hofsommer Collection.

Burlington Northern, the formation of which in 1970 triggered the great merger movement in the West, also was on the prowl for new properties. Senior officers of the company conducted a thorough investigation of the Missouri Pacific and were greatly impressed with its operations, the physical condition of the property, its customer base, and its substantial revenue stream. They recommended a merger, but Louis W. Menk, chairman, overruled them, insisting, instead, that Burlington Northern make a run at the 4,626-mile St. Louis–San Francisco. The St. Louis–based company, Menk affirmed, possessed a diverse traffic mix that included wheat, flour, feed grains, soybeans, cotton, vegetable oils, processed food, construction materials, pulp, paper, motor vehicles, coal, metals, chemicals, and piggyback. It also had impressive Missouri customers, such as Metal Container (a division of Anheuser-Busch) at Tenbrook and a ConAgra pet-food-processing mill at Rolla. A merger application was filed on December 28, 1977, and although initially no fewer than fifteen other railroads contested the Burlington Northern–Frisco merger, the Interstate Commerce Commission nonetheless gave its blessing. After the merger went into effect on November 21, 1980, Burlington Northern possessed a 29,226-mile rail system that stretched across the American West and South all the way from Pacific Coast outlets at Portland and Seattle to the Gulf of Mexico at Pensacola,

Winds of Change

FIGURE 6.8.
St. Louis–San Francisco would become part of Burlington Northern in 1980. On October 21, 1975, Frisco train #39 skirted the Meremac River Bluffs west of Valley Park, Missouri. Jeff Schmid photograph, Don L. Hofsommer Collection.

Florida. The enlarged company served customers in twenty-five states and a pair of Canadian provinces and now included Frisco tracks that formed a big X across Missouri, with one leg extending from St. Louis to Dallas/Fort Worth and the other from Kansas City to the Gulf Coast of Florida. As if to emphasize the new system's potential, Burlington Northern train *PBF* departed Portland on December 1, 1980, on its way to Birmingham, Alabama, a distance of 3,076 miles via Missouri's Kansas City and Springfield.[17]

* * *

Burlington Northern and Frisco were hardly the only partners riding the region's merger carousel. On January 8, 1980, Union Pacific and Missouri Pacific announced that they had agreed in principle to a merger just weeks after John Reed of Santa Fe declined to meet Missouri

Pacific's Downing Jenks to discuss a possible combination of those two properties. That astonishing news was followed almost immediately by another announcement from Union Pacific—that it also sought control of the Western Pacific with its important Salt Lake City–Bay Area corridor. If approved, "MoP-UP," as the combination came to be nicknamed, would spread Union Pacific's influence across a vast domain that extended from Portland, Oakland, and Los Angeles on the West Coast to Chicago, St. Louis, Houston, and New Orleans in mid-America. "MoP-UP," said Union Pacific, would improve existing competition by opening new routes that would make its rail service more efficient and economical. The argument was compelling. Moreover, argued Union Pacific, its combination with Missouri Pacific and Western Pacific would give parity with those western railroads that already enjoyed two-carrier transcontinental opportunities via Chicago, St. Louis, Memphis, or New Orleans. These included, of course, Burlington Northern, Santa Fe, and Southern Pacific—all of which blasted the proposed Union Pacific–Missouri Pacific–Western Pacific merger as anticompetitive and otherwise contrary to the public interest[18]

As Interstate Commerce Commission regulators wrestled with the merits of the Union Pacific case, a new variable appeared on the western railroad landscape. On May 15, 1980, directors of Southern Pacific and Santa Fe Industries announced that they had jointly embraced a memorandum of intent to merge Southern Pacific into Santa Fe. Casual discussions between Benjamin Biaggini and Santa Fe's John S. Reed had gone on before, but the campaign by Union Pacific to enlarge its dominion with acquisition of Missouri Pacific and Western Pacific now forced these ancient rivals to embrace. Santa Fe Industries and its railroad were more profitable than Southern Pacific and its rail holdings, although the combination of the latter's rail and nonrail properties boasted larger gross revenues and net assets. Santa Fe would be the survivor if the merger were approved by shareholders and government regulators. The initial reaction to the merger proposal on Wall Street, however, was not flattering. Nevertheless, Biaggini thought the creation of Burlington Northern, soon followed by its acquisition of Frisco and then the massive Union Pacific merger proposal, made the matter academic. "There would be no use in leaving the Southern Pacific alone and the Santa Fe alone to compete with railroads the size" of Burlington Northern and "MoP-UP," he explained.[19]

The obvious need to unite in the face of significant railroad restructuring across the states west of the Mississippi River notwithstanding, major obstacles to a Santa Fe–Southern Pacific merger remained. One centered on Southern Pacific's persistent interest in acquiring much of Rock Island's Golden State Route, and, even as Santa Fe and Southern Pacific managers studied their overall merger proposition, the Interstate

Commerce Commission gave its permission for the $57 million Golden State Route acquisition on June 10, 1980.

Southern Pacific's Cotton Belt, which had been providing directed service over the Golden State Route since March 24, found that business on its new acquisition, both local and overhead, was initially slack. The sole train dispatched from Kansas City on April 1, for instance, handled only thirty-five cars, of which more than half were empty. There was no disputing the potential of the route through New Mexico, however, and that autumn Cotton Belt committed itself to a massive rehabilitation program, using some funds generated internally and obtaining the remainder from a federal loan. This activity presented Southern Pacific and its potential merger partner, Santa Fe, with a conundrum. Southern Pacific management saw the revitalized Golden State Route as essential to survival if the merger with Santa Fe failed, but Santa Fe's John Reed was "horrified" at the prospect of sinking money into what he considered a redundant line should the merger be completed. To make it the high-speed route that Southern Pacific envisioned would require an expenditure of millions of dollars that, said Reed, was "not economically justified."[20]

Southern Pacific's determination to follow through not only with acquisition but also rehabilitation of the Golden State Route was hardly the sole problem plaguing merger negotiations. In fact, both companies issued terse statements on September 12, announcing that they had mutually determined to end such discussions. Biaggini cited several reasons: the management of nonrail properties, benefit programs for company officers, and accounting problems. Outsiders pointed to another element: the clash of corporate as well as individual egos.[21]

Although they might not be able to agree to merge, Southern Pacific and Santa Fe commonly viewed the prospect of a strengthened Union Pacific as abhorrent to their individual business interests. Both asked the Interstate Commerce Commission to reject the Union Pacific–Missouri Pacific–Western Pacific combination. Southern Pacific estimated its annual loss, if federal regulators approved the merger, to be $100 million, and Santa Fe expected annual losses of $92 million. Nevertheless, the Interstate Commerce commission granted Union Pacific's wishes on September 13, 1982. Southern Pacific immediately filed suit to halt the merger because, in its view, the combination would "destroy railroad competition in the West." This legal action and that initiated by other rail carriers was of no avail. MoP-UP became a very impressive component of the newly redrawn American transportation landscape when Omaha-based Union Pacific more than doubled its size as a railroad on December 22, 1982. "DONE!" boasted the Union Pacific in full-page newspaper advertisements.[22]

Southern Pacific was not the only rail carrier subject to altered conditions as a result of Union Pacific's dramatic expansion. Denver & Rio Grande Western had prospered by handling overhead business to and from the Missouri Pacific connection at Pueblo; Chicago, Burlington & Quincy and Rock Island at Denver; and Western Pacific at Salt Lake City. These opportunities shrank, however, when the Chicago, Burlington & Quincy became an integral part of Burlington Northern, when Rock Island disappeared, and when Western Pacific and Missouri Pacific extended the reach of Union Pacific, the Denver & Rio Grande Western's historic competitor. Meanwhile, Southern Pacific became Rio Grande's premier connection, and that important association predictably matured as Southern Pacific lost its own traditional Overland Route partner at Ogden, Utah, and as Union Pacific diverted traffic to itself from the former Western Pacific at Salt Lake City and away from Missouri Pacific's Pueblo gateway. Fortunately for both the Denver & Rio Grande Western and Southern Pacific, the former railroad gained trackage right concessions along Missouri Pacific tracks east from Pueblo to Kansas City following the new Union Pacific combination. This implied long-haul opportunities for the Denver-based carrier and routing alternatives for Southern Pacific.[23]

FIGURE 6.9. Southern Pacific officials took great delight in initiating Cotton Belt rights over former Missouri Pacific tracks between Kansas City and St. Louis—hence the staged meet between Southern Pacific's office train and *BSM* on January 7, 1983. Jim Johnson photograph, Don L. Hofsommer Collection.

Winds of Change 215

Another consequential trackage rights concession to result from the Union Pacific proceedings was gained by Southern Pacific's Cotton Belt. This one gave the St. Louis Southwestern the right to close the strategic gap between Kansas City and St. Louis by way of Missouri Pacific rails. Cotton Belt trains, of course, already threaded their way along the recently acquired Rock Island tracks between Missouri's bookend cities. In truth, however, that cross-state route completed in 1904 was an underwhelming prize because it had originally been poorly engineered and was now in wretched physical condition, and across Missouri its builders had managed to avoid every sizeable center of population.

Indeed, Southern Pacific estimated that rehabilitation of the former Rock Island route would cost at least $100 million and add capacity to a rural right-of-way already adequate for the meager traffic it carried. Cotton Belt willingly agreed to service industrial zones on either end of the line near Kansas City and St. Louis. But when spurred by the Union Pacific–Missouri Pacific–Western Pacific combination, Cotton Belt initiated through service on its former Rock Island route across Missouri on January 7, 1983. In a move that foretold the future abandonment of its dubious acquisition, the first train to take advantage of the Golden State Route between East St. Louis and Los Angles via El Paso, Texas, was the Cotton Belt's famous *Blue Streak Merchandise*, but on its way west from St. Louis to Kansas City it sped along the Missouri Pacific's well-maintained right-of-way and avoided the tracks it had acquired from Rock Island.[24]

*   *   *

As Missouri underwent this traumatic 1960s and 1970s period of shakeout and restructuring, national legislators put finishing touches on two vitally important pieces of legislation that at last sought to give American railroads entrepreneurial opportunity relatively free of federal and state overreach. The "4Rs Act" of 1976, among other things, permitted greater flexibility in ratemaking; streamlined Interstate Commerce Commission procedures, including its historic oversight of merger applications; and prohibited state and local tax practices that discriminated against rail carriers. The Staggers Rail Act of 1980—named for West Virginia Congressman Harley O. Staggers, who sponsored the legislation—built on the legacy of the 1976 measure and during the coming years would become widely regarded as a truly monumental contribution to the history of American railroads. Signed into law by President Jimmy Carter on October 14, 1980, the Staggers legislation stopped short of wholesale deregulation of America's rail carriers, but it substantially eased their regulatory burden and significantly changed the process of ratemaking, legalized contract rates, established modern accounting principles, and further eased abandonment and merger standards.[25]

These proved difficult changes to implement. Most railroad companies were inadequately prepared for the new environment. As the chief executive of one road confessed, his company "was strong for the principle of deregulation, but weak on the practice." Competition, especially for contract business, proved exceptionally keen, and although ton miles increased among most roads, net profits deteriorated. Traffic managers for major shippers were bemused by the bumbling manner in which railroads sought to cope in the newly deregulated climate. One said, "If a railroad moves freight at a loss today, it is usually because it is deliberately implementing a short-range strategy to capture traffic or because it is not yet used to competing in the market place." There were additional complications. Single-line service, always desirable from the carriers' point of view, became even more so under provisions of the Staggers Act. Previously, railroads had been protected from antitrust action in the process of making joint rates, but under deregulation they had reason to worry about prosecution by the Justice Department when they sought to negotiate rates on point-to-point shipments. The easiest way to avoid such legal difficulty was, of course, to own the track from origin to destination. Short of this, and in an attempt to force shippers to accept, as much as possible, single-carrier service, large railroads closed traditional gateways and raised rates via others. Customers grew justifiably nervous, and eventually rail carriers modified their stance. Still, competition remained intense.[26]

*   *   *

Competition was not restricted to other rail companies. Most competition, in fact, was with other modes of transportation. The volume of intercity freight traffic moved by rail carriers had dropped from 74.9 percent in 1929 to a disappointing 35.8 percent in 1982, although the number of tons carried had nearly doubled during those same years. Trucks, waterway operators, and pipelines exacted devastating tolls on the railroads. The Staggers Rail Act of 1980, of course, significantly reduced artificial restrictions on the inherent efficiency of steel wheels on steel rails, but modal competition clearly was not going to vanish just because Congress had enacted a constructive and much-needed piece of legislation. Railroads had dieselized, purchased thousands of high-capacity cars, dumped their money-losing passenger service, and trimmed lightly trafficked branches. Yet they continued to be an asset-rich, cash-poor, high-labor-cost industry with clearly inadequate returns on investment. Other than gaining productivity-enhancement contracts from the railroad brotherhoods or reducing investment in property, the only immediate opportunity for improvement seemed to be additional merger activity.[27]

Ironically, as the number of major roads serving Missouri declined, the number of Show-Me State short lines expanded. The multiplication resulted primarily from the determination of the largest, or Class I, railroads to shed what they regarded as low-density lines with marginal long-term profitability. Newcomers ranged from tiny 1.89-mile-long Railroad Switching Service of Missouri (formerly Illinois Terminal/N&W) and 5.8-mile Semo Port Railroad (formerly Union Pacific/Missouri Pacific) to the 139.5-mile Arkansas & Missouri (formerly Burlington Northern/Frisco) and 560-mile Missouri & Northern Arkansas (formerly Union Pacific/Missouri Pacific). Short lines, which could operate with lower labor costs and fewer work rule restrictions, offered shippers a more personalized and customized service and in that way regained traffic or even secured new business. If all went well, owners of short lines would prosper, shippers and on-line communities would smile, and connecting major roads would see a handsome increase in interline volumes. Good fortune did follow for Arkansas & Missouri and Missouri & North Arkansas, but eighteen-mile-long Jackson & Southern (formerly Union Pacific/Missouri Pacific) failed to prosper and ceased running trains in 1992. In a very real way, the phenomenon of the modern short-line railroad was an additional benefit conferred by the Staggers Rail Act.[28]

*   *   *

Major carriers faced mounting costs of labor and aggressive competition, which closely followed the advent of interstate highways, big trucks, federally subsidized inland waterways, and major pipeline systems. The Interstate Highway Act of 1956 fostered the creation of a new nationwide network of super roads that served to increase railroad woes. Their managers understandably sought ways to reduce labor costs and implement more efficient work rules. Organized labor predictably resisted. By 1983, average total earnings and fringe levels exceeded those paid to workers in all other transportation modes. During the era of regulation, those rates of compensation were generally passed along to customers, but that was no longer the case after 1980 and passage of the Staggers Act. Furthermore, mushrooming growth of wages and benefits was not accompanied by simultaneous gains in productivity. In other words, railroads generated more ton miles per train mile by way of more powerful locomotives, larger cars, and longer trains, but higher wages, increased benefits, and counterproductive work rules negated any gain in net production. Managers and workers gradually, if grudgingly, agreed to substantial alterations in the modus operandi. By far the most visible change was the gradual removal of cabooses from freight trains. That was followed by the elimination of second brakemen on road trains and the eventual whittling of road crew size from five men to two and lengthening crew districts so that distance traveled equaled a full day's work for operating employees.[29]

During the decade following its creation in 1970, Burlington Northern poured millions of dollars into infrastructure and equipment. The rewards were disheartening—at least in the short term. "We are not . . . satisfied with our company's return on equity," admitted management. Burlington Northern's return had been 2.3 percent in 1971, the first full year of operation under the merger, rising only to 3.2 percent in 1975 and 4.2 percent in 1976. By 1979, Burlington Northern had spent $1 billion to upgrade its coal-carrying capacity (which increased by 400 percent during the 1970s), and in 1978 and 1979 strong overseas demand for grain—amounting to 264,356 carloads in 1979, or nearly 20 percent of all grain loaded in the United States—further stretched Burlington Northern's capacity. Nevertheless, profit margins remained, as company management complained, "less than satisfactory." Indeed, in 1979, Burlington Northern's return on equity was 8.7 percent, but only 3.8 percent came from its railroad because of impressive performances by the company's forest products and resources divisions. "Of all our assets, the railroad offers the best opportunity for growth," said management, "but it also provides the greatest test of Burlington Northern's ability to excel as a company. We cannot be content with allowing the strength of other activities to bolster weak earnings performance by the railroad," shareholders were bluntly advised. A new management team clearly was more interested in Burlington Northern's energy, forest products, and real estate assets at the expense of its railroad. The timing of the management shift was curious and ironic given Burlington Northern's expanded ability to tap the flourishing Sun Belt, including Gulf Coast ports, and the much-brightened prospect for railroads because of the Staggers Act. Nevertheless, in 1981 the railroad was reborn as Burlington Northern Incorporated to signal its primary interest in its nonrail holdings, which in 1984 accounted for 36 percent of total operating income.[30]

For Burlington Northern, the decade of the 1980s would be one of constant inner turmoil and change. Longtime senior managers retired and were replaced with outsiders who had no background in or little knowledge of the rail industry and came with an avowed plan to grow Burlington Northern's natural resource ventures by cost-cutting on the rail side. In August 1981, holding-company staff relocated from the railroad's historic headquarters in St. Paul, Minnesota, to Seattle, Washington. Its marketing arm moved to Fort Worth, Texas, and operating departments to Overland Park, Kansas, near Kansas City. Employment dropped from 59,000 in 1980 to 35,000 in 1986. The integration of Frisco into Burlington Northern was not without its bumps and bruises—"a tough merger," one insider called it. Rates on early coal movement contracts provided inadequate returns. Morale at the railroad sagged.[31]

Elsewhere, Chicago & North Western profited greatly from the collapse of both the Milwaukee Road and Rock Island. "I think it is fair to conclude that of the three big, historically marginal prairie granger roads, North Western is clearly the survivor and will be both the major architect and beneficiary of the restructured Midwestern railroad system," asserted that road's president. Indeed, Chicago & North Western had won the prized grain-gathering lines in Iowa along with the former Rock Island Mid-Continent Minneapolis–Des Moines–Kansas City artery. Chicago & North Western was, of course, interested in hauling more than corn and soybeans. Pledging to convert its new north–south thoroughfare into a high-speed, high-capacity strategic route for great tonnage as well as time-sensitive lading, management observed that the former Rock Island route was "more direct and energy-efficient than the existing C&NW line," meaning the former Chicago Great Western route from Des Moines south through St. Joseph to Kansas City. The implication was clear: the Des Moines–Kansas City corridor had one too many options. The route via former Chicago Great Western tracks perished in April 1985.[32]

*   *   *

Then there was Conrail, birthed on April 1, 1976, with the federal government serving as midwife, and suckled with federal dollars and beneficial legislation. It was also a political conundrum. Conrail served America's densely populated Northeast, historically a prime manufacturing region, but one that suffered wrenching dislocation as the American economy changed course. In addition, during its early years Conrail struggled to deal with changes and dislocations that included onerous labor requirements and harsh winters. Many leaders in manufacturing, transportation, and government doubted the carrier's long-term success and, in fact, freely predicted its early demise.

Policy planners in the Reagan administration found Conrail an acute embarrassment, an awful contradiction to their firm devotion to marketplace solutions. Not surprisingly, enactment of the Northeast Rail Services Act of 1981 enabled Conrail to cease functioning as an instrument of social policy and—like all other rail carriers under the Staggers Act—to respond to traditional business needs and challenges. The unshackling gave heart to an invigorated Conrail management team, and shippers soon reported improved performance. Politicians remained impatient. Secretary of Transportation Elizabeth Dole announced that bids would be received for the property, but she was disappointed because the early show of interest came only from Conrail's own employees. Then, during the summer of 1984, came several offers with varying caveats and conditions. One of the two large railroads operating east of the Mississippi River, CSX, proposed a split-up of Conrail. Its primary competitor, Norfolk Southern, on the other hand, proposed to acquire Conrail in its entirety.[33]

In the end, the federal government on March 26, 1987, sold its ownership interest in Conrail in what ranked as the largest initial public stock offering in American history. Alas, Conrail had imposed surcharges and closed gateways and optional routings, and it also instituted single-line rates over its own routes that did little, if anything, to reduce shipper costs but required customers, in many cases, to deal with it in a captive way. Within its own system, Conrail focused on main routes, slimming down as best it could by abandonments or line sales. As an example, Conrail favored the former Pennsylvania route across Illinois to East St. Louis over the former New York Central line, which it allowed to atrophy before removing the tracks.[34]

The merger-and-acquisitions merry-go-round remained fully in motion, and speculation as to the next combination remained rife. For example, rumors circulated that Southern Pacific intended to acquire all, or at least a substantial portion, of Illinois Central Gulf; that it would purchase Denver & Rio Grande Western; that it would merge with Burlington Northern; or that CSX would purchase Southern Pacific. Many observers predicted that the next round of mega-mergers would result in the nation's first truly transcontinental railroad, but others agreed with Hayes T. Watkins of CSX, who saw no financial advantage to such an arrangement—"although that may eventually come." However, none doubted the combination with Missouri Pacific and Western Pacific had so improved Union Pacific's economy of scale that another round of rail mergers was inevitable. Security analysts uniformly agreed that Southern Pacific and its allied railroads had been especially hurt by "MoP-UP." Indeed, many referred to the expanded Union Pacific as "an unstoppable monster." Santa Fe, too, had been hurt by MoP-UP, and John Schmidt, chairman and chief executive officer, admitted late in 1982 that Santa Fe Industries was "taking a hard look" at merging its historic Atchison, Topeka & Santa Fe franchise with another railroad. He predicted early action on the matter. At Southern Pacific a comprehensive merger study undertaken for the company by an outside firm was completed in the same year.[35]

There was only modest surprise on September 27, 1983, when Southern Pacific Company and Santa Fe Industries announced plans to create a new holding company—Santa Fe Southern Pacific Corporation, which would unite "complementary" properties and, most importantly, be a "merger of equals." The proposed combination represented a very impressive $5.2 billion plan that would create, among other things, a twenty-five-thousand-mile railroad—third in size behind Burlington Northern and CSX Corporation. *Fortune* called it "the biggest deal of all" for 1983. But it was not to be. The Interstate Commerce Commission on July 25, 1986, astonished almost everybody by saying that the merger was monopolistic and turned it down. The issue was not the new holding company, which remained firmly in place, but rather the railroads, one of which would have to be jettisoned. The one cast adrift would be Southern Pacific, shorn of its nonrail assets and forced to face a very uncertain future. For that matter, could Santa Fe itself stand alone in a frighteningly intense and competitive transportation marketplace?[36]

*　*　*

Railroads of the United States had recorded major accomplishments during the 1980s within the partially deregulated environment provided for under the Staggers Act. Indeed, in 1990 the railroads' share of transportation ton miles was the highest since 1981, and Wall Street took note as investors anticipated even greater gains during the following decade. Not all, to be sure, was moonlight and roses. In 1980 through 1989, the industry also saw its share of the national transportation dollar continue to shrink, from 13.1 percent to 9.1 percent. Water and pipeline shares dropped also, but air rose from 1.9 percent to 3.6 percent, and intercity truck lines increased their overwhelming supremacy from 73.9 to 77.8 percent, aided in no small measure by the rapidly growing national network of interstate superhighways. The Interstate Commerce Commission reported that in 1989 only Burlington Northern and Norfolk Southern were "revenue adequate" (meaning that their rates of return on investment were at least matched by the cost of capital).[37]

In pursuit of increased market share and revenue adequacy, railroad companies persisted in seeking strategic advantage. In 1987, Chesapeake & Ohio vanished into CSX, and Seaboard System was also merged into CSX. In the same year, Illinois Central Gulf sold 631 miles of former Gulf, Mobile & Ohio line from Joliet, Illinois, to Kansas City and East St. Louis to a start-up company called Chicago, Missouri & Western, but the new rail enterprise soon failed and filed for Chapter 11 protection. In 1988 Union Pacific gobbled up Missouri–Kansas–Texas, but as a concession, Kansas City Southern gained what had been Katy's right to access Iowa grain markets. Kansas City Southern chose to have Union Pacific handle such traffic on a haulage basis (billing in Kansas City Southern cars moved by Union Pacific trains). Kansas City Southern, of course, had its own line serving poultry producers of Arkansas and Oklahoma and continuing farther south to Gulf Coast ports. Moreover,

FIGURE 6.10.
Rio Grande Industries acquired sprawling Southern Pacific, but there was no loss of pride in the *Blue Streak*. Jim Johnson photograph, Don L. Hofsommer Collection.

KCS proved to be an aggressive player, not just in the grain business but generally under a management team that sniffed out all kinds of opportunities opened by congressional passage of the North American Free Trade Agreement (NAFTA) legislation. In that same year, 1988, Rio Grande Industries, which owned Denver & Rio Grande Western, acquired the sprawling Southern Pacific empire, and during the following year, a Southern Pacific puppet corporation gained direct access to the Chicago gateway by taking possession of the seemingly marginal Joliet–East St. Louis leg of the former Gulf, Mobile & Ohio, while one of the Midwest's new start-ups, Gateway Western, picked up the 461-mile Kansas City–East St. Louis line via Roodhouse, Illinois.[38]

The economic vitality of any rail company is typically a reflection of the economic vitality of its service area. That relationship was especially true at this time for carriers serving Missouri and the Midwest and looking for sustenance therefrom, but the correlation meant less so to those roads also serving the Sun Belt or the West. The picture, then, was blurred in the 1980s. John F. Due, a respected professor of business at the University of Illinois, worried in 1981 that railroads were an endangered species, noting wretched rates of return for the industry. James W. McClellan of Norfolk Southern was not as somber but noted in mid-decade that, on an industrywide basis, rail ton miles had grown by nearly a quarter between 1971 and 1984, but during the same period national industrial production had grown by nearly half—"indicating

Winds of Change 223

that rail transportation has significantly lagged the national economy." Moreover, added William H. Dempsey of the Association of American Railroads, "competition is more intense than ever, creating a rate compression of troubling proportions." This compression was the result of several factors, including truck deregulation leading to the creation of "thousands of new motor competitors who are largely low-cost, non-union carriers," the consequence of "safe" rail markets that were not growing as they had previously, and partly because railroads were competing "more with each other than ever before." At Chicago & North Western, James R. Wolfe complained that outmoded labor agreements shackled the industry in its difficult struggle to address highway, air, water, and pipeline competition. Chicago & North Western's struggle was not unique. Soo Line, recent recipient of Milwaukee Road property, stumbled. "The position of rail lines has changed dramatically in the past 10 years," observed LaVerne W. Andreessen, professor of accounting at the University of Northern Iowa. "It will change again because of mergers and consolidations," Andreessen forecast, "but it also will be related in no small part to the habits of the shipping public. If the grain trade and other large volume shippers continue to use the rails, the rails will remain."[39]

By the end of the 1980s, however, the railroad industry expressed greater optimism. "American railroads have left stagnation behind and are trying many new things," said an expansive Darius W. Gaskins at Burlington Northern. "We have changed our way of thinking about what we do. We no longer say we are in the railroad business; we say that we are in the transportation and distribution business." As examples, Gaskins pointed to double-stack cars carrying two layers of easily loaded and unloaded freight containers—blending rail and road for domestic use and adding ocean for transport to distant destinations. Railroad managers were finally adjusting to and taking advantage of the freedoms and opportunities afforded by the Staggers Act and other federal legislation that allowed railroads a reasonably fair chance to compete among themselves and with other modes of transportation. Innovative labor contracts allowed carriers to shed cabooses, reduce crew size, and introduce advantageous work rules. A broad expression of optimism finally spread across the faces of railroad managers, and in 1989, a writer for *Insight* observed that "the industry appears to be moving under a full head of steam." But, he cautioned, "razor-thin margins remain under pressure from competing modes and from costly labor arrangements. Even in the midst of signs of health, recession worries stalk the railroads." To be sure, in 1988 only Kansas City Southern and Union Pacific earned more than 10 percent returns on investment. Nevertheless, industry performance during the next decade would be impressive.[40]

If there was anything constant about the rail landscape of the 1990s, that constant was change. Chicago & North Western had turned in a mixed record during the 1980s and had found itself subject to a hostile takeover. The railroad dodged this bullet, but only by favoring a "white knight" consortium that added appreciable debt to its balance sheet. The company shuddered, pared down to a system of forty-three hundred miles—just 40 percent of its size in 1972—and pressed on. But not for long as an independent. Chicago & North Western had earlier swallowed Chicago Great Western and assorted other Midwestern rail carriers, but it was about to discover that what goes around comes around. Omaha-based Union Pacific, historically the North Western's reliable partner on the Overland Route to California and its recent financial collaborator in tapping lucrative Wyoming coalfields, purchased a sizeable block of Chicago & North Western stock and in 1995 gained authority to acquire the remainder. The historic railroad that had long served the Upper Midwest region disappeared into Union Pacific's expansive network on April 25, 1995.[41]

Union Pacific approached its Chicago & North Western acquisition with an arrogance seemingly endemic among takeover victors—throwing aside tradition and convention and dismissing managers who knew and understood North Western customers and the road's peculiarities. Union Pacific altered or reduced service and appeared to thumb its nose at shippers, employees, and public figures alike. The "Omaha knows best" mentality reaped an ugly reward. Union Pacific's president was obliged to admit late in 1995 that many customers were "experiencing unprecedented problems with service provided by our railroad"—acute candor that likely hastened his departure. "UP has cut back in warm bodies and when you call you rarely get a person who knows anything," growled one irate shipper. "It has been about the ugliest operational situation I have seen since I have been around railroads," chimed in a representative of Farmland Industries. Service disruptions backed up freight at Chicago, Kansas City, and other gateways, and the result was delayed deliveries, clogged yards, and irritated railroad connections. Several customers switched to truck, while others diverted their shipments to other railroads.[42]

Burlington Northern more than any other road serving Missouri stood to gain at Union Pacific's expense, but Burlington Northern experienced its own trials. The road had pumped prodigious amounts of cash into infrastructure upgrades to meet growing traffic demand, but return on these investments had been frankly disappointing—and for investors frustrating. A new management team early in the 1980s determined to emphasize Burlington Northern's lucrative natural resources holdings over its railroad assets. The company's acquisition and improvement money went for pipelines plus oil-and-gas purchases. Critics complained that the railroad had become the "cash cow" that supplied dollars for nontransport ventures. In 1988, Burlington Northern was carved up—Burlington Resources departing one way with all nonrail assets and Burlington Northern Incorporated taking away but one principal subsidiary: the railroad. And rail managers rightly groaned that the railroad shouldered "the substantial debt load remaining after the sign-off of Burlington Resources." As one senior executive put it, "Burlington Resources got the gold and we got the shaft." Indeed, the railroad inherited most of the old company's debt and was saddled with a 76 percent debt-to-capital ratio. The railroad struggled to put on a happy face: "The fundamentals are now in place to create an environment of expanded opportunities for Burlington Northern and its shareholders." The company clearly had returned to its roots as a railroad. It certainly owned a marvelous franchise, but the debt it was freighted with meant a very tough slog for Burlington Northern.[43]

Santa Fe, too, had its tribulations. The combination of Santa Fe Industries and Southern Pacific Company had occurred on December 23, 1983, and Santa Fe Southern Pacific Corporation, the resulting holding company, fully expected Interstate Commerce Commission regulators to approve the merger of Atchison, Topeka & Santa Fe and Southern Pacific, the holding-company railroad subsidiaries. Neither Santa Fe nor Southern Pacific, went the argument, could stand alone against the giants Union Pacific and Burlington Northern. Likely, but the Interstate Commerce Commission in 1986 turned thumbs down on their merger application and left both railroads to fend for themselves as best they could. Meanwhile, unfriendly parties raided the holding company, which responded by shedding assets so that by 1991 the Atchison, Topeka & Santa Fe was by far the largest component of the corporation. Santa Fe, too, returned to its roots, and, under the dynamic guidance of Robert D. Krebs, the slimmed-down railroad fairly oozed competitive instincts—focusing on high-speed, high-capacity arteries from Chicago to the Gulf and to the California coast.[44]

Union Pacific, now shorn of its resource business and basically a railroad company once again, closed in on and captured sprawling Southern Pacific, the West's odd man out. Southern Pacific, of course, was Union Pacific's longtime partner on the western segment of the historic Overland Route between Chicago and the West Coast. Early in the twentieth century, the two railroads had been corporately aligned until the United States Supreme Court untied the knot in its 1912 "trust-busting" decision. With Chicago & North Western and Southern Pacific under its belt, Union Pacific boasted single-line ownership from Chicago, St. Louis, Memphis, and New Orleans west to Seattle, Portland, Oakland, and Los Angeles as well as a powerful north-south presence from Duluth/

Superior down through Des Moines and Kansas City to the Texas and Louisiana Gulf Coast—not to mention vital gateways to Mexico. Withal, Union Pacific was a formidable giant—the largest rail system in North America after its Southern Pacific acquisition on September 11, 1996. Its track network blanketed the West and totaled thirty-six thousand route miles. However, the operating problems that had bedeviled the Union Pacific earlier as it sought to digest its Chicago & North Western acquisition seemed insignificant when compared to the headaches that resulted from its gaining Southern Pacific. A monumental service melt-down frightened and exasperated shippers, regulators, politicians, and employees, who wondered openly and angrily why Union Pacific had not learned anything from its bruising experience following its Chicago & North Western acquisition.[45]

∗   ∗   ∗

Hardly a tear was shed on December 31, 1995, when the Interstate Commerce Commission breathed its last. The federal regulatory agency had badly botched the Rock Island–Southern Pacific–Union Pacific case and had bungled other rail matters over the years. The ossified bureaucracy, the oldest of all federal regulatory bodies (established in 1888), proved painfully slow to respond to changing transportation patterns within the United States and seemingly remained convinced that American rail carriers maintained the vigorous modal monopoly of its early years. The Interstate Commerce Commission would be replaced by the Surface Transportation Board (STB), which presumably would take a more reasoned approach to rail regulation.[46]

The happy surprise railroad among Missouri's carriers was the Kansas City–based Kansas City Southern, which despite its relatively small size and limited route structure proved surprisingly agile. The holding company of which it was a part thought seriously about disposing of the railroad, but after it hired Michael Haverty as president, it changed its mind. Nevertheless, conventional wisdom had Kansas City Southern passing soon to one of the West's rail giants. Instead, it pressed ahead aggressively on its own as it expanded in Texas and created an impressive anchor in Mexico with a subsidiary railroad. Kansas City Southern likewise expanded within Missouri by picking up the Gateway Western, the former Gulf, Mobile & Ohio line across the state, which provided it access to St. Louis. In 2000 Mike Haverty was named "Railroader of the Year" by *Railway Age*.[47]

Elsewhere, Soo Line's acquisition of Milwaukee Road in 1985 had produced embarrassing and staggering net losses ($60,510,000 for the three-year period 1985–1987) and an intolerable operating ratio of 108.1 for 1986. Soo's response was to concentrate on its "core"—identified

The Rock Crumbles

Predecessors and surrogates of the Chicago, Rock Island & Pacific had cobbled together railroad bits and pieces during the years 1881–1904 to complete a cross-state corridor between St. Louis and Kansas City. At 295.8 miles long, the new Rock Island route was slightly longer than Missouri Pacific's Sedalia line (282.4 miles) and its "river line" (292 miles), longer than Wabash (278.7 miles), and longer than Chicago, Burlington & Quincy (279.0 miles). An additional disadvantage was the line's jagged profile on its eastern end, which featured a ruling grade of 1 percent eastward plus four tunnels. A senior locomotive engineer recalled that "we were constantly running uphill and then downhill." To access downtown St. Louis, Rock Island used Terminal Railroad tracks east to Union Station and the Carrie Avenue Yard from the end of its own tracks that stopped thirteen miles outside the city at Lackland. To access Kansas City Union Station and a massive classification yard at Armourdale, Rock Island used Frisco tracks from Leeds Junction to Sheffield, Kansas City Terminal beyond.*

Rock Island bid fair to challenge all comers for intrastate Missouri business, but more importantly, the St. Louis gateway option expanded its strategic reach—especially for traffic between the Missouri metropolis and the West. This was reflected by

FIGURE 6.2.1. When Extra 1201 passed through Pleasant Hill, Missouri, on August 3, 1954, the Rock Island still looked like a "mighty fine" line. Steve Patterson Photo.

the road's *St. Louis-Colorado Express*, which offered passengers a St. Louis–Denver sleeper, a "lounge club," chair cars, and a diner en route to the Centennial State or to connections beyond.†

The company was successful in attracting an impressive collection of freight customers near St. Louis at Lackland. These included, among others, Weyerhaeuser Lumber, Horner Box, Owens-Corning, Johnson Wax, Celanese, US Gypsum, and Johns Manville. Kingsford Charcoal offered considerable tonnage at Belle, as did another backyard grill charcoal producer at Meta. A large railroad-tie-treating plant near Leeds Junction provided for Rock Island's needs. At intervening stations between St. Louis and Kansas City could be found a sprinkling of smaller customers—lumberyards, grain elevators, feed mills, feed and coal yards, propane dealers, ammonia purveyors, oil and gas bulk plants, brick and tile producers, and plant food manufacturers.‡

Traffic patterns and demand predictably changed over time. By 1945 passenger service had dwindled to a plodding, day-long "motor" train over the line—later abbreviated to Belle–Kansas City and then discontinued. In 1956 Rock Island carded double-daily freight trains plus locals to serve on-line customers. Like other roads,

FIGURE 6.2.2. Weeds reclaim Rock Island's abandoned track across Missouri. Don L. Hofsommer Collection.

the Chicago, Rock Island & Pacific gradually embraced piggyback operations that included trailers-on-flat-cars as well as movement of automobiles on multilevel carriers. With that traffic in mind, it added a trailers-on-flat-cars ramp and made other improvements to its Carrie Yard and enlarged three tunnels to allow passage of triple-level auto cars. There followed an aggressive campaign to win long-haul traffic between St. Louis and Texas, Colorado, and California destinations.§

Sad to say, of course, Rock Island was coasting into hard times and eventual oblivion. Between 1972 and 1976, billings from Kansas City dropped from 34,999 carloads annually to 22,478 and in St. Louis from 11,982 to 6,435. On-line business remained stable at Owensville, Belle, and Eldon but dropped significantly at Union—from 2,887 carloads in 1972 to only 650 in 1976. St. Albans neither received nor dispatched cars during the same four-year period. Indeed, prospects for business at many stations was at best bleak. In addition, maintenance along much of the line had fallen off as Rock Island fortunes deteriorated.¶

As it developed, Southern Pacific, through its St. Louis Southwestern subsidiary, acquired Rock Island's "Golden State Route" west of Kansas City as well as the rapidly decaying Kansas City–St. Louis route, which Southern Pacific asserted was a "dog" and would cost at least $100 million to rehabilitate—and even then it would likely continue to create operating headaches. Yet it might serve as a useful pawn in the rail industry's ongoing strategic chess game played out across Missouri. However, as a concession resulting from Union Pacific's acquisition of Missouri Pacific, the Southern Pacific's Cotton Belt gained operating rights over the former Missouri Pacific main line between St. Louis and Kansas City and thereby sealed the fate of the ex–Rock Island line across the state. Except for industrial districts at the route's bookend cities, which Cotton Belt trains continued to serve, most of the track was "abandoned in place," left to the weeds and other ravages of nature, and eventually dismantled.#

* William Edward Hayes, *Iron Road to Empire: The History of the Rock Island Lines* (New York: Simmons Boardman, 1853), 162–63, 174; Chicago, Rock Island & Pacific, Missouri-Kansas Division 2nd District, *Timetable No. 5* (September 9, 1956), 1–2; Robert Huff, interview, July 26, 2019.

† *Official Guide*, January 1930, 982, 989; William K. Kratville, *Steam, Steel and Limiteds* (Omaha: self-published, 1962), 249.

‡ Chicago, Rock Island & Pacific, *Station Earnings for the Year 1976*, passim.

§ *Official Guide*, June 1941, 899; ibid., November 1950, 927; Chicago, Rock Island & Pacific, *Annual Report, 1963*, 7; Chicago, Rock Island & Pacific, *Annual Report, 1969*, 7, 9; Chicago, Rock Island & Pacific, *Annual Report, 1971*, 9.

¶ Chicago, Rock Island & Pacific, *Station Earnings for the Year 1976*, passim.

Gregory L. Schneider, *Rock Island Requiem: The Collapse of a Mighty Fine Line* (Lawrence: University Press of Kansas, 2013), 182, 184, 265; Don L. Hofsommer, *Southern Pacific, 1901–1985* (College Station: Texas A&M University Press, 1986), 295–30.

as "main arteries which connect the Canadian border with Chicago, Kansas City, and Louisville." Beyond that, said Soo, "branch lines must feed traffic to the main lines profitably or they will be sold." As it developed, however, Soo itself would not call that shot. Canadian Pacific, which already owned 56 percent of Soo Line stock, decided in 1990 to purchase the rest. Its purpose, said Canadian Pacific, was to create "an expanded transcontinental railway with a major U.S. presence able to compete aggressively for growing international trade and for increased north-south traffic under the Canada-U. S. Free Trade Agreements." That did not include former Milwaukee lines toward Kansas City, which with other lines were conveyed to the newly born Iowa & Minnesota Rail Link (IMRL) in 1997.[48]

As Canadian Pacific vacated the scene, its archrival Canadian National came riding in. For more than three-quarters of a century, Canadian National had been a sleepy Crown Corporation, a ward of the national government larded with inefficiency and redundant trackage. But more recently Canadian National had muscled up, been privatized in 1995, and become an astonishingly nimble and energetic company that boldly announced its determination to become "a truly North American railway" poised to take every advantage afforded by the creation of NAFTA. Illinois Central—the "Main Line of Mid-America"—became Canadian National's quarry. Particularly tantalizing was Illinois Central's prize arterial speedway south from Chicago through Memphis to the Gulf Coast port of New Orleans and with a branch to East St. Louis, which, when coupled to traffic alliances forged with Kansas City Southern, would create, Canadian National beamed, "a NAFTA network" from Canada across the United States to Mexico. Illinois Central disappeared under Canadian National's broad banner on July 1, 1999, to join a very long list of "fallen flags" departed from Missouri's rail landscape.[49]

For Burlington Northern, the 1980s and into the next decade were additional years of trauma and tribulation—the merger with Frisco followed by "Friscoization," three successive CEOs without railroad experience, disaggregation of headquarters from St. Paul (the executive branch going to Seattle, Washington, operations to Overland Park, Kansas, and marketing to Fort Worth, Texas), upheaval and constant churning of corporate culture, intense labor unrest, and separation of nonrail assets from the railroad, but the railroad left saddled with a mountain of debt. That it performed as well as it did during these years was vivid testimony to the innate strength of the franchise.[50]

Stability for Burlington Northern would come, ironically, out of even more upheaval—in this instance, merger with Atchison, Topeka & Santa Fe, a deal consummated on September 22, 1995, with Robert Krebs (late of Southern Pacific and then Santa Fe) becoming chief executive officer. As it happened, unfriendly parties had raided the Santa Fe Southern

Pacific holding company, which then responded by shedding assets so that by 1991 the Atchison, Topeka & Santa Fe Railway was by far the largest component of the corporation. Santa Fe went back to its roots—a slimmed-down railroad fairly oozing competitive instincts and focused on its high-speed, high-capacity arteries extending from Chicago to the Gulf and to California. The new company, Burlington Northern Santa Fe—and Krebs insisted that it *was* a new company—blended the best of two great railroads. Moreover, it was a new company with a new corporate culture independent of previous allegiances that would be headquartered at a striking new campus on the northern edge of Fort Worth. There would be predictable pulling and hauling as the new company took form and matured, but Krebs was determined to maximize its full potential. "We have a strong franchise, resourceful employees, and the momentum to fulfill our merger promise," he affirmed. In 1996 Burlington Northern Santa Fe planned a capital program approaching $1.7 billion, adequate to fund a massive program of track betterment, new locomotives and cars, and a plan to "rebuild from the ground up" Argentine Yard at Kansas City, Kansas. Krebs likewise promised to make even better "intermodal service through Midwestern gateways like Chicago, Kansas City and St. Louis to both the Pacific Northwest and California" and to take full advantage of trackage rights from Houston to Memphis and St. Louis—a concession gained as a result of the recent Union Pacific–Southern Pacific merger. Not surprisingly, the two rail giants that now dominated the trans-Mississippi West—Burlington Northern Santa Fe and Union Pacific—continued to spar for advantage in Missouri.[51]

For that matter, Burlington Northern Santa Fe sought to dramatically broaden its reach by combining with Canadian National to forge an end-to-end amalgamation that would create a fifty-thousand-mile colossus and employ sixty-seven thousand people. The timing proved awkward, however, with many shippers, analysts, and politicians recalling the woes that Norfolk Southern and CSX had in their joint purchase and carving up of Conrail and the stumbling and bumbling of Union Pacific in seeking to digest Chicago & North Western and then Southern Pacific. Other carriers—CSX, Norfolk Southern, Canadian Pacific, and Union Pacific—coalesced in opposition, and a federal court upheld a fifteen-month moratorium on rail mergers. Burlington Northern Santa Fe and Canadian National called off their proposed marriage.[52]

Splitting Conrail between CSX and Norfolk Southern and the corporate indigestion that followed not only played a part in derailing the Burlington Northern Santa Fe–Canadian National combination but also impacted the national rail network, including carriers serving Missouri. As it developed, the ex–New York Central routes eastward from St. Louis to Cleveland, Buffalo, New York City, Boston, and Montreal went to CSX.

There were delays in implementation, however, and although Conrail's last "official" day was [Au]gust 22, 1998, CSX and Norfolk Southern did not assume Conrail['s] operations until June 1, 1999. Even then there would be service[. The switch]ip from Conrail to CSX was not the only such Change of [corporate?] scene. The former Milwaukee Road line through alteration o[...]nd Excelsior Springs to Kansas City had passed to Gault, Ch[...] [I]owa & Minnesota Rail Link, and on July 30, 2002, Soo Li[...] [Io]wa, Chicago & Eastern. Interestingly, Kansas City Soo Li[ne] had bid on those lines, and it did so again in 2002— beca[...][54]

S[...] the salient alteration in railroad freight carriage in the [...] of the twentieth century was the development and even-[...]ve growth of the intermodal business. New York Central [...] were aggressive proponents in the 1960s, and Burlington [...]d Grand Trunk Western later proudly teamed with *Expeditor* trains between Detroit and St. Louis. Norfolk Southern insti-[...] *dRailer* operation on its Detroit–St. Louis (formerly Wabash) [...]or in July 1986, but the great surge in growth awaited the inven-[...]on of double-stack cars to efficiently handle a flood of containerized imports arriving from Asia at West Coast ports. Another breakthrough came in 1989 when Santa Fe gained the confidence of J. B. Hunt, the country's biggest truckload carrier. Taken together with deregulation and enterprising managers, the race was on to put new business on the rails. And it was a successful contest.[55]

*   *   *

What of the iconic Union Stations at St. Louis and Kansas City in all of this corporate tugging and pulling? In 1969, even as a handful of passenger trains still rumbled into and out of the train shed at St. Louis, railroad officials and local politicians sought to address Union Station's "long, lingering death." The Terminal Railroad Association itself commissioned a study done by an area architectural firm, which suggested the building's future use as an amusement park, convention center, or even terminal for short-takeoff-and-landing aircraft. Politicians initially embraced the convention-center concept but eventually warmed to the notion of an industrial park. A headline writer for the *St. Louis Globe-Democrat* labeled Union Station "St. Louis' Great White Elephant." He got it wrong. Union Station was reborn, not as a railroad facility but rather as a very attractive hotel and a modern commercial center—righ[t] fully winning acclaim as a preservation showcase. The story was m[uch] the same for Kansas City, where the city's imposing Union Station f[ound] itself abandoned by Amtrak, atrophied, and probably destined to

FIGURE 6.11.
New Amtrak cars were intended to lure passengers back to the rails. Don L. Hofsommer collection.

wrecking ball. That structure, too, happy to say, was reborn and emerged all polished up, sporting a splendid science museum, restaurants, and the return of Amtrak trains. As the pride of Kansas City, it became a metropolitan icon.[56]

It is not too much to suggest that the positive outcomes that resulted from the repurposing of the Kansas City and St. Louis Union Stations during the final years of the twentieth century provide an appropriate metaphor for the nation's rail industry—the two great edifices down on their knees, the industry down on its knees, prognosticators predicting the demise of both, but then redemption for all parties, which could look to the future with guarded optimism.

In 1885 CP made history by connecting a country; in 2023 CP and KCS made history again by connecting a continent. . . . Kansas City, Missouri, is the heart of our network.

—*CPKC 2023 Annual Report*, a celebration of the merger of two railroads with a rich history: Canadian Pacific and Kansas City Southern

There were delays in implementation, however, and although Conrail's last "official" day was August 22, 1998, CSX and Norfolk Southern did not assume Conrail's operations until June 1, 1999. Even then there would be service blips.[53]

Change of ownership from Conrail to CSX was not the only such alteration on the local scene. The former Milwaukee Road line through Gault, Chillicothe, and Excelsior Springs to Kansas City had passed to Soo Line, then to Iowa & Minnesota Rail Link, and on July 30, 2002, became part of Iowa, Chicago & Eastern. Interestingly, Kansas City Southern in 1997 had bid on those lines, and it did so again in 2002—losing each time.[54]

Without doubt the salient alteration in railroad freight carriage in the latter portion of the twentieth century was the development and eventually explosive growth of the intermodal business. New York Central and Santa Fe were aggressive proponents in the 1960s, and Burlington Northern and Grand Trunk Western later proudly teamed with *Expeditor* piggyback trains between Detroit and St. Louis. Norfolk Southern instituted *RoadRailer* operation on its Detroit–St. Louis (formerly Wabash) corridor in July 1986, but the great surge in growth awaited the invention of double-stack cars to efficiently handle a flood of containerized imports arriving from Asia at West Coast ports. Another breakthrough came in 1989 when Santa Fe gained the confidence of J. B. Hunt, the country's biggest truckload carrier. Taken together with deregulation and enterprising managers, the race was on to put new business on the rails. And it was a successful contest.[55]

* * *

What of the iconic Union Stations at St. Louis and Kansas City in all of this corporate tugging and pulling? In 1969, even as a handful of passenger trains still rumbled into and out of the train shed at St. Louis, railroad officials and local politicians sought to address Union Station's "long, lingering death." The Terminal Railroad Association itself commissioned a study done by an area architectural firm, which suggested the building's future use as an amusement park, convention center, or even terminal for short-takeoff-and-landing aircraft. Politicians initially embraced the convention-center concept but eventually warmed to the notion of an industrial park. A headline writer for the *St. Louis Globe-Democrat* labeled Union Station "St. Louis' Great White Elephant." He got it wrong. Union Station was reborn, not as a railroad facility but rather as a very attractive hotel and a modern commercial center—rightfully winning acclaim as a preservation showcase. The story was much the same for Kansas City, where the city's imposing Union Station found itself abandoned by Amtrak, atrophied, and probably destined to face a

FIGURE 6.11.
New Amtrak cars were intended to lure passengers back to the rails. Don L. Hofsommer Collection.

wrecking ball. That structure, too, happy to say, was reborn and emerged all polished up, sporting a splendid science museum, restaurants, and the return of Amtrak trains. As the pride of Kansas City, it became a metropolitan icon.[56]

It is not too much to suggest that the positive outcomes that resulted from the repurposing of the Kansas City and St. Louis Union Stations during the final years of the twentieth century provide an appropriate metaphor for the nation's rail industry—the two great edifices down on their knees, the industry down on its knees, prognosticators predicting the demise of both, but then redemption for all parties, which could look to the future with guarded optimism.

In 1885 CP made history by connecting a country; in 2023 CP and KCS made history again by connecting a continent. . . . Kansas City, Missouri, is the heart of our network.

—*CPKC 2023 Annual Report*, a celebration of the merger of two railroads with a rich history: Canadian Pacific and Kansas City Southern

7

Rail Industry Survivors Face an Uncertain Future

The railroad industry of the United States during the last two decades of the twentieth century underwent seismic shifts—partial deregulation, mega-mergers, fallen flags, significant line abandonments, and, ironically, the birth of a new generation of short lines and regional carriers. Observers of the industry might logically conclude that a period of extended calm would follow. But the winds of change proved inexorable. Missouri's railroad landscape would not be spared.

Securities analysts, shippers, journalists, and other observers took a measured view of the industry as the new century unfolded. There was more than a hint of pessimism. "Not being able to supply a service appropriate to a modern economy," wrote one analyst, "the freight railroads are relegated to a smaller and smaller chunk of the 'captive' economy, like chemical plants and utilities and auto plants." Another argued that "the future of railroading does not depend on further consolidation that inevitably will lead to a North American duopoly." Rather, he continued, "it depends on growing the railroad industry's traffic base." Mergers, he continued, "have relied on achieving earnings growth through cost cutting"—indeed, "mergers have not yet produced a railroad business organization that is interested in developing and instituting a true growth strategy." Observed the president of United Parcel Service, "We haven't seen any tangible customer service from any railroad merger." Raymond C. Burton at TTX Company noted with great concern that railroad ton miles were rising much faster than revenue miles.[1]

Union Pacific, still smarting from monumental service failures in the wake of acquiring Chicago & North Western and then Southern Pacific and seeking to repair its badly bruised corporate image, reported a 4 percent growth in traffic during the year 2000 over 1999 and said it was making progress in the area of "customer satisfaction." The Union Pacific traffic commodity revenue mix was energy, 21 percent; industrial,

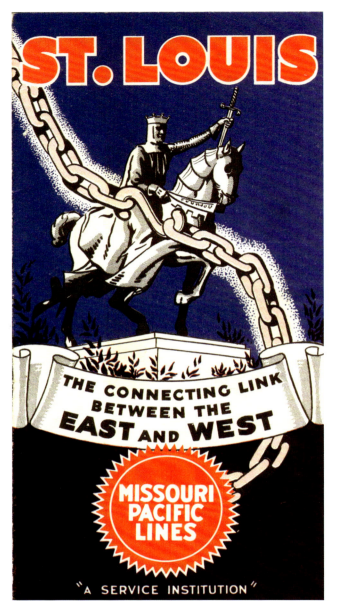

FIGURE 7.1.
Whether describing it as a link between East and West or as a continental crossroads, the Missouri Pacific brochure cover emphasized the geographical centrality of Missouri. Schwantes-Greever-Nolan Collection.

19 percent; intermodal, 19 percent; chemicals, 16 percent; agricultural, 14 percent; and automotive, 11 percent.[2]

Burlington Northern Santa Fe, with 33,500 route miles sprawled across twenty-eight states and two Canadian provinces, experienced bumps and bruises of its own, which were partly explained by a surge in business that resulted from Union Pacific's continuing trials. Revenue was up slightly in 2000 over 1999, yet railroad net income was down. A bright spot was intermodal, with revenue up by 6 percent and volume by 7 percent. Indeed, intermodal led in revenue, followed by carload coal, agricultural commodities, and automotive. In a bit of surprise, following the failure of the proposed BNSF/Canadian National merger, Rob Krebs opted for early retirement and was succeeded by Matthew K. Rose.[3]

Norfolk Southern, having become a 21,800-mile giant that served twenty-two states and the Canadian province of Ontario, owned a splendid horizontal thoroughfare (former Wabash) that extended west across Missouri to Kansas City. Norfolk Southern served the Ford assembly plant at Claycomo (north and east of Kansas City) and the General Motors plant at Wentzville (west of St. Louis), which gave it multiple long-haul options for parts and set-up automobiles as well. The railroad took special pride in its emphasis on workplace safety and earned many accolades in that regard. Its operating revenue in 2000 topped that in 1999, but like other rail carriers Norfolk Southern saw its net income slump.[4]

On July 13, 2000, Kansas City Southern Industries began trading as just a transportation company after it had spun off its financial holdings to create Stilwell Financial. With the return to its transportation roots, the rail company dropped "industries" from its corporate name. Indeed, KCS among Missouri's major railroads proved to be particularly innovative, willing to take risks, banking heavily on the prospect of North American Free Trade Agreement (NAFTA) benefits, but not ignoring

238   Missouri Railroads

FIGURE 7.2. Norfolk Southern boasted a splendid horizontal thoroughfare in Missouri from Hannibal and St. Louis to Kansas City. On this bright day in 2014, a manifest freight parades in front of the famous Gateway Arch in St. Louis. Norfolk Southern photograph.

other possibilities. In 1997 the takeover of the Gateway Western, the former Chicago & Alton/Gulf, Mobile & Ohio line that linked East St. Louis and Springfield, Illinois, with Kansas City, had been approved by the Surface Transportation Board, and the Gateway acquisition soon resulted in impressive traffic alliances with various eastern rail carriers and continued as a bridge for Burlington Northern Santa Fe to operate a Kansas City route to St. Louis via a haulage agreement. Kansas City Southern also forged a marketing agreement with I&M Rail Link, the old Milwaukee Road/Soo Line trackage that joined Minneapolis with Chicago and Kansas City, a move that enabled KCS to gain traffic originating within the grain-rich states of Iowa and Minnesota. In 1995 Kansas City Southern acquired a financial stake in the Texas Mexican (Tex-Mex) Railway, which operated 151 miles from Corpus Christi to Laredo. Tex-Mex then leveraged trackage rights over Union Pacific between Beaumont and Corpus Christi as a condition of the Union Pacific/Southern Pacific merger. The new arrangement linked Kansas City Southern with its Tex-Mex line to the Mexican border, a linkup

Terminal Railroad Today

The Terminal Railroad Association of St. Louis has a simple mission—to provide top-level service to its transportation partners and its customers. Although its operations and infrastructure are constantly evolving to meet the needs of those same owners and patrons, its core purpose has not changed since its founding in 1899—to connect the St. Louis region to the nation and to the rest of the world.

FIGURE 7.1.1.
Two locomotives of the Terminal Railroad Association proudly displayed against the dramatic background formed by the Gateway Arch of St. Louis on the opposite bank of the Mississippi River. Terminal Railroad Association of St. Louis.

The accelerating change of pace in the domestic rail industry during the first two decades of the twenty-first century predictably impacted the Terminal Railroad Association. In particular, the embrace of "Precision Scheduled Railroading" among Class I roads has resulted in them pressing to increase network velocity and lower car dwell times. All of that has spelled opportunity for intermediate switching carriers such as the Terminal Railroad when its Class I partners moved away from doing much of their own switching and blocking of cars. Indeed, the Terminal Railroad has seen substantial increased demand for such service.

The Terminal Railroad's own customer base slowly eroded over several decades, but it has enjoyed a most pleasant resurgence during the last few years. United States Steel, for instance, remains a valued asset within the rail network, and the Terminal Railroad has seen growing demand for transload and storage-in-transit service. In addition, unprecedented growth of the Mississippi River barge transfer/loadout facilities has earned St. Louis Harbor the title of "Ag Coast of America," and this, too, has added to the Terminal Railroad's traffic mix and volumes.

Two massive infrastructure projects have taken, and will continue to take, massive resources. In 2006, the railroad launched a program to replace each end of the

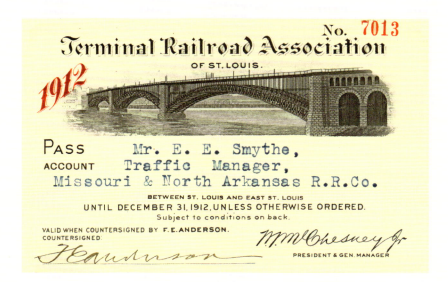

FIGURE 7.1.2. Terminal Railroad pass featuring Eads Bridge. One perk enjoyed by rail employees was their pass, which gained them free travel on many passenger trains around North America. Among the assets of the Terminal Railroad Association was the Eads Bridge, completed across the Mississippi River in 1874 to link Missouri rails for the first time to tracks covering the eastern half of the United States. Previously, rail cars had to be ferried across the river. Schwantes-Greever-Nolan Collection.

Merchants Bridge, a vital link across the Mississippi River, and ten years later it rebuilt the west approach using a technique that encapsulated the old bridge structure in lightweight but durable concrete. In 2019 work began to replace the three main river spans, encase their four piers for seismic and barge strike protection, and rebuild the bridge's eastern approach. The $220 million package was completed in 2022. Before that, the MacArthur Bridge, too, received attention. In 2020/2021 the Terminal Railroad replaced the Broadway Truss on the bridge's west approach in downtown St. Louis, and in 2022/2023 it replaced the main span floor.

Another appreciable cash outlay has been mandated for Terminal Railroad's "Positive Train Control" along its "Amtrak hosted routes." On its own the rail line determined to expand the upgrade to include all of its centralized traffic control main routes. This was completed in 2021. Human capital, too, received attention with the Terminal Railroad's hiring additional train and engine crews as well as personnel in its signal department. All the system upgrades reflect increased demand for transportation services and the never-ending deployment of technology required to run a modern and efficient railroad.*

---

* Mike McCarthy to Don L. Hofsommer, September 1, 2019.

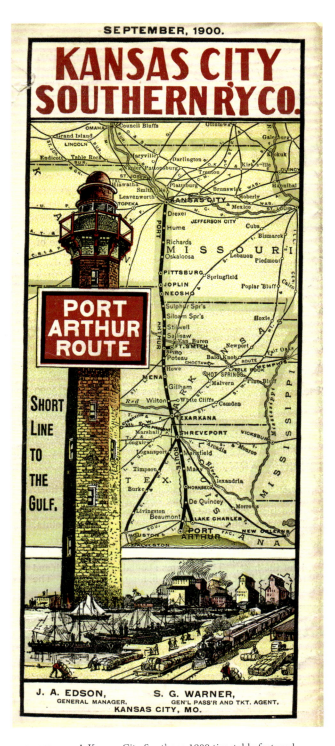

FIGURE 7.3. A Kansas City Southern 1900 timetable featured a cover map. Straight as the crow flies? The colorful advertising ignored the reality of tracks that wound gently through the Ouachita Mountains, which define the borderlands between Oklahoma and Arkansas. Schwantes-Greever-Nolan Collection.

that made the Kansas City railroad and its Mexican partner, Grupo TMM, S. A., legitimate bidders on south-of-the-border railway concessions as the government-owned railroad in Mexico was privatized.

Even earlier, in 1993, Kansas City Southern had taken control of Mid-South Railroad between Shreveport, Louisiana, and Meridian, Mississippi—the most direct rail route between the southeastern and the southwestern United States—and through alliances with Norfolk Southern moved cross-country domestic traffic as well as gained Norfolk Southern and Canadian National access to Mexican markets. In 1998, Canadian National and Kansas City Southern entered into a marketing agreement that allowed traffic to flow between both carriers within the United States and, even more importantly, encouraged NAFTA traffic among Canada, the United States, and Mexico. Consequently, after the Canadian National marketing agreement, Kansas City Southern proudly and enthusiastically dubbed itself the "NAFTA Railway."

Even as Kansas City Southern expanded internationally, it likewise took pride in serving existing accounts in Missouri, such as trackside grain elevators in Kansas City and two Kansas City Power & Light plants on its Gateway Line that received low-sulfur unit coal trains from the Power River Basin. It shipped Ford trucks produced in Claycomo from the new Center Point–Kansas City Southern Intermodal Center at the International Freight Gateway, a facility designed to handle intermodal, automotive, and warehouse traffic at the former Richards Gebaur Memorial

Airport in Belton, a Missouri community on the KCS main line south of Kansas City.[5]

Early in the twenty-first century, Union Pacific announced that it had developed a recyclable racking system to ship auto parts between St. Louis and Mexico, that it now carried 80 percent of finished vehicles in the western United States, and that it was teaming with CSX to expedite food and perishables from Roseville, California, to Chicago and St. Louis and then to destinations farther east. In 2003 Union Pacific shed its remaining nonrail assets—becoming, once again, a "pure" railroad. Norfolk Southern notched down its operating ratio from 91.8 percent in 2000 to 86.2 percent a year later, a positive development, and announced that it had gained new revenue by handling DaimlerChrysler vehicles from Detroit to St. Louis. At the same time, Burlington Northern Santa Fe entered into separate marketing agreements with both Kansas City Southern and Canadian National (following the failure of the proposed Burlington Northern Santa Fe/Canadian National merger) to expand "market reach" for all parties. Also in 2003, Burlington Northern Santa Fe completed its second "flyover" on the Kansas City Terminal Railway to expedite transcontinental trains that operated through Kansas City by means of Kansas City Terminal tracks. The first was at Union Pacific Junction on the west end of the terminal railroad's trackage, and the second was over Union Pacific and Kansas City Southern trackage at Sheffield junction on the east end of the terminal rail line. In 2003 Burlington Northern Santa Fe's Argentine Yard handled a daily average of 1,814 cars and ranked as the railroad's busiest classification facility.[6]

Kansas City Southern continued its expansive growth under the aggressive leadership of Michael Haverty: the railroad moved into a historically designed new corporate headquarters in Kansas City in 2002, took 100 percent control of the Texas Mexican Railway, and acquired 80 percent of Transportation Ferroviaria Mexicans after buying out Mexican partner Grupo TMM in 2005 and then changing its name at the end of the year to Kansas City Southern de Mexico. A year later it gained the Mexican government's 20 percent stake in the Kansas City Southern de Mexico concession in a settlement with the government won by Kansas City Southern de Mexico. KCS rebuilt the former ninety-mile Southern Pacific "Macaroni Line" between Rosenberg and Victoria, Texas, which Surface Transportation Board regulators forced Union Pacific to sell to Tex-Mex in 2000 in order to alleviate congestion on the Sunset Route through Texas. Indeed, with ownership of both the Texas Mexican Railway and Transportation Ferroviaria Mexicans and the rebuilt Macaroni Line, Kansas City Southern de Mexico became a genuine competitor with Union Pacific in reaching intermodal and motor vehicle plants in Mexico and opening the prospect of moving American corn and soybeans into Mexico. The result was a dramatic

FIGURE 7.4.
Map of Kansas City
Southern's international
network before its merger
with Canadian Pacific.
Don L. Hofsommer
Collection.

increase in cross-border traffic. "Those critics who originally questioned KCS's investment in Mexico," insisted Haverty, "have long ago fallen silent and have been replaced by those who correctly championed the progress of TFM and the NAFTA rail concept."[7]

During the next few years, the American rail industry gained self-confidence. Union Pacific—with 32,426 route miles, 8,226 locomotives, and a whopping 106,743 pieces of rolling stock—reported in 2005 that its intermodal business was 19 percent of commodity revenue and that its operating ratio was a healthy 86.8. As for the other western rail giant, Burlington Northern Santa Fe boasted that it handled more intermodal traffic than any other railroad in the world, that it had committed to double tracking its entire Chicago–Kansas City–Los Angeles artery, that its motive power stable included 5,790 locomotives, that its rolling stock encompassed 81,981 cars of all types, and that its "40,000 people demonstrate . . . the tremendous value that our rail franchise brings to the entire U.S. supply chain." Gutsy Kansas City Southern revealed that the holding company for its Texas Mexican line had been consolidated into the parent company and that the Transportation Ferroviaria Mexicans name had been changed to Kansas City Southern de Mexico—"an integral component of the total KCS international rail network." The "traffic potential," insisted Kansas City Southern, "is enormous." Compared to Union Pacific and Burlington Northern Santa Fe, the rolling stock of Kansas City Southern—331 locomotives and 14,939 leased and owned cars—seemed miniscule but adequate.[8]

A new contender to enter Missouri's railroad landscape was Canadian Pacific. In 2000 Canadian Pacific was a diversified company active in transportation, energy, and hotels, but during the following year it separated into five businesses, one of which was Canadian Pacific Railway. Six years later the Canadian giant gained Dakota, Minnesota & Eastern, which in 2002 had itself acquired I&M Rail Link and transformed that carrier into Iowa, Chicago & Eastern. As a result of years of reshuffling the viable segments of failed railroads, the former Milwaukee Road line to Kansas City now resided under the Canadian Pacific banner.[9]

*   *   *

"Rail Renaissance" was a flattering term widely touted during the first several years of the twenty-first century. Indeed, America's rail industry often struggled to meet demand, and, despite record levels of investment by railroad companies, more would be needed, argued observers of the country's transportation network. During the previous few decades, rail managers had faced constant pressure to fill lines with traffic. Now it seemed a matter of handling the right business at the right price. With congested highways, a shortage of truck drivers, and improvements in rail efficiency, shippers found railroads to be an increasingly attractive option. Rail carriers also prospered from a surge in imports from Asia, which typically flowed to destinations on long-haul trains. Moreover, said Michael Ward at CSX, "rails aren't as cyclical as they used to be and can prosper over the long term."[10]

Not surprisingly, investors took notice. BNSF Railway Company, the new official title that the Burlington Northern Santa Fe Railway adopted in January 2005, saw its share price surge from 2004 into 2005. Berkshire Hathaway took an 11 percent stake in BNSF in what the *Wall Street Journal* early in 2007 hailed as "the latest sign that the resurgence in railway stocks has some strength over the long haul." And, said one approving analyst, "the whole railroad industry is transitioning from cost cutting to growth."[11]

The economy hit a rough spot in 2008, and that predictably was reflected in the rail industry. Union Pacific reported, for example, that in the second quarter it suffered a 3 percent decrease in carloads but an increase in net income. Transportation of auto parts, lumber, and building materials in general sagged, but demand for coal, metals, and agricultural commodities held up. Managers took a measured view. Matt Rose at BNSF said his company was engaged in a "ten-year review on risk analysis . . . on risk by what we haul, by what we buy, by the world we live in." Meanwhile, the Surface Transportation Board determined that in 2006 Norfolk Southern, BNSF, and Kansas City Southern all earned a return on investment that surpassed the cost of capital. That seemed to energize forces arguing for re-regulation, although during the decades that followed the passage of the Staggers Act in 1980, rail rates had dropped by 50 percent in inflation-adjusted terms and in real terms by nearly 10 percent. An independent study showed that railroads needed to invest $148 billion by 2035 if they were to carry their share of an increasingly heavy national transportation package. Jim Young at Union Pacific noted that customers often complained about high rates, but at the same time they demanded expanded capacity. Prognosticators focused tightly on Kansas City as the Heartland's future "growth crossroads."[12]

*　　*　　*

The economic downturn in 2008 caused rail carriers to furlough employees—2,000 at BNSF and 3,150 at Union Pacific. Most of these workers would be recalled later, but the size of the rail workforce had shrunk substantially over the years with the demise of passenger service, mechanized track work, closed local stations, and the disappearance of less-than-carload business. Missouri railroads in 1950 had employed 48,979 persons, but by 2004 they needed only 7,992. Those who remained were well compensated; in 2008, the average freight railroad employee across the nation earned $71,300 in wages and $27,200 in fringe benefits—for a total compensation of $98,500 versus an average total compensation of $62,600 per full-time American employee.[13]

BNSF, whose largest shareholder was Warren Buffet's Berkshire Hathaway, in 2008 surpassed Union Pacific to become the country's biggest railroad in annual sales. Thus, it was not a complete shock when Berkshire Hathaway on February 12, 2010, acquired full control of Burlington Northern Santa Fe Corporation and its BNSF Railway Company subsidiary. Buffet's tradition was to give his managers extensive leeway, and now Matt Rose could push BNSF forward without nettlesome securities analysts questioning every detail in a quarterly report. This meant increased freedom of movement for BNSF in a highly competitive transportation field.[14]

Railroad renaissance? During the years from the end of World War II to 1968, rail's share of domestic intercity freight traffic had declined from 69 percent to 41 percent, and from 1968 to 1978 it dropped to 36 percent. Partial deregulation in 1980 enabled railroads to price business competitively, and mergers afforded them the opportunity to rationalize plant and upgrade mainline networks needed to handle cross-country intermodal traffic as well as the surge in demand to move low-sulfur coal from Wyoming's Powder River. Those hauls grew increasingly longer—from an average of 161 miles in 1980 to 919 miles in 2010. During that same year, America's railroads moved a ton of freight an average of 484 miles on one gallon of fuel, and nationwide, each freight rail job supported 4.5 jobs elsewhere in the economy. A positive outcome was that operating ratios dropped—Norfolk Southern's declined to 71.9 percent and Union Pacific's to 70.66 percent. Returns on investment were impressive: 10.25 percent at BNSF, 10.02 percent at Union Pacific, 9.44 percent at Norfolk Southern, and 8.43 percent at Kansas City Southern.[15]

Intermodal was increasingly the bright, shining star in the railroad traffic galaxy. All major rail carriers devoted themselves to large accounts—United Parcel and FedEx, for example—and eagerly sought business moving five hundred miles or more. The reward at Norfolk Southern for its efforts in 2010 was 10 percent growth in its haulage of containerized freight. "The Company's intermodal growth continued at an accelerated pace," said Kansas City Southern, "and is giving no hint of slowing down anytime in the near future." Indeed, Kansas City Southern's "fastest growing intermodal component" was its cross-border service. "Offering the only single-line cross border intermodal service between the U.S. and Mexico," Kansas City Southern volumes grew by 56 percent in 2011, and revenues increased by 76 percent.[16]

An important new element in the traffic mix derived from the boom in oil and natural gas production—the result of hydraulic fracturing of wells, particularly in North Dakota and Texas but at other locations as well. For its part, Union Pacific noted that the "increasing development of oil production in various domestic shale formations is providing an emerging market opportunity for rail with shipments of inbound frac sand and pipe, and outbound crude oil." All of this proved to be a double-edged sword, however, since many utilities quickly rushed to fire boilers with cleaner and often less expensive natural gas and eschewed coal.[17]

Some of this oil patch traffic would find its way to Kansas City Southern, which credibly claimed that "no other railroad can offer KCS' breadth of service options connecting the three North American countries." Said Kansas City Southern, "Through our interchange with Canadian National in Jackson, Mississippi, KCS can offer customers service from central Mexico to Chicago, the Upper Midwest and Canada." Moreover, "New York and the Mid-Atlantic are only one connection away with hand off of traffic to Norfolk Southern in Meridian, Mississippi," and "the connection with Canadian Pacific in Kansas City extends our reach into the upper Midwest and Western Canada." There was more: "Connections with CSX in East St. Louis, Illinois, and New Orleans, Louisiana, allow us to access the Midwest and Southern regions of the United States," while "our interchanges with Union Pacific and BNSF facilitate the movement of cargo between Mexico and the western half of the United States."[18]

*   *   *

Canadian Pacific, with which Kansas City Southern had a primary connection at Kansas City, found itself under attack in 2012 by Bill Ackman, a take-no-prisoners activist, and his Pershing Square Capital Management crew, which acquired a large stake in Canadian Pacific and then threatened "nuclear winter" if the railroad did not agree to his suggested management changes. In the end Ackman forced out Canadian Pacific's chief executive officer and several board members and installed E. Hunter Harrison as the railroad's top gun. Harrison, best known for an innovative operating concept he labeled "precision scheduled railroading," had retired at Canadian National in 2009, where he cultivated the notion that he had "turned the company around." At Canadian Pacific he promised to reduce bureaucracy, cut costs, change the corporate culture, and run longer and fewer trains, the latter a key feature of "precision scheduled railroading." Share prices doubled. Canadian Pacific, claimed Harrison, was "driving change . . . to become the best railroad in North America, while creating long-term value for shareholders."[19]

Hunter Harrison's name dominated conversations among railroaders of all stripes and others, too, well beyond the industry. He pumped money into plant, fired personnel left and right, developed at Canadian Pacific a culture that employed fear and intimidation as motivators, rankled labor and customers alike, and, as the operating ratio fell, earned the admiration of Wall Street. Late in 2014 Harrison proposed a merger between Canadian Pacific and CSX, arguing that a coast-to-coast railroad such as he envisioned would improve customer service, increase network capacity, and relieve congestion in places such as Chicago. Nothing came of it. But Harrison quickly made another merger proposal—this time with Norfolk Southern and based on a similar set of arguments. Harrison's approach seemed to be, as one observer put it, "go big, or go home." Many wondered if he simply wanted to precipitate "the final round of mergers in the railroad industry." Harrison's proposed Canadian Pacific–Norfolk Southern marriage also foundered.[20]

*   *   *

By the middle of the second decade of the twenty-first century, the traffic mix of major railroads in Missouri was relatively stable. Coal traffic remained prominent. In 1969, Missouri Pacific had sealed a contract to haul coal from southern Illinois mines to a new power plant at West Labadie, Missouri, but the great coal surge came later, mostly from Wyoming. Coal accounted for 16 percent of revenue at Union Pacific in 2015, 1.7 million carloads of it two years earlier, but BNSF moved even more, 2.2 million carloads in 2014. Loadings in the future were certain to decline, however, because of market forces and government regulations favoring natural gas in fueling generating plants. On a happier note, growth in intermodal billings was remarkable. When he was at Santa Fe, Michael Haverty had clinched a deal with the long-haul trucking firm of J. B. Hunt, and subsequently Hunt had shifted resources away from its own over-the-road operations. By 2014, Hunt moved 1.7 million intermodal loads. In 2006, another long-haul trucker, Schneider National, commissioned its own train between Marion, Ohio, and Kansas City via CSX and Kansas City Southern. BNSF in 2013 opened its 1.5-million-lift Logistics Park Kansas City at Edgerton, Kansas.

Railroad traffic patterns reflected a mix of traditional and new sources. Intermodal cargo accounted for 16 percent of Kansas City Southern revenues and 20 percent at Union Pacific. The growth of motor vehicle assembly in Mexico favored Kansas City Southern and Union Pacific in the movement of auto parts and set-up machines. Rack design included Union Pacific's ninety-foot AutoFlex, an innovation developed by the railroad's own personnel and built at the company shop in De Soto, Missouri. Automotive-related traffic in 2015 accounted for 11 percent of Union Pacific revenues and 9 percent at Kansas City Southern. For Missouri railroads, agriculture has always been an important revenue component, accounting for 15 percent of Union Pacific's total in 2015, for instance. Burlington Northern in the 1990s had adopted pricing policies for moving grain by unit train in 286,000-pound covered hoppers. Its successor BNSF continued and expanded "shuttle" trains. A new variable came with the growing importance of ethanol as a renewable fuel and a product that cannot be shipped practically by pipeline. Ethanol distillers' dried grains, remains of corn after fermentation, proved important as animal feed. Not surprisingly, all major carriers serving Missouri profited from massive shipments of ethanol and distillers' dried grains—much of it moving across the state to more distant destinations.[21]

*   *   *

Hunter Harrison, late of Canadian National and then Canadian Pacific, took his "precision scheduled railroading" concept to CSX early in 2017, where, as expected, he promised to cut costs and improve operations by running fewer trains, using fewer locomotives and cars, closing classification yards, trimming employment numbers, and driving down the operating ratio. Investors rejoiced. The price of CSX securities rose to impressive new heights. Shippers and labor were less enthusiastic. "There will be a little pain and suffering," Harrison admitted. One survey showed that 24 percent of rail customers rated CSX service during Harrison's brief tenure as "poor." The Surface Transportation Board frowned. Harrison died unexpectedly on December 16, 2017, but CSX management vowed to "stick with" his strategies. Harrison left a mixed legacy, revered by many but reviled by others. One respected observer affirmed that Harrison was a "genius at railroad operations" but was not "a genius at running a railroad."[22]

Nevertheless, Harrison's reach extended beyond the grave. Investors and securities analysts remained enthralled by his devotion to low operating ratios, and many of his acolytes attained senior positions at every major railroad except BNSF. "Rail maverick's legacy inspires rivals," asserted the *Wall Street Journal*, noting that Union Pacific was adopting Harrison's "strategy to speed its freight trains." For Union Pacific this was a dramatic shift because until recently it had been adding locomotives and crews; now it cut back on both. Union Pacific asserted that it was devoted to "building long-term value for our key stakeholders—shareholders, communities, customers, and employees," but it was not clear how that would square with Harrison's values. As one observer put it, "Shippers are agitated that Precision Scheduled Railroading—a strategy to reduce operating ratios, boost profit and hike stock price—is degrading service quality."[23]

Matt Rose was not bashful in staking out the position of BNSF:

> Trying to be more precise-like in scheduling isn't something new at BNSF. We have a history of trying to do just that. Growth in customer business is our focus. Cost cutting as a PSR theme only goes so far. Yes, "sweating out the assets" has to be part of a balancing act, but BNSF balances its management of the railroad toward benefits shared by employees, customers, investors, and the community at large. A PSR method that seeks . . . cost savings from every thousand employees cut isn't thinking long term, as it often ignores service disruptions to customers. . . . As a required goal, BNSF seeks continued traffic growth in volume. This is essential. . . . BNSF needs to grow units, not just yield. Disengaging from our customers to change internal cost savings is not good long-term business strategy. De-marketing tactics can result in unanticipated but logical bad policy outcomes. There's nothing wrong with being a low-cost supplier, but ignoring your customers until you hit a wall on costs can have undesirable longer-term consequences.

BNSF, insisted Rose, preferred a "balanced approach" to operations: "Growing traffic units and operating income is a better way to increase revenues that figure into the operating ratio." Clearly, there was a significant difference of philosophy among senior railroad managers as to ultimate goals and objectives. How it would play out to the satisfaction of all stakeholders remained a question.[24]

"Precision scheduled railroading," its exact definition, and ways in which each railroad might implement it remain fluid. The same remains true for Harrison's legacy as a railroad guru with operating ideas worth implementing.

* * *

Sixty years after the modern merger movement began, and forty years after the Staggers Rail Act of 1980 streamlined the merger process, Class I freight railroading had rationalized into seven carriers. As if to underscore Missouri's continuing central role, all seven—BNSF, Canadian National, Canadian Pacific, CSX, Kansas City Southern, Norfolk Southern, and Union Pacific—serve the state. (Technically, the tracks of Canadian National and CSX do not enter the state, but both railroads maintain yards and intermodal facilities just east of the Mississippi River in Illinois within the St. Louis terminal district.)

CSX and Norfolk Southern serve mainly the eastern states; BNSF and Union Pacific serve mainly the west; two of the carriers are primarily Canadian, but with a significant United States presence—and then there was Missouri's own Kansas City Southern, which chose to go its own way, as it always had, until Canadian Pacific acquired it in 2023. The spatial dimensions of the rail giants raised the intriguing possibility of a last round of mergers, each of them combining an eastern railroad, a western carrier, and one of the Canadian systems. Indeed, BNSF and Canadian National proposed a merger in 1999. Shippers protested, however, mindful of the near-meltdown of the national network in the wake of the 1996 Union Pacific–Southern Pacific merger. The Surface Transportation Board, which assumed the Interstate Commerce Commission's merger oversight role effective with the Staggers Act, imposed a cooling-off period for the deal, after which BNSF and Canadian National called off their merger plans. Still, it is not hard to imagine what might have happened if they had consummated their proposed union: Canadian Pacific and Union Pacific might have had little choice but to join forces, after which each of the new US-Canadian systems might have teamed up with an eastern carrier.

Mexico could have been the subject of still more consolidations. Union Pacific, with a 26 percent stake in Ferrocarril, or Ferromex, would have brought that partnership to any merger it undertook with United States and Canadian carriers. In response, BNSF might have made a play for Kansas City Southern, which operated a network through Mexico's industrial heart, stretching from Nuevo Laredo to San Luis Potosi, Monterrey, Mexico City, and Guadalajara. Like Ferromex, Kansas City Southern de Mexico served ports on both the Caribbean and the Pacific coasts.

*   *   *

Crystal-ball gazing is often hazardous to a historian's reputation. That said, while consolidations of the kind just described remain possible, most industry observers regarded them as unlikely. Every consolidation in the round of mergers that took place more than twenty years ago led to significant service disruptions that severely impacted hundreds of shippers and could have threatened the national economy. Moreover, the carriers and shippers seem to have made their peace with the status quo, since they often have a choice of routings and interchange partners, no matter how limited that choice may be. And choice means competition, which encourages responsiveness, innovation, and—most pleasing to shippers—lower pricing.

The rail networks of North America and Missouri appear unlikely to witness major changes. A stable network generally means stable traffic flows, but coal could be a notable exception: production declined by more than one-third from 2008 to 2016 as a number of electric power plants switched to less-expensive and cleaner-burning natural gas, lately made more abundant with the rise of hydraulic fracturing. Analysis by the United States Energy Information Administration suggests that coal demand may tumble an additional one-third by 2040. As of this writing, however, coal remains a strong commodity for Missouri railroads: Some 358,800 carloads of coal were terminated in the state in 2018, more than any other class of traffic, and represented fully 44.3 percent of all carloads delivered. Hundreds of thousands of additional carloads transit Missouri en route to power plants located in southeastern states.[25]

Unlike coal, the future of intermodal traffic in Missouri seems assured. The state has been home to the United States population center in every census since 1980, and its transportation infrastructure reflects that fact. Some 3,862 route-miles of railroad lie within its borders, along with 1,386 miles of interstate highways. Intermodal traffic is thus an important part of the rail-freight mix, representing 61.8 percent of Missouri's originating carloads and 34 percent of its terminations. For consumer goods especially, but also for manufacturing, intermodal offers the economy of rail for the long-haul portion of a shipment, combined with the door-to-door flexibility of trucks. Consumer goods from Asia and automobile manufacturing alike benefit from intermodal, to name just two market segments. Other commodity groups, particularly those related to agriculture, are almost a given for Missouri railroads, as they always have been.[26]

Rail employment stood at 7,272 in Missouri in 2018, but this is another area that could witness significant change. Technology has facilitated a dramatic reduction in train-crew sizes since 1980. The five-person crew is completely unknown in the twenty-first century, and the two-person train crew is now the norm. With the advent of fail-safe positive train control systems, however, which enforce movement authorities and speed restrictions when the engineer fails to do so, the industry has begun a push for one-person train crews. Organized labor has understandably resisted such a move, thus far successfully, but the handwriting is on the wall. It is not unreasonable to expect that this issue will be resolved in the same way that train crews have been reduced in the past—through labor agreements that grandfather existing employees and then eliminate their jobs through attrition. The impetus for one-person crews will likely grow should driverless trucks come into widespread use, which in one stroke could solve the motor-freight industry's perpetual staffing needs and take valued intermodal shipments off the rails.

We are fully aware that the march of technology could render this discussion moot within a few years of publication, but we offer it as a snapshot of the challenges facing the industry during the third decade of the twenty-first century.

* * *

FIGURE 7.5. The splendidly clad conductor was boss of the train and a familiar figure to generations of rail travelers. As essential as his watch was to accident-free train operations, it offered no clue as to the future fate of the industry. Schwantes-Greever-Nolan Collection.

Expect the unexpected. Early in 2021 Canadian Pacific and Kansas City Southern agreed to a takeover of the Missouri-based company, a $25 billion deal that would create the first-ever rail network running from Canada across the United States and into Mexico, a roughly twenty-thousand-mile system with CP's Keith Creel as chief executive officer. The issue went before the Surface Transportation Board, which, by statute, requires major transportation matters to be in the public interest and to enhance competition. Canadian National then poked its nose into this merger tent with a $30 billion counteroffer for Kansas City Southern, a bid that agitated negotiations but was ultimately rejected by KCS.[27]

Canadian Pacific, seemingly a bit rattled for the moment, went on the offensive. CP's Creel enthusiastically pointed out that the combination of CP and KCS would be an end-to-end arrangement that would stimulate competition, take trucks off the highway, and benefit the environment.[28]

Competitors took exception. Norfolk Southern complained that a combined CP-KCS would harm its valued Meridian Speedway (Meridian, Mississippi, to Shreveport, Louisiana), while METRA, Chicago's commuter operation, argued that increased freight movements by CP-KCS would certainly interfere with and delay commuter trains on lines owed by CP-KCS and shared with METRA. And certain Chicago suburbs fussed that an increase in the number of freight trains would degrade neighborhood quality of life.[29]

Despite these and other irritations and complaints, Canadian Pacific and Kansas City Southern prevailed, with the Surface Transportation Board authorizing CP to exercise control of KCS effective April 14, 2023. The United States headquarters were located in Kansas City.[30]

Nearly four decades earlier, a greatly disappointed Grand Trunk Western's John H. Burdakin wryly observed that his company had "prettied up" only to pass to Soo Line instead of to Grand Trunk Western. One might have expected a similar response from Michael R. Haverty, who more than any other had "prettied up" Kansas City Southern and now would see it submerged into CPKC. Not so. Said Haverty, "I strongly support the CP/KCS merger" because it creates a "transcontinental railroad that is the only one . . . that operates in all three North American countries." Moreover, in Haverty's view, "Keith Creel is the best CEO of any railroad in North America. . . . He may have trained under Hunter Harrison, but he is growth oriented and not just focused on reducing costs to improve the operating ratio." Haverty noted that Kansas City Southern had faced many attempts at takeover during his "tenure," and "none were successful as we squelched them all. I may have gotten the reputation that I would fight to the death to keep KCS independent. But that was not the case. I was committed to doing what was in the best interest of KCS shareholders." Yes, he affirmed, "I strongly support the CP/KCS merger." Expect the unexpected.[31]

The future is usually murky, filled with a combination of factors known and unknown and obliging railroaders to place their bets using the best information available. As we have seen in these pages, it was ever thus. Railroad construction, finance, and regulation were seldom accomplished in neat and orderly ways, especially during the early days, but the result is beyond dispute: railroads have done as much as any industry to shape Missouri's destiny, to foster the rise of its cities and farms, and to boost the economy of the state and nation. Indeed, modern Missouri and its railroads have long been joined at the hip—a symbiotic relationship if ever there was one. Each has changed and been changed by the other. The future will be no different.

Publishing Missouri's Railroads

American railroads were prodigious publishers, especially during the span of eighty years from the early 1880s through the 1950s, and Missouri lines were no exception. Their annual outpouring of paper documents encompassed millions of public timetables, calendars, and promotional brochures. Determined to give these documents maximum eye appeal, they embraced color printing and lavish and imaginative cover images, especially after technological advances in color printing during the late 1890s made these visual enhancements possible.

Most brochures could be sorted into three broad categories: promotion of vacation travel, land settlement, or the railroad itself. In the latter category were publications that saluted improved safety, smoother roadbed and track, and new passenger trains and their onboard amenities. We end our second volume of Missouri railroad history with a representative sampling of publishing intended to boost Missouri and its railroads.

FIGURE 7.2.1. Missouri Pacific's eye-catching advertisement saluted its large fleet of long-distance trains. Schwantes-Greever-Nolan Collection.

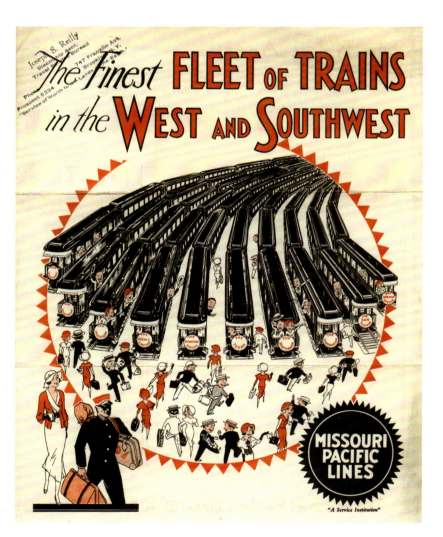

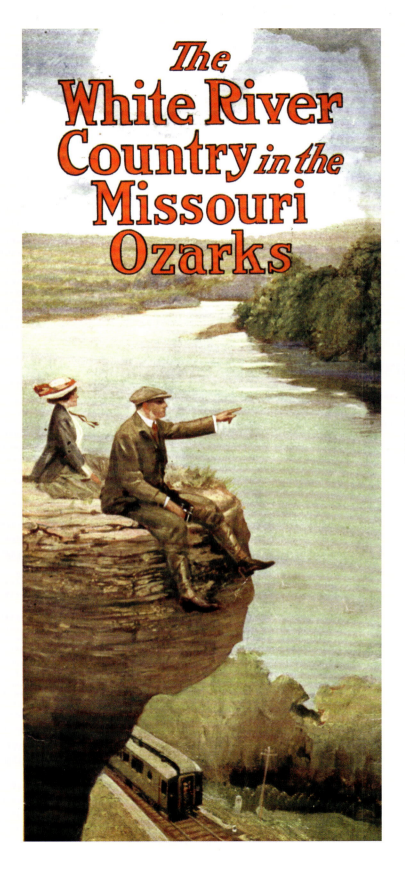

FIGURE 7.2.2. Missouri Pacific's Ozarks promotional brochure cover. Railroads used commercial art to direct public attention to vacation and settlement opportunities along their tracks. Schwantes-Greever-Nolan Collection.

FIGURE 7.2.3. Frisco tracks crisscrossed southern Missouri and blessed residents of Kansas City and other communities with through travel to Florida. Schwantes-Greever-Nolan Collection.

FIGURE 7.2.4. Union Pacific, until its acquisition of Missouri Pacific and Katy properties, was not a major player within Missouri, but through passenger trains did connect Kansas City with exotic western destinations like Yellowstone National Park. Residents of the St. Louis area could join the journey aboard through Pullman cars. This example shows the value of whimsical themes in advertising. Schwantes-Greever-Nolan Collection.

FIGURE 7.2.5. The Missouri-based St. Louis Southwestern issued this brochure early in the twentieth century to promote development in East Texas. Its optimistic message and its eye-catching cover artwork were typical of this type of publication, which railroads of the United States issued by the millions. Schwantes-Greever-Nolan Collection.

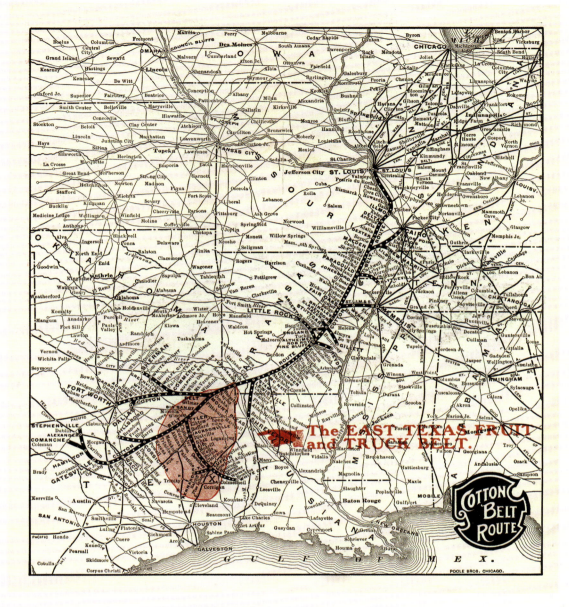

FIGURE 7.2.6. A map was an essential feature of railroad publications issued to inform the public, and this included their timetables. Schwantes-Greever-Nolan Collection.

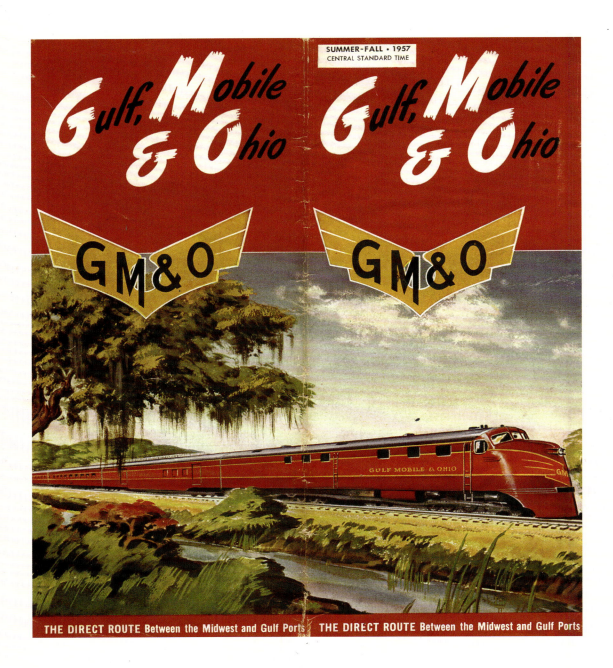

FIGURE 7.2.7 AND 7.2.8. We conclude this book with a question that will elicit a variety of answers. Displayed here are two timetables from 1957. These railroads, which served Missouri destinations, still took passenger travel seriously. Which cover image is your personal favorite? Schwantes-Greever-Nolan Collection.

Notes

Overview and Acknowledgments

1. Peter A. Hansen, Don L. Hofsommer, and Carlos Arnaldo Schwantes, *Crossroads of a Continent: Missouri Railroads, 1851–1921* (Bloomington: Indiana University Press, 2022).

Introduction

1. Harland Bartholomew, "The Future Transportation Requirements of St. Louis," *Proceedings of the St. Louis Railway Club* (April 8, 1921), 33.

2. Peter A. Hansen, Don L. Hofsommer, and Carlos Arnaldo Schwantes, *Crossroads of a Continent: Missouri Railroads, 1851–1921* (Bloomington: Indiana University Press, 2022).

1. Spirit of St. Louis

1. Chicago, Rock Island & Pacific, *Public Timetable* (October 1929), 13, 24–25. By this date, the Rock Island's motor trains no longer ran through but broke their daily runs in Eldon, where they halted for the night. The through trains required slightly more than eight hours to complete their overnight journeys between St. Louis and Kansas City.

2. The engineer of the express train apparently failed to notice the signal to stop.

3. James J. Horgan, *City of Flight: The History of Aviation in St. Louis* (Gerald, MO: Patrice, 1984).

4. Daniel L. Rust, *Flying across America: The Airlines Passenger Experience* (Norman: University of Oklahoma Press, 2009).

5. *Automobile*, September 10, 1904, 303.

6. Steven Watts, *The People's Tycoon: Henry Ford and the American Century* (New York: Vintage Books, 2006); James J. Flink, *The Car Culture* (Cambridge: MIT Press, 1975); Warren James Belasco, *Americans on the Road: From Autocamp to Motel, 1910–1945* (Cambridge: MIT Press, 1979); David McCullough, *The Path between the Seas: The Creation of the Panama Canal, 1870–1914* (New York: Simon and Schuster, 1977).

7. Carlos A. Schwantes, "The West Adapts the Automobile: Technology, Unemployment, and the Jitney Phenomenon of 1914–1917," *Western Historical Quarterly* (1985), 307–26.

8. The origin of the name *jitney* is obscure, but one explanation is that it derived from a low-value French coin called a *jeton* and having the value of approximately five American cents. See Schwantes, "West Adapts the Automobile," for a detailed account of the jitney phenomenon.

9. Robert A. Smith, *A Social History of the Bicycle: Its Early Life and Times in America* (New York: American Heritage, 1972); David V. Herlihy, *Bicycle: The History* (New Haven, CT: Yale University Press, 2004).

10. John A. Jakle and Keith A. Sculle, *Supplanting America's Railroads: The Early Auto Age, 1900–1940* (Knoxville: University of Tennessee Press, 2017).

11. Julia D. Cowles, "The Good Roads Convention at St. Louis," *World To-Day*, June 1903, 761.

12. Cowles, "Good Roads Convention," 762.

13. Cowles, "Good Roads Convention," 766.

14. *Good Roads Magazine*, October 1904, 498. The railroad's monthly publication was titled *Frisco System Magazine*. The September 1904 issue featured a broad array of articles, including "Southwest Missouri as a Woman Sees It" and "An Ode to the Hen." It also included an essay on the St. Louis World's Fair, a seemingly obligatory topic in 1904 for every magazine published in the United States.

15. Cowles, "Good Roads Convention," 762.

16. John K. Brown, *The Baldwin Locomotive Works, 1831–1915* (Baltimore: Johns Hopkins University Press, 1995), 223–25.

17. James J. Flink, *America Adopts the Automobile, 1895–1910* (Cambridge: MIT Press, 1970).

18. Michael L. Berger, *The Devil Wagon in God's Country: The Automobile and Social Change in Rural America, 1893–1929* (Harden, CT: Archon Books, 1979).

19. Phil Patton, *Open Road: A Celebration of the American Highway* (New York: Simon and Schuster, 1986); Earl Swift, *The Big Roads: The Untold Story of the Engineers, Visionaries, and Trailblazers Who Created the American*

265

Superhighways (Boston: Houghton Mifflin Harcourt, 2011).

20. George W. Hilton and John F. Due, *The Electric Interurban Railways in America* (Stanford: Stanford University Press, 1960.

21. Albro Martin, *Enterprise Denied: Origins of the Decline of American Railroads, 1897–1917* (New York: Columbia University Press, 1971); Robert E. Gallamore and John R. Meyer, *American Railroads: Decline and Renaissance in the Twentieth Century* (Cambridge, MA: Harvard University Press, 2014).

22. Stephen B. Goddard, *Getting There: The Epic Struggle between Road and Rail in the American Century* (1994; repr., Chicago: University of Chicago Press, 1996); Donald M. Itzkoff, *Off the Track: The Decline of the Intercity Passenger Train in the United States* (Westport, CT: Greenwood, 1985).

2. The Dark Decade

1. Carlos A. Schwantes, *Going Places: Transportation Redefines the Twentieth Century West* (Bloomington: Indiana University Press, 2003), 144.

2. Samuel O. Dunn, "A Revolution in Railroading," *World's Work* 53 (1927): 419–26; G. Andrews, "War among the Railroads," *Nation*, August 12, 1925, 184–86.

3. Frederick Lewis Allen, *Since Yesterday: The 1930s in America* (New York: Harper and Row, 1939), 2–15; Peter Fearon, *War, Prosperity and Depression: The U.S. Economy, 1917–1945* (Lawrence: University Press of Kansas, 1987), 90–97, 1110, 173; *Railway Age*, January 27, 1934, 155–59; Alfred D. Chandler Jr., *The Visible Hand: The Managerial Revolution in Business* (Cambridge, MA: Harvard University Press, 1977), 496.

4. David B. Danbom, *Born in the Country: History of Rural America* (Baltimore: Johns Hopkins University Press, 1995), 197–202; Fearon, *War, Prosperity and Depression*, 101–7; Lester V. Chandler, *America's Greatest Depression, 1921–1941* (New York: Harper and Row, 1970), 53–67.

5. *Railway Age*, November 23, 1929, 1177–78, 1201–3; *Railway Age*, January 4, 1930, 9; *New York Times*, November 20, 1929, January 29, 1930.

6. Roger Biles, *A New Deal for the American People* (DeKalb: Northern Illinois University, 1991), 23–24.

7. *New Republic*, January 14, 1931, 231–32; George W. Anderson, "Salvaging our Railroads," *Atlantic Monthly*, December 1932, 710–17; *New York Times*, September 18, 1932; Earl Latham, *The Politics of Railroad Coordination, 1933–1936* (Cambridge, MA: Harvard University Press. 1959), 1–34.

8. Herbert Spero, *Reconstruction Finance Corporation Loans to Railroads, 1932–1937* (Boston: Bankers, 1929), 1–4, 18–41, 132–50, 163–65; *Wall Street Journal*, February 15, 1933, May 6, 1933; Churchill Rodgers and Littleton Groom, "Reorganization of Railroad Corporations under Section 77 of the Bankruptcy Act," *Columbia Law Review* 33 (1933): 571–616; Edward T. Paxton, "Railroad Receiverships and Reorganization," *Editorial Research Report* 10 (1933): 23–36.

9. *Moody's Manual of Investments: Railroad Securities* (New York: Moody's Investors Services, 1945), a13–a24. Hereinafter cited as *Moody's Manual*.

10. "The Railways in 1933 and 1934," *Railway Age*, January 27, 1934, 93–136.

11. James H. Lemly, *The Gulf Mobile and Ohio: A Railroad That Had to Expand or Expire* (Homewood: Richard D. Irwin, 1953), 167, 183–91; Gene V. Glendinning, *The Chicago & Alton Railroad: The Only Way* (DeKalb: Northern Illinois University Press, 2002), 182–229; Don L. Hofsommer, *The Southern Pacific, 1901–1985* (College Station: Texas A&M University Press, 1986), 183–88.

12. *Official Guide*, January 1930, 331, 333.

13. *Railway Age*, January 4, 1930, 55; *Railway Age*, January 20, 1934, 178; *Railway Age*, January 27, 1934, 135–36.

14. *Official Guide*, March 1920, 984–85; ibid., May 1940, 1157; George W. Hilton and John F. Due, *The Electric Interurban Railways in America* (Stanford: Stanford University Press, 1960), 366–69; H. Roger Grant, *Electric Interurbans and the American People* (Bloomington: Indiana University Press, 2016), 137–39.

15. Allen, *Since Yesterday*, 226; *Wall Street Journal*, June 19, 1996; *Business Week*, November 30, 1932, 15–15; *Business Week*, December 30, 1933, 24.

16. Chicago, Rock Island & Pacific, *Annual Report, 1931*, 8.

17. H. Roger Grant, "Hard Times," *Rails across America: A History of Railroads in North America* (New York: Smithmark Books, 1993), 130–47; *Official Guide*, March 1930, 15; ibid., June 1934, 24, 28, 455, 732; ibid., May 1930, 15, 16; ibid., December 1933, 42; ibid., July 1930, 4; ibid., February 1930, 7; ibid., July 1932, 33; ibid., May 1933, 34; Wabash, *Timetable* (November 1932), 31–32; *Terminal Railroad Association of St. Louis Historical and Technical Society (Bulletin)* 6 (August 1992): 2–25.

18. *Official Guide*, May 1932, 44; ibid., August 1932, 57; ibid., May 1933, 34; ibid., August 1934, 41.

19. *Official Guide*, July 1935, 24; ibid., June 1936, 30; ibid., December 1936, 43; ibid., August 1937, 29.

20. *Official Guide*, June 1936, 29; ibid., March 1937, 40; ibid., November 1938, 49; ibid., August 1935, 27; ibid., April 1937, 44; ibid., April 1939, 42; ibid., June 1936, 30; ibid., May 1937, 45.

21. *Official Guide*, May 1934, 41; ibid., June 1936, 29; ibid., March 1937, 41; ibid., April 1939, 41–42.

22. The American Association of Railroad Superintendents, *Committee Reports 1946*, 30.

23. *Police Guide and Directory of St. Louis* (1884), 31–34; *Official Railway Guide of St. Louis* 5 (September 1875): 21; *Official Guide*, July 1904, 701; *Traveler's Railway Guide Western Section*, October 1904, 13; *Proceedings of the . . . Convention . . . American Railway Engineering Association* 24 (1923): 863–66; *St Louis Globe-Democrat* March 18, 1933; Terminal Railroad Association, *Timetable 217*, January 20, 1939; Terminal Railroad Association, *Timetable 263*, September 24, 1939; Terminal Railroad Association, *Timetable 5-B*, November 1, 1942.

24. *Railway Age*, October 25, 1930, 870; *Official Guide*, October 1924, 14; ibid., January 1930, xxxii; ibid., August 1935, 25; H. Roger Grant, *Transportation and the American People* (Bloomington: Indiana University Press, 2019), 183–218.

25. *Official Guide*, January 1930, 790, 989, 1026, 1051; ibid., March 1935, 397; ibid., August 1938, 980; *Railway Age*, January 4, 1930, 100–101; Edmund Keilty, *Doodlebug*

Country: The Rail Motor Car on the Class I Railroads of the United States (Glendale: Interurban Press, 1982), 22–28, 51–56, 57–60, 67, 83; Edmund Keilty, *Interurbans without Wires: The Rail Motor Car in the United States* (Glendale: Interurban Press, 1979), 12, 138–44.

26. G. W. Marriott, "In One Year—a 4,000-Mile System," *Railway Age*, February 22, 1930, 518–20; Richard C. Overton, *Burlington Route: History of the Burlington Lines* (New York: Alfred A. Knopf, 1965), 353, 406; Glendinning, *Chicago & Alton Railroad*, 193–95.

27. *Moody's Manual* (1941), a9–a10.

28. Hofsommer, *Southern Pacific*, 184; "Operating a Co-ordinated Rail-Motor Truck Service," *Railway Age*, April 26, 1930, 1014–18; Overton, *Burlington Route*, 416; Chicago, Burlington & Quincy, *Annual Report, 1935*, 12.

29. Chicago, Rock Island & Pacific, *Annual Report, 1936*, 44; "More Cattle Move by Truck," *Railway Age*, March 1, 1930, 543; *Moody's Manual* (1941), a10–a43.

30. "Wabash Poultry Age," *Railway Age*, April 5, 1930, 843; "A Close-Up of Perishable Handling," *Railway Age*, December 20, 1930, 1306–7; Broadus Mitchell, *The Depression Decade from the New Era through the New Deal, 1929–1941* (New York: Holt, Rinehart and Winston, 1947), 190; "A 27-Car Beer Train," *Railway Age*, April 14, 1934, 557; Scott Muskopf, "The Beer Baron's Railway," in *The Manufacturers Railway Company* (St. Louis: Terminal Railroad Association Historical Society, 2009), 28.

31. *Official Guide*, March 1935, 645; ibid., October 1936, 66; ibid., April 1938, 640, 661, 960, 961; ibid., May 1938, 49.

32. Hofsommer, *Southern Pacific*, 185; *Official Guide*, August 1938, 863.

33. *Railway Age*, June 30, 1934, 954; Overton, *Burlington Route*, 403; Chicago, Burlington & Quincy, *Annual Report, 1933*, 30; Chicago, Milwaukee, St. Paul & Pacific, *Annual Report, 1939*, 64.

34. Chicago, Rock Island & Pacific, *Annual Report, 1931*, 7–8; Chicago, Milwaukee, St. Paul & Pacific, *Annual Report, 1930*, 4; "Railways to Operate over St. Louis Municipal Bridge," *Railway Age*, August 30, 1930, 449–50; "First Train over St. Louis Municipal Bridge," *Railway Age*, October 4, 1930, 718; "4,000,000 Bridge Building Program to Increase Railroad Terminal Facilities at St. Louis," *Manufacturers Record*, June 30, 1932, 14–15; M. H. Doyne, "St. Louis Municipal Bridge Is Ready for Use," *Railway Age*, December 16, 1939, 923–25; *St. Louis Post-Dispatch*, August 14 and 18, 1939; "New KCS Line Completes Ownership to Gulf Ports," *Railway Age*, April 19, 1930, 907–8; *Railway Age*, November 8, 1930, 1011; Chicago, Milwaukee, St. Paul & Pacific, *Annual Report, 1936*, 24; Chicago, Milwaukee, St. Paul & Pacific, *Annual Report, 1939*, 15.

35. *Official Guide*, January 1930, 1294, 1393; ibid., May 1940, 654, 675, 895, 933, 997, 1150, 1154, 7189; *Moody's Manual* (1941), 66–67, 214, 263.

36. Chicago, Burlington & Quincy, *Annual Report, 1935*, p. 8; Chicago, Burlington & Quincy, *Annual Report, 1936*, 8; *Moody's Manual* (1941), 7.

37. Mitchell, *Depression Decade*, 33; *Moody's Manual* (1953), a49.

38. *Moody's Manual* (1953), a4; John F. Stover, *American Railroads* (Chicago: University of Chicago Press, 1961), 212–13, 238.

39. *Moody's Manual* (1941), a4; Stover, *American Railroads*, 186.

40. Allen, *Since Yesterday*, 332–34; *Official Guide*, November 1939, 51; ibid., May 1940, 43, 45.

3. Of War and Peace

1. Frederick Lewis Allen, *Since Yesterday: The 1930s in America* (New York: Harper and Row, 1939), 332–34.

2. Eliot Janeway, *The Struggle for Survival: A Chronicle of Economic Mobilization in World War II* (New Haven, CT: Yale University Press, 1951), 181–84, 234–39, 275–76; John F. Stover, *American Railroads* (Chicago: University of Chicago Press, 1961), 200–202; Richard C. Overton, *Perkins/Budd: Railway Statesmen of the Burlington* (Westport: Greenwood, 1982), 201–2.

3. *Railway Age*, January 5, 1929, 18–19; *Railway Age*, January 4, 1930, 57, 75, 85; Chicago, Rock Island & Pacific, *Annual Report, 1931*, 8; John F. Stover, *History of the Baltimore & Ohio Railroad* (West Lafayette: Purdue University Press, 1987), 304.

4. Janeway, *Struggle for Survival*, 275–76; Overton, *Perkins/Budd*, 201–2.

5. James F. Willis and Martin L. Primack, *An Economic History of the United States* (Englewood Cliffs: Prentice-Hall, 1989), 391, 393; A. J. Baine, *The Arsenal of Democracy: FDR, Detroit, and the Epic Quest to Arm an America at War* (Boston: Houghton-Mifflin, 2014), 87, 107, 113, 135–36, 197, 209. See also John W. Jeffries, *Wartime America: The World War II Home Front* (Lanham: Rowman and Littlefield, 2018).

6. Association of American Railroads, Circular No. T&T 329, May 27, 1942.

7. John F. Stover, *History of the Illinois Central Railroad* (New York: Macmillan, 1975), 356; James H. Lemly, *The Gulf, Mobile & Ohio: A Railroad That Had to Expand or Expire* (Homewood: Richard B. Irwin, 1953), 175–76; Gene V. Glendinning, *The Chicago Alton Railroad: The Only Way* (DeKalb: Northern Illinois University Press, 2002), 219; Don L. Hofsommer, *The Quanah Route: A History of the Quanah, Acme & Pacific Railway* (College Station: Texas A&M University Press, 1991), 122–25.

8. James E. Valle, *The Iron Horse at War* (Berkeley: Howell-North, 1977), 143; Keith L. Bryant Jr., *History of the Atchison, Topeka & Santa Fe Railway* (New York: Macmillan, 1974), 272.

9. Bryant, *Atchison, Topeka & Santa Fe Railway*, 273; Don DeNevi, *America's Fighting Railroads: World War II Pictorial History* (Missoula: Pictorial Histories, 1996), 106.

10. Stover, *American Railroads*, 202–5; *Official Guide*, March 1941, 35; ibid., May 1941, 40; ibid., September 1941, 48. Other Missouri military installations included Camp Clark (Nevada), Camp Crowder (McElhany), Jefferson Barracks (St. Louis), O'Reilly General Hospital (Springfield), Quartermaster Depot (Kansas City), Richards Field (Kansas City), Rosecrans Field (St. Joseph), and St. Louis Medical Depot (St. Louis).

11. Terminal Railroad Association, "Statement . . . Passenger Trains and Cars Crossing Eads, Merchants, Municipal . . . ," ended June 30, 1942; "Why St. Louis Is No Bottle-neck," *Railway Age*, October 24, 1942, 655–60; *Railway Age*, October 3, 1942, 519; *Official Guide*, August

1942, 65; ibid., July 1942, 60; ibid., December 1942, 49–51.

12. *Official Guide*, January 1943, 51, 53; Patrick E. Purcell, "St. Louis Union Station," *Bulletin* (NRHS) 37, no. 4 (1972): 16.

13. Stover, *American Railroads*, 204–5; S. Kip Farrington, *Railroads at War* (New York: Coward-McCann, 1944), 296; *Official Guide*, March 1944, 13.

14. Donald J. Heimburger and John Kelly, *Trains to Victory: America's Railroads in World War II* (Forest Park: Heimburger House, 2009), 111. See also Joseph R. Rose, *American Wartime Transportation* (New York: Crowel, 1953).

15. *Official Guide*, February 1945, 14; ibid., June 1945, 14; ibid., July 1945, 14–15; ibid., August 1945, 13–15; *St. Louis Globe-Democrat*, March 7, 1945.

16. *St. Louis Globe-Democrat*, February 29, 1944.

17. *St. Louis Globe-Democrat*, May 11, 1944.

18. *Missouri Pacific Lines Magazine*, September 1944, 3.

19. L. O. Hand, "Railway Express Agency Services and Problems," *Annals of American Political and Social Science* 230 (1943): 101–9; *St. Louis Star*, July 3, 1945; *Railway Age*, March 4, 1939, 363, 365–72; Margaret Farrand Thorp, *America at the Movies* (New Haven, CT: Yale University Press, 1939), 1–25.

20. Bryant, *Atchison, Topeka & Santa Fe Railway*, 312–14; Chicago, Rock Island & Pacific, *Annual Report, 1942*, 37; *Railway Age*, November 11, 1950, 67; David P. Morgan, *Diesels West: The Evolution of Power on the Burlington* (Milwaukee: Kalmbach, 1963), 86–95; Eugene L. Huddleston, "The Production Board and Diesels," *Railfan and Railroad*, January 1986, 6–44; Chicago, Burlington & Quincy, *Annual Report, 1944*, 10.

21. Chicago, Burlington & Quincy, *Annual Report, 1943*, 8; Chicago, Rock Island & Pacific, *Annual Report, 1942*, 65; Freeman Hubbard, *Encyclopedia of North American Railroading: 150 Years of Railroading in the United States and Canada* (New York: McGraw-Hill, 1981), 359; Stover, *Illinois Central Railroad*, 367.

22. DeNevi, *America's Fighting Railroads*, 73; Glendinning, *Chicago Alton Railroad*, 220; Stover, *Illinois Central Railroad*, 354; Chicago, Rock Island & Pacific, *Annual Report, 1942*, 2; August Derleth, *The Milwaukee Road: Its First Hundred Years* (New York: Creative Age, 1948), 256; Chicago, Burlington & Quincy, *Annual Report, 1944*, 7.

23. Frank W. Fox, *Madison Avenue Goes to War: The Military Career of American Advertising, 1941–1945* (Provo: Brigham Young University Press, 1975), 25–91; Mark H. Leff, "The Politics of Sacrifice on the American Home Front in World War II," *Journal of American History* 77 (1991): 1296–318; Raymond Rubicam, "Advertising," in *While You Were Gone*, ed. Jack Goodman (New York: Simon and Schuster, 1946), 437–39; Freeman Hubbard, "Wartime Rail Advertising," *Railroad Magazine*, May 1943, 8–60.

24. *Railway Age*, December 16, 1944, 942; Chicago, Burlington & Quincy, *Timetable* (April–May 1942), 26; Chicago, Rock Island & Pacific, *Timetable* (November 1942), 1, 13, 35.

25. *Railway Age*, January 6, 1945, 1, 5; *New York Times*, March 19, 1945; Richard R. Lingeman, *Don't You Know There's a War On? The American Home Front, 1941–1945* (New York: G. P. Putnam's Sons, 1970), 351–53.

26. *Railway Age*, May 12, 1945, 835–39; *Railway Age*, May 19, 1945, 874–77, 907–9; *New York Times*, May 27, June 17, and July 15, 1945.

27. *New York Times*, August 15–18, 1945; *Railway Age*, August 25, 1945, 344–45.

28. *Railway Age*, September 15, 1945, 452; *Railway Age*, November 17, 1945, 789–93; *Railway Age*, December 22, 1945, 1058–62.

29. *New York Times*, December 17 and 23–27, 1945; *St. Louis Globe-Democrat*, December 15 and 22, 1945; *Official Guide*, January 1946, xv.

30. Heimburger and Kelly, *Trains to Victory*, 103, 111–15, 339–40.

31. Stover, *Illinois Central Railroad*, 367; Stover, *Baltimore & Ohio Railroad*, 324.

32. *Moody's Manual of Investments: Steam Railroads, 1945* (New York: Moody's Investor Service, 1945), a3–a24; *New York Times*, February 12, 1946; *Official Guide*, January 1946, xv; "The Railways in Transition," *Railway Age*, January 5, 1946, 1–2; Julius H. Parmelee, "Railway Operations in 1945," *Railway Age*, January 5, 1946, 69–78.

33. *Official Guide*, January 1946, xv; Kent T. Healy, *Performance of the U.S. Railroads since World War II* (New York: Vantage, 1985), 7; *Moody's Manual* (1945), a3–a12; Joseph C. Goulden, *The Best Years, 1945–1950* (New York: Atheneum Books, 1976), 120–27; Joseph Finkelstein, *The American Economy: From the Great Crash to the Third Industrial Revolution* (Arlington Heights: Harlan Davidson, 1992), 51–60.

34. David A. Shannon, *Twentieth Century America: The United States since the 1890s* (Chicago: Rand McNally, 1969), 508–514.

35. *Des Moines Register*, May 9, 1948.

36. Keith L. Bryant Jr. and Henry C. Detloff, *History of American Business* (Englewood Cliffs: Prentice Hall, 1990), 133–49, 297–99.

37. Stover, *Baltimore & Ohio Railroad*, 284, 317; *Moody's Manual* (1945), 39, 256, 352, 371, 389, 441, 1074.

38. "President Harry S. Truman Bridge Dedicated," *Milwaukee Magazine*, June 1945, 6–8; *Moody's Manual* (1945), 39, 446; Richard C. Overton, *Burlington Route: A History of the Burlington Lines* (New York: Alfred A. Knopf, 1965), 518–19, 522; S. Kip Farrington, *Railroading from the Rear End* (New York: Coward-McCann, 1946), 38–39, 158–61; S. Kip Farrington, *Railroads of Today* (New York: Coward-McCann, 1949), 95–98.

39. Farrington, *Railroading from the Rear End*, 394–97; *Moody's Manual* (1945), 446.

40. Overton, *Burlington Route*, 516–17; L. L. Waters, *Steel Trails to Santa Fe* (Lawrence: University of Kansas Press, 1950), 89–90, 371–73; William Edward Hayes, *Iron Road to Empire: The History of the Rock Island Lines* (New York: Simmons Boardman, 1953), 162–64, 174; *St. Louis Post-Dispatch*, January 15, 1931; *New York Journal of Commerce*, January 29, 1931; *St. Louis Post-Dispatch*, November 10, 1946.

41. Stover, *American Railroads*, 203; American Association of Railroad Superintendents, *Committee Reports, 1946*, 29, 31–34, 45, 66.

42. American Association of Railroad Superintendents, *Committee Reports, 1946*, 46–55.

43. *Official Guide*, May 1946, 13; ibid., July 1946, 13–14; ibid., April 1948, 6; *Modern Railroads*, July 1947, 12–20; *Modern Railroads*, January 1948, 59; *Official Guide*,

August 1948, xiii; ibid., March 1946, xiv; ibid., May 1948, 6; ibid., September 1949, 13; *Modern Railroads*, May 1949, 48–51; *Modern Railroads*, February 1949, 49–52, 57.

44. *St. Louis Star Times*, March 11, 1946; *Moody's Manual* (1945), 901; *Moody's Manual* (1950), 290; *St. Louis Globe-Democrat*, June 10, 1945.

45. *St. Louis Globe-Democrat*, June 10, 1946; *Official Guide*, December 1947, 26–60; Arthur D. Dubin, *More Classic Trains* (Milwaukee: Kalmbach Books, 1974), 93.

46. *St. Louis Globe-Democrat*, November 26, 1946; *Terminal Railroad Association of St. Louis Historical Society Bulletin* 4 (1990): 14; *Official Guide*, January 1947, 14; *St. Louis Star-Times*, March 11, 1946; *St. Louis Globe-Democrat*, July 10, 1945; Terminal Railroad Association, *Timetable 16-C* (August 15, 1948); Terminal Railroad Association, *Timetable 19* (September 25, 1949).

47. *Official Guide*, December 1947, 243, 680, 699, 711, 724, 820, 920, 934, 975, 1001, 1016.

48. Farrington, *Railroading from the Rear End*, 134–35; Farrington, *Railroads of Today*, 46–48, 136–43.

49. *Official Guide*, December 1947, 686, 704, 728–29; Dubin, *More Classic Trains*, 244–53; Farrington, *Railroading from the Rear End*, 400–407.

50. Bob Withers, *The President Travels by Train: Politics Pullmans* (Lynchburg: TLC, 1996), 179–87, 200–203, 225–26, 232; *Des Moines Register*, September 16 and 19, 1948; Walter Fitzmaurice, "President Truman's Campaign Special," *Trains*, March 1949, 19–22; Phillip White, *Whistle Stop* (Lebanon: University Press of New England, 2014), 154–59, 229, 240, 314.

51. Farrington, *Railroading from the Rear End*, 186–87, 225–42, 342–43, 392–93; Farrington, *Railroads of Today*, 147–53, 248–49, 270–72, 281, 393; Hofsommer, *Quanah Route*, 133.

52. Stover, *American Railroads*, 194, 212–15; Overton, *Burlington Route*, 537–40.

4. A Fluid State

1. *Official Guide*, November 1950, 174, 259, 266, 394, 534, 630, 642, 696, 709, 724, 822, 936, 1076, 1003, 1026, 1196.

2. Ibid.

3. Lucius Beebe and Charles Clegg, *The Trains We Rode*, vol. 1 (Berkeley: Howell-North, 1965), 15–135, 266–75, 286–95; Beebe and Clegg, *Trains We Rode*, vol. 2 (Berkeley: Howell-North, 1966), 522–95, 696–703, 790–883; Arthur D. Dubin, *Some Classic Trains* (Milwaukee: Kalmbach, 1964), 212–49, 262–81, 364–67; Arthur D. Dubin, *More Classic Trains* (Milwaukee: Kalmbach, 1974), 190–213, 244–63, 368–73; Stan Repp, *Super Chief . . . Train of the Stars* (San Marino: Golden West Books, 1980), passim.

4. *Official Guide*, November 1951, 13; ibid., June 1952, xiv; ibid., August 1952, xiii; ibid., May 1953, 14; *Illinois Central Magazine*, July 1952, 7; *Illinois Central Magazine*, June 1954, 208; *Modern Railroads*, April 1950, 5, 30–34, 47–48; S. Kip Farrington, *Railroads of the Hour* (New York: Coward-McCann, 1958), 26–27, 100–105, 138–41.

5. USPOD, *Schedule of Mail Routes*, Fifteenth Division (June 3, 1955), 113; USPOD, *Schedule of Mail Routes*, Chicago Region (February 15, 1958), 21, 144; Bryant Alden Long and William Jefferson Dennis, *Mail by Rail:*

The Story of the Postal Transportation Service (New York: Simmons-Boardman, 1951), app. 1.

6. S. Kip Farrington, *Railroads of Today* (New York: Coward-McCann, 1949), 48–54; Edward M. DeRouin, *Moving Mail and Express by Rail* (LaFox: Pixels, 2007), 121–27, 136–42, 155–59, 167–70, 172–77, 181–8s, 185–88. See also Gordon Strachan, "RMS: The Story of the Railway Mail Service," *Santa Fe Magazine*, June 1946, 1–24; and Charles B. Castner, "Mail by Rail: The First 100 Years," *L&N Magazine*, July 1964, 2–5.

7. V. S. Roseman, *Railway Express: Overview* (Denver: Ricky Mountain, 1992). 4–9; "Union Station Expansion Nearly Completed," *Official Proceedings of St. Louis Railway Club* 34 (1929): 27–30.

8. Freeman Hubbard, *Encyclopedia of North American Railroading* (New York: McGraw Hill, 1981), 10–11. See also Klink Garrett, *Ten Turtles to Tucumcari: Personal History of the Railway Express Agency* (Albuquerque: University of New Mexico Press, 2003).

9. *St. Louis Globe-Democrat*, September 13, 1961. See also John Ferguson Moore, *The Story of the Railroad "Y"* (New York: Association Press, 1930).

10. *Official Guide*, March 1958, 689; *Railway Age*, September 25, 1961, 38–39.

11. *Official Guide*, November 1950, 766.

12. Chicago Great Western, *Directory of Industries*, 1957, 84–87, 92; Chicago, Burlington & Quincy, *Annual Report, 1961*, 12–13; Chicago, Burlington & Quincy, *Annual Report, 1965*, 9, 11; St. Louis–San Francisco, *Annual Report, 1966*, 7.

13. Chicago, Burlington & Quincy, *Annual Report, 1961*, 9; Chicago, Burlington & Quincy, *Annual Report, 1962*, 9, 11; H. Roger Grant, *Follow the Flag: A History of the Wabash Railroad Company* (DeKalb: Northern Illinois University Press, 2004), 237

14. H. Roger Grant, "Piggyback Pioneer," *Trains*, January 1986, 31–34; *Railway Age*, August 11, 1958, 9–10; *Railway Age*, August 24, 1959, 8–9; *Railway Age*, June 26, 1961, 40–41; Farrington, *Railroads of the Hour*, 42–43; Chicago, Burlington & Quincy, *Annual Report, 1962*, 8–11; Chicago, Burlington & Quincy, *Annual Report, 1967*, 5; Atchison, Topeka & Santa Fe, *Annual Report, 1962*, 8–9; Atchison, Topeka & Santa Fe, *Annual Report, 1963*, 8.

15. David P. Morgan, "Fast Freight," *Trains*, November 1949, 44–49; *Railway Age*, June 2, 1952, 77–81; Steve Patterson, "In a Race with Missouri Pacific's Red Balls, Cotton Belt Goes Like a Blue Streak," *Trains*, November 1962, 18–27; Farrington, *Railroads of the Hour*, 53–59; Don L. Hofsommer, *The Quanah Route: A History of the Quanah, Acme & Pacific Railway* (College Station: Texas A&M University Press, 1991), 169–71; Grant, *Follow the Flag*, 237.

16. Patterson, "In a Race," 23.

17. *Official Guide*, March 1958, 116, 676, 678, 686, 714, 716–17, 813.

18. Richard C. Overton, *Burlington Route: A History of the Burlington Lines* (New York: Alfred A. Knopf, 1965), 558; St. Louis–San Francisco, *Annual Report, 1966*, 11–13; Farrington, *Railroads of the Hour*, 178–80.

19. Farrington, *Railroads of the Hour*, 45; *Moody's Manual of Investments: Railroad Securities* (New York: Moody's Investors Services, 1950), 39; Overton, *Burlington Route*, 561.

20. Don L. Hofsommer, "Getting to Know Her," in *Railroad History Millennium Special* (2000), 100–109.

21. *St. Louis Globe-Democrat*, January 14, 1951; *Official Guide*, May 1952, 7; ibid., February 1953, 14–15; ibid., March 1954, 10; ibid., April 1955, 10; ibid., September 1957, 13, 15; ibid., December 1957, 14; ibid., June 1958, 26; ibid., December 1958, 22; ibid., November 1959, 18; *Illinois Central Magazine*, February 1956, 37; *Illinois Central Magazine*, November 1956, 3–5; *Illinois Central Magazine*, June 1958, 20–21; *Illinois Central Magazine*, March 1959, 12–13; *Terminal Railroad Association of St. Louis Historical Society (Bulletin)* 6 (1992): 4–5, 21–15; *St. Louis Globe-Democrat*, October 4, 1959.

22. Peter T. Maiken, *Night Trains: The Pullman System in the Golden Years of American Rail Travel* (Chicago: Lakme, 1989), 159–73, 229–37; *Official Guide*, November 1950, passim.

23. *Illinois Central Magazine*, October 1953, 2–4; *Illinois Central Magazine*, October 1954, 15; Dubin, *More Classic Trains*, 3; *Moody's Manual* (1953), 6; ibid. (1958), a7; *New York Times*, January 3, 1955; Carlos A. Schwantes, *Going Places: Transportation Redefines the Twentieth-Century* (Bloomington: Indiana University Press, 2003), 196, 279, 281–82, 306, 358; R. D. McKenzie, *Metropolitan Community* (New York: McGraw-Hill, 1933), 140–43, 270–75, 311–18.

24. *St. Louis Globe-Democrat*, January 14 and July 3, 1945, and December 1, 1951; *St. Louis Post-Dispatch*, May 25, 1959; *Official Guide*, September 1946, 18; *L&N Magazine*, March 1950, 45; *Modern Railroads*, July 1950, 79–80.

25. *Official Guide*, December 1950, xiv; *Illinois Central Magazine*, December 1954, 12–13; *Illinois Central Magazine*, December 1958, 10–11.

26. USPOD, *Schedule of Mail Routes, Fifteenth Division* (June 3, 1955), 113; USPOD, *Schedule of Mail Routes, Chicago Region* (February 15, 1958), 21, 144; Long and Dennis, *Mail by Rail*, app. 1.

27. American Association of Railroad Superintendents, *Proceedings and Committee Reports 1954*, 23–29; *Modern Railroads*, November 1953, 20; *St. Louis Globe-Democrat*, April 1, 1953; *Illinois Central Magazine*, January 1955, 2–4; Atchison, Topeka & Santa Fe, *Annual Report, 1962*, 9.

28. *Official Guide*, October 1960, 799, 836; *Illinois Central Magazine*, June 1961,17; *Illinois Central Magazine*, December 1962, 17.

29. *Official Guide*, May 1953, 10; *Illinois Central Magazine*, October 1953, 2–4; *Illinois Central Magazine*, October 1954, 15; Dubin, *More Classic Trains*, 93; *St. Louis Globe-Democrat*, April 9, 1958, January 2 and 5, 1959; *Official Guide*, September 1959, 21.

30. *New York Times*, August 29, 1957, April 19, 1958; *U.S. News & World Report*, October 3, 1958, 36–39; *Railway Age*, October 26, 1953, 15–16; *Illinois Central Magazine*, October 1953, 2–5; *Illinois Central Magazine*, January 1955, 2–4; Kent T. Healy, *Performance of the U. S. Railroads since World War II* (New York: Vantage, 1965), 46–50; David P. Morgan, "Who Shot the Passenger Train?," *Trains*, April 1959, 14–51; Schwantes, *Going Places*, 306–8, 326, 330.

31. H. Roger Grant, *The Corn Belt Route: A History of the Chicago Great Western Railroad Company* (DeKalb: Northern Illinois University Press, 1984), 160–61; *The National Limited* (St. Louis: Terminal Railroad Association Historical Society, 2018), 143, 168.

32. Tom Parkinson and Charles P. Fox, *The Circus Moves by Rail* (Boulder: Pruett, 1978), 60, 383; Chicago, Burlington & Quincy, *Flyer*, April 29, 1962; Chicago, Burlington & Quincy, *Annual Report, 1962*, 16; Chicago, Burlington & Quincy, *Annual Report, 1963*, 18–19.

33. *Mixed Train* (2018–11), 3; Bob Withers, *The President Travels by Train* (Lynchburg: TLC, 1996), 364–73; *St. Louis Globe-Democrat*, December 6, 1961, and November 15, 1962; *Illinois Central Magazine*, November 1967, 10; *St. Louis Post-Dispatch*, February 13, 1966.

34. Chicago, Burlington & Quincy, *Annual Report, 1967*, 3; Chicago, Burlington & Quincy, *Annual Report, 1968*, 11; Illinois Central, *Annual Report, 1968*, 31; W. David Randall and Alan R. Lind, *Monarchs of Mid-America* (Park Forest: Prototype, 1973), 227, 231; Harry Stegmaier, *Baltimore & Ohio Passenger Service, 1945–1971*, vol. 1, *The Route of the National Limited* (Lynchburg: TLC, 1993), 43–59, 95–100; *Illinois Central Magazine*, January 1968, 16; *St. Louis Globe-Democrat*, December 17, 1961, December 2, 1967, February 19, April 18, and November 28, 1969; Don L. Hofsommer, *The Southern Pacific, 1901–1985* (College Station: Texas A&M University Press, 1986), 271. See also Joe Welsh and Bill Howes, *Travel by Pullman: A Century of Service* (St. Paul: MBI, 2004); and Fred W. Frailey, *Twilight of the Great Trains* (Bloomington: Indiana University Press, 1998).

35. Hofsommer, *Southern Pacific*, 293.

36. *Moody's Manual* (1953), a9; *Harpers*, August 1950, 17; *Business Week*, April 8, 1950, 86–87, 90; *Business Week*, February 23, 1952, 166–68, 170, 172; *Business Week*, October 17, 1953, 62, 64, 66, 68; *Railway Age*, October 26, 1953, 23.

37. *Newsweek*, February 13, 1950, 56, 59–60; M. W. Clement, "Whither the Railroads," *Vital Speeches*, July 1, 1950, 573–75.

38. *Moody's Manual* (1945), a26–a27; ibid. (1958), a71; John F. Stover, *American Railroads* (Chicago: University of Chicago Press, 1961) 210–16, 237–38; *Railway Age*, November 15, 1930, 1021–24; McKenzie, *Metropolitan Community*, 92–93.

39. *New York Times*, January 3 and April 29, 1955; *Moody's Manual* (1958), a6, a9–a20; Benjamin F. Fairless, "The First Freedom: Railroads Have Been Denied the Freedom to Compete," *Vital Speeches*, September 15, 1954, 731–34; *Forbes*, January 1, 1954, 32–41; *New York Times*, September 21, 1955; Missouri–Kansas–Texas, *Annual Report, 1966*, 3.

40. *U.S. News & World Report*, April 20, 1956, 110–24; *Business Week*, August 11, 1956, 52–56; *Forbes*, January 1, 1957, 93–98; Edward T. Thompson, "What Hope for the Railroads," *Fortune*, February 1958, 137–39, 146–48; Lawrence T. King, "Railroads in Crisis," *Commonweal*, June 6, 1958, 253–55; *New York Times*, January 4, 1958.

41. *U.S. News & World Report*, November 14, 1960, 88–89; H. Roger Grant, *Erie Lackawanna: Death of an American Railroad, 1938–1992* (Stanford: Stanford University Press, 1994), 72.

42. E. F. Thompkins, "A Senate Objective: Rescuing the Railroads," *American Mercury*, May 1958, 26–30; *U.S. News & World Report*, December 20, 1957, 95–97; *New York Times*, January 9, 1959; Perry N. Shoemaker, "What's Wrong with the Railroads," *Fortune*, January

1960, 118–19, 168–76; Gilbert Burck, "A Plan to Save the Railroads," *Fortune*, August 1958, 82–86.

43. William B. Chafe, *The Unfinished Journey: America since World War II*, 2nd ed. (New York: Oxford University Press, 1991), 177; David A. Shannon, *Twentieth Century America: The United States since the 1890s*, 2nd ed. (Chicago: Rand McNally, 1969), 623–61.

44. Chicago, Rock Island & Pacific, *Annual Report, 1964*, 4; Chicago, Rock Island & Pacific, *Annual Report, 1965*, 4, 9; Chicago, Rock Island & Pacific, *Annual Report, 1966*, 4.

45. *Barron's*, March 25, 1963, 28–29; Chicago Great Western, *Annual Report, 1963*, 4; Chicago Great Western, *Annual Report, 1964*, 10; Chicago Great Western, *Annual Report, 1967*, 1, 13; Chicago, Milwaukee, St. Paul & Pacific, *Annual Report, 1967*, 4; Illinois Central, *Annual Report, 1960*, 2; Illinois Central, *Annual Report, 1967*, 3; Chicago, Burlington & Quincy, *Annual Report, 1968*, 23.

46. Hofsommer, *Southern Pacific*, 252.

47. Stover, *American Railroads*, 230–31; Chicago, Burlington & Quincy, *Annual Report, 1962*, 29; Illinois Central, *Annual Report, 1963*, 21; Chicago Great Western, *Annual Report, 1964*, 8; Atchison, Topeka & Santa Fe, *Annual Report, 1965*, 16–17.

48. Chicago, Milwaukee, St. Paul & Pacific, *Annual Report, 1960*, 10; Chicago, Burlington & Quincy, *Annual Report, 1967*, 4.

49. Illinois Central, *Annual Report, 1960*, 9; Chicago, Burlington & Quincy, *Annual Report, 1962*, 22; Chicago, Rock Island & Pacific, *Annual Report, 1963*, 7; Chicago, Rock Island & Pacific, *Annual Report, 1965*, 14; Atchison, Topeka & Santa Fe, *Annual Report, 1965*, 9; Atchison, Topeka & Santa Fe, *Annual Report, 1967*, 11; Chicago Great Western, *Safety News*, September–October 1963, 1–2; Chicago Great Western, *Safety News*, September–October 1966, 1; Missouri–Kansas–Texas, *Annual Report, 1965*, 7.

50. Chicago Great Western, *Annual Report, 1967*, 2.

51. *Trains*, November 1990, 22–47; Chicago & North Western, *Annual Report, 1967*, 18–19; Chicago, Rock Island & Pacific, *Annual Report, 1969*, 4; Hofsommer, *Southern Pacific*, 262–63.

52. Hofsommer, *Southern Pacific*, 263–65.

53. Ibid., 265–68; Maury Klein, *Union Pacific: The Rebirth, 1894–1969* (New York: Doubleday, 1989), 514–31.

54. Illinois Central, *Annual Report, 1962*, 20; Illinois Central Industries, *Annual Report, 1963*, 5; Katy Industries, *Annual Report, 1969*, 3; Atchison, Topeka & Santa Fe, *Annual Report, 1969*, 12–13; Illinois Central Industries, *Annual Report, 1968*, passim; Northwest-Industries, *Annual Report, 1968*, passim.

5. Debilitated and Downsized

1. Northwest Industries, *Annual Report, 1970*, 2–3; Chicago, Milwaukee, St. Paul & Pacific, *Annual Report, 1970*, 2–3; Illinois Central Industries, *Annual Report, 1970*, 2–3.

2. Richard Saunders, *Merging Lines: American Railroads, 1900–1970* (DeKalb: Northern Illinois University Press, 2001), 377–78, 414–15; B. F. Biaggini, "Nationalization versus Rationalization: What's the Future for the Railroads?" (speech before the National Press Club, Washington, DC, December 14, 1970).

3. *Moody's Transportation Manual, 1973* (New York: Moody's Investors Service, 1973), 802; *Fortune*, June 15, 1968, 214–15; Chicago, Rock Island & Pacific, *Annual Report, 1969*, 4; Chicago, Rock Island & Pacific, *Annual Report, 1970*, 3–4, 7–9; *Official Guide*, November 1970, 6; *Rocket*, November–December 1970, 8–9.

4. *Minneapolis Tribune*, February 3, 1970; *Chicago Tribune*, March 3, 1970; David P. Morgan, "Farewell, CB&Q, GN, NP, and SP&S; Hello Burlington Northern," *Trains*, June 1970, 24–28; Don L. Hofsommer, "Hill's Dream Realized: Burlington Northern's Eight Decade Gestation," *Pacific Northwest Quarterly* 79 (1988): 138–49; Burlington Northern, *Annual Report, 1970*, 3–5.

5. Burlington Northern, *Annual Report, 1970*, 2; Chicago, Rock Island & Pacific, *Annual Report, 1970*, 19.

6. Lucius Beebe and Charles Clegg, *The Trains We Rode*, 2 vols (Berkeley: Howell-North, 1965), 1:8; David P. Morgan, "The Super Trains," *Trains*, June 1970, 20–23; *Official Guide*, April 1971, 68–69, 122, 169, 264, 324, 396–97, 441.

7. James W. McClellan, "Reflections on Deregulation," *Railroad History*, Autumn 2001, 16–19; *Illinois Central Magazine*, April 1971, 8–9; *Chicago Tribune*, May 1, 1971; Amtrak, *Timetable* (May 1, 1971), 17, 21–24. See also Harold A. Edmonson, ed., *Journey to Amtrak: The Year History Rode the Passenger Train* (Milwaukee: Kalmbach, 1972); William E. Thoms, *Reprieve for the Iron Horse: The Amtrak Experiment—Predecessors and Prospect* (Baton Rouge: Claitor's, 1973).

8. Union Pacific Corporation, *Annual Report, 1970*, 2; Union Pacific Corporation, *Annual Report, 1971*, 18–19; Union Pacific Corporation, *Annual Report, 1973*, 8; Chicago Milwaukee Corporation, *Annual Report, 1971*, 4; Chicago Milwaukee Corporation, *Annual Report, 1972*, 5; William J. Quinn to Stockholders, March 23, 1975; Burlington Northern, *Annual Report, 1973*, 2–3; Chicago & North Western, *Annual Report, 1973*, 1; John McClaughty, "Employee Ownership: A New Way to Run a Railroad," *Business and Society Review/Innovation*, Spring 1974, 34–37; H. Roger Grant, *The North Western: A History of the Chicago & North Western Railway System* (DeKalb: Northern Illinois University Press, 1996), 119–220.

9. Michael A. Verespej, "'Doctors' Split on Relief for Railroads' Ills," *Industry Week*, July 21, 1975, 24–32; Union Pacific Corporation, *Annual Report, 1975*, 2; *Trains*, November 1990, 22–47; Richard Saunders, *The Railroad Mergers and the Coming of Conrail* (Westport, CT: Greenwood, 1978), 301, 305, 309, 315, 319, 324–25; Alexander L. Morton, "How to Revive the Railroads," *Challenge*, November–December 1974, 32–37.

10. *Rocket*, July–August 1970, 3–8; *Rocket*, May–June 1972, 8–10; Chicago, Rock Island & Pacific, *Annual Report, 1971*, 6; Chicago, Rock Island & Pacific, *Annual Report, 1972*, 7; Chicago, Rock Island & Pacific, *Annual Report, 1973*, 7–8; *Wall Street Journal*, August 25, 1972; *Modern Railroads*, June 1983, 28; N. J. Nessen to Don Hofsommer, October 3 and 16, 1974.

11. Norfolk & Western, *Annual Report, 1973*, 7; William A. Martin to Don Hofsommer, September 24 and October 11, 1974; Illinois Central Industries, "Fact File" (July 1974); D. W. McLeod to Don Hofsommer, November 26, 1974; Chicago Milwaukee Corporation, *Annual*

Report, 1972, 4–5; Norfolk & Western, *Annual Report, 1973*, 7; Illinois Central Industries, "Fact File" (July 1974).

12. Burlington Northern, *Annual Report, 1970*, 9; Burlington Northern, *Annual Report, 1975*, 3; Burlington Northern, *Annual Report, 1978*, 3, 5; Burlington Northern, *Annual Report, 1979*, 5.

13. Don L. Hofsommer, *The Quanah Route: A History of the Quanah, Acme Pacific Railway* (College Station: Texas A&M University Press, 1991), 172–74; Santa Fe Industries, *Annual Report, 1973*, 7; Burlington Northern, *Annual Report, 1977*, 12; Burlington Northern, *Annual Report, 1978*, 7; St. Louis–San Francisco, *Annual Report, 1973*, 5; St. Louis–San Francisco, *Annual Report, 1974*, 5; St. Louis–San Francisco, *Annual Report, 1979*, 7; Chicago, Rock Island & Pacific, *Annual Report, 1972*, 7.

14. Jimmy M. Skaggs, *Prime Cut: Livestock Raising and Meatpacking in the United States, 1607–1983* (College Station: Texas A&M University Press, 1986), 60 129, 144–46; Dominic A. Pacygia, *Slaughterhouse: Chicago's Union Stock Yard and the World It Made* (Chicago: University of Chicago Press, 2015), 158–69; William Cronon, *Nature's Metropolis: Chicago and the Great West* (New York: Norton, 1991), 207–59. See also Wilson J. Warren, *Tied to the Great Packing Machine: The Midwest and Meatpacking* (Iowa City: University of Iowa Press, 2007).

15. Charles B. Kuhlmann, *The Development of the Flour Milling Industry in the United States* (Boston: Houghton Mifflin, 1929), 84–85, 183–99; Atchison, Topeka & Santa Fe, *Annual Report, 1967*, 46–47; Santa Fe Industries, *Annual Report, 1973*, 7.

16. Keith L. Bryant, *History of the Atchison, Topeka and Santa Fe Railway* (New York: Macmillan, 1974), 296, 371–72; Jim McClellan, *Life with Trains: Memoir of a Railroader* (Bloomington: Indiana University Press, 2017), 166; Santa Fe Industries, *Annual Report, 1970*, 7; Santa Fe Industries, *Annual Report, 1973*, 8; Hofsommer, *Quanah Route*, 180; Burlington Northern, *Annual Report, 1971*, 7; St. Louis–San Francisco, *Annual Report, 1973*, 7.

17. Santa Fe Industries, *Annual Report, 1970*, 5, 9; Santa Fe Industries, *Annual Report, 1973*, 9; St. Louis–San Francisco, *Annual Report, 1973*, 8; St. Louis–San Francisco, *Annual Report, 1974*, 10; St. Louis–San Francisco, *Annual Report, 1977*, 14; Burlington Northern, *Annual Report, 1977*, 6, 12.

18. St. Louis–San Francisco, *Annual Report, 1971*, 9; St. Louis–San Francisco, *Annual Report, 1973*, 32; St. Louis–San Francisco, *Annual Report, 1977*, 14; Chicago, Burlington & Quincy, *Annual Report, 1962*, 30; Missouri–Kansas–Texas, *Annual Report, 1974*, 7.

19. Illinois Central Industries, *Annual Report, 1975*, 3.

20. Don L. Hofsommer, *The Southern Pacific, 1901–1985* (College Station: Texas A&M University Press, 1986), 281; Maury Klein, *Union Pacific, The Reconfiguration: America's Greatest Railroad from 1969 to the Present* (New York: Oxford University Press, 2011), 77–95.

21. Albro Martin, *Railroads Triumphant: The Growth, Rejection and Rebirth of a Vital American Force* (New York: Oxford University Press, 1992), 387; Albro Martin, *Enterprise Denied: Origins of the Decline of American Railroads* (New York: Columbia University Press, 1971), 354, 361, 369, 372–73.

22. Union Pacific Corporation, *Annual Report, 1974*, 2; Illinois Central Industries, *Annual Report, 1974*, 3; Chicago Milwaukee Corporation, *Annual Report, 1974*, 2, 6.

23. Chicago, Rock Island & Pacific, *Annual Report, 1971*, 2–5; Chicago, Rock Island & Pacific, *Annual Report, 1972*, 2–5; Chicago, Rock Island & Pacific, *Annual Report, 1973*, 2–5; Chicago, Rock Island & Pacific, *Annual Report, 1974*, 2, 3, 10, 12; *Wall Street Journal*, March 17–19, 1975. See also Gregory L. Schneider, *Rock Island Requiem: The Collapse of a Mighty Fine Line* (Lawrence: University Press of Kansas, 2013).

24. *Wall Street Journal*, March 3 and December 20, 1977; Chicago, Milwaukee, St. Paul & Pacific, *Annual Report, 1975*, 8; Chicago, Milwaukee, St. Paul & Pacific, *Annual Report, 1977*, 1–13.

25. James F. Willis and Martin L. Primack, *An Economic History of the United States*, 2nd ed. (Englewood Cliffs: Prentice-Hall, 1989), 419–32; Jonathan Hughes, *American Economic History*, 3rd ed. (Glenview: Scott Foresman/Little, Brown, 1990), 578–79.

26. Chicago, Rock Island & Pacific, *Annual Report, 1977*; *Wall Street Journal*, March 16 and August 29, 1977.

27. *Wall Street Journal*, March 14, 1979; Chicago, Milwaukee, St. Paul & Pacific, press release, April 23, 1979.

28. *Wall Street Journal*, September 25, 1978.

29. Chicago, Rock Island & Pacific, *News Bulletin*, February 10, 1978, May 16, 1979; *Wall Street Journal*, August 29 and 30, 1979.

30. *Wall Street Journal*, September 20, 21, 24, 26, and 27, October 4, 8, 11, 19, and 24, and November 16 and 19, 1979.

31. McClellan, *Life with Trains*, 230, 234.

32. Don Sarno, Norbert Shacklette, and Mike Schafer, "St. Louis, Part III: The Amtrak Era," *Passenger Train Journal* 21 (1990): 33–40; *St. Louis Globe-Democrat*, August 2, October 31, and November 1, 1978; *Trains*, November 1990, 39, 41.

6. Winds of Change

1. George D. Moss, *America in the Twentieth Century*, 3rd ed. (Upper Saddle River, NJ: Prentice Hall, 1997), 511–20; John O'Sullivan and Edward F. Keuchel, *American Economic History: From Abundance to Constraint* (New York: Franklin Watts, 1981), 219–32; Jonathan Hughes, *American Economic History*, 3rd ed. (Glenview, IL: Scott Foresman/Little, Brown, 1990), 578–79, 592.

2. Moss, *America in the Twentieth Century*, 551–74; Hughes, *American Economic History*, 593–96.

3. James F. Willis and Martin L. Primack, *An Economic History of the United States*, 2nd ed. (Englewood Cliffs, NJ: Prentice Hall, 1989), 435; Hughes, *American Economic History*, 593; Moss, *America in the Twentieth Century*, 573; *Statistical Abstract of the United States, 1990* (Washington, DC: US Department of Commerce, 1990), 740–41.

4. H. Craig Miner, *The Rebirth of the Missouri Pacific, 1956–1983* (College Station: Texas A&M University Press, 1983), xiii, 3, 19, 28, 30, 52, 86, 101, 209.

5. Chris Faulk, "Union Pacific's Gibbon Cut Off in the Modern Era: 1980 to Present," *Streamliner*, Summer 2018, 14–24.

6. *Wall Street Journal*, September 27, 1979, April 17, 1980; *Railway Age*, October 29, 1979, 8–9; *Traffic World*, March 24, 1980; Chicago, Rock Island & Pacific to All Contract Employees of All Crafts at All Locations, March 24, 1980. See also Michael Conant, "The Future of

the Rock Island Railroad," *ICC Practitioners' Journal* 44 (1976): 5159.

7. John W. Ingram, "Branchlining: Cure for the Railroads?" (remarks before the Western Railway Club, April 21, 1975); *Des Moines Register*, September 17 and 30, October 26, December 9, 1979, January 27 and 30, 1980; *Wall Street Journal*, January 31, 1980; Gregory L. Schneider, *Rock Island Requiem: The Collapse of a Mighty Fine Line* (Lawrence: University Press of Kansas, 2013), 225–75; Michael R. Haverty to Don L. Hofsommer, June 5, 2019.

8. *Des Moines Register*, March 17, 1980; *Traffic World*, March 24, 1980, 13; Chicago & North Western, *Annual Report, 1980*, 2, 4, 5; Chicago & North Western, *Annual Report, 1983*, 2–4; Richard J. Lane, "Liquidating the Rock," *Railroad History*, Autumn 1999, 103–12.

9. *Wall Street Journal*, August 6, 13, 27, and 28, September 27, 1979.

10. *Wall Street Journal*, November 5, 1979, January 2, February 1, 5, and 26, 1980. See also Michael Conant, "The Failure of the Milwaukee Road," *ICC Practitioners' Journal* 45 (1978): 280–90.

11. Don L. Hofsommer, *Grand Trunk Corporation: Canadian National Railways in the United States, 1971–1992* (East Lansing: Michigan State University Press, 1995), 95–111; Wallace W. Abbey, *The Little Jewell: Soo Line Railroad and the Locomotives That Make It Go* (Pueblo: Pinon Productions, 1984), 182–89; Soo Line, *Annual Report, 1984*, 1–3; Soo Line, *Annual Report, 1985*, 2–3, 6, 12.

12. *Wall Street Journal*, April 20 and 23, 1984; Dan Rottenberg, "The Last Run of the Rock Island Line," *Chicago*, September 1984 197–201, 234–37.

13. *Wall Street Journal*, September 27, 1979, April 17, 1980; *Traffic World*, March 24, 1980, 9–10, 13–14; Chicago, Rock Island & Pacific, *Annual Report, 1902*, 11–12; Oliver Philip Byers, "Early History of the El Paso Line of the Chicago, Rock Island & Pacific Railway," in *Collections of the Kansas State Historical Society, 1919–1922*.

14. Southern Pacific, *Annual Report, 1978*, 9.

15. 363 ICC 320–599; Southern Pacific, *Annual Report, 1979*, 21–22.

16. Illinois Central Industries, *Annual Report, 1977*, 7; Illinois Central Industries, *Annual Report, 1978*, 3; Illinois Central Industries, *Annual Report, 1979*, 2; Illinois Central Industries, *Annual Report, 1981*, ii, 6, 23; *Trains*, November 1981, 82; *Wall Street Journal*, February 4, 1982; Miner, *Rebirth of the Missouri Pacific*, 115–36, 145. On Illinois Central Industries, see Frank J. Allston, *Conglomerate: A Case Study of IC Industries under William B. Johnson* (Naperville: Illumina Concepts, 1992).

17. Earl J. Currie, *Building Burlington Northern: The Lorentzen Years, 1970–1980* (self-published, 2015), 26; Burlington Northern, *Annual Report, 1978*, 9; Burlington Northern, *Annual Report, 1980*, 10; "Merger Special," *Burlington Northern News*, 1–8.

18. *Trains*, December 1982, 3; *Railway Age*, August 9, 1982, 9; Miner, *Rebirth of the Missouri Pacific*, 216–29; Burlington Northern, *Annual Report, 1981*, 19. Union Pacific, it should be noted, did have a two-carrier transcontinental option with Norfolk & Western via Kansas City; Michael R. Haverty to Don L. Hofsommer, June 5, 2019.

19. *San Francisco Examiner*, May 15, 20, and 22, 1980; *San Francisco Chronicle*, May 17, 1980; *Sacramento Union*, May 18, 1980.

20. Southern Pacific, *Annual Report, 1980*, 18, 39; *Herington Times*, October 9, 1980.

21. *San Francisco Chronicle*, September 13, 1980; *Wall Street Journal*, September 15, 1980.

22. Miner, *Rebirth of the Missouri Pacific*, 215–29; *Railway Age*, August 9, 1982, 9; *Topeka Capital-Journal*, July 23, 1982; Santa Fe Industries, *Annual Report, 1981*, 3; *New York Times*, September 14, 1982; *San Francisco Examiner*, September 14, 1982; 366 ICC 458–819; *Wall Street Journal*, December 23, 1982; Union Pacific, *Annual Report, 1982*, 5–9; *Wall Street Journal*, January 4, 1983.

23. *Wall Street Journal*, September 15, 1982, January 4, 1983; Rio Grande Industries, *Annual Report, 1982*, 11; *Traffic World*, February 13, 1984, 13–14; *San Francisco Chronicle*, February 29, 1984.

24. *Kansas City Times*, July 16, 1981; *South East Missourian*, January 7, 1983.

25. John F. Stover, *American Railroads* (Chicago: University of Chicago Press, 1997), 245–46, 252–53.

26. *Railway Age*, August 30, 1982, 29–35; *Fortune*, September 20, 1982, 22, 24, 28, 32, 36, 38; *Journal of Commerce*, June 17, 1982, March 22, 1983; *Wall Street Journal*, February 22, July 13, 1983.

27. Robert Roberts, "Deregulation: The Turning Point," *Modern Railroads*, December 1980, 58–62; F. Stewart Mitchell, "Loosening the Grip," *Modern Railroads*, April 1981, 34–35; Frank D. Shaffer, "We Now Have the Tools," *Modern Railroads*, April 1981, 36–39; Frank Malone, "Contract Rates Are Catching On," *Railway Age*, February 22, 1982, 42–44; Gus Welty, "Change!," *Railway Age*, January 1984, 37–44.

28. Edward A. Lewis, *American Shortline Railway Guide* (Waukesha: Kalmbach, 1996), 28, 29–30, 203–4, 260, 358; *Burlington Northern Viewpoint* (Second Quarter 1987), 1–4.

29. *New York Journal of Commerce*, September 20, 1984; "The Productivity Dilemma," *Progressive Railroading*, June 1985, 37–38; *Trains*, July 1985, 3–4; *Railway Age*, November 1984, 31–34; Frank N. Wilner, *Railroads and Productivity: A Matter of Survival* (Washington: Association of American Railroads, 1985), 1–25; "The End of the Line," *Burlington Northern News*, May 1985, 11, 12.

30. Burlington Northern, *Annual Report, 1979*, 4, 7; Burlington Northern, *Annual Report, 1980*, 1, 3, 5, 7, 9, 11; Burlington Northern, *Annual Report, 1984*, 1.

31. *Business Week*, March 8, 1982, 8–19; *Business Week*, August 3, 1987, 66–67; *New York Times*, April 16, 1982; Tom Shedd, "Burlington Northern: Aggressive, Innovative—and Thoroughly Non-traditional," *Modern Railroads*, November 1986, 20–23; Earl J. Currie, *BN-Frisco: A Tough Merger* (self-published, 2010), passim; Burlington Northern, *Annual Report, 1988*, 1–2, 20; Dan Piller, "BN Inc. Returns to Railroading," *Modern Railroads*, November 1989, 27–31.

32. *Des Moines Register*, November 7, 1981, June 30, November 13, 1983; *Journal of Commerce*, February 7, March 21, July 1, 1983; *Wall Street Journal*, June 22, 1983; Chicago & North Western, *Annual Report, 1983*, 2, 4, 5, 18.

33. Gus Welty, "The Meaning of Merger," *Railway Age*, July 1984, 73–76.

34. *New York Times*, June 17, 1985; Conrail, *Annual Report, 1986*, 1–2; Richard Saunders Jr., *Main Lines: Rebirth of the North American Railroads, 1970–2002*

(DeKalb: Northern Illinois University Press, 2003), 112, 203.

35. *Chicago Tribune*, October 16, 1983; *Wall Street Journal*, July 13, 1983; *San Francisco Chronicle*, March 10, 1983; *San Francisco Examiner*, May 20, 1983; *New York Journal of Commerce*, May 20, 1983.

36. *San Francisco Examiner*, September 27, 1983; *Chicago Tribune*, September 28, 1983; *Wall Street Journal*, December 27, 1983; *Traffic World*, January 2, 1984, 8–10; *Fortune*, January 23, 1984, 20–26; *Los Angeles Times*, November 9, 1986.

37. *Traffic World*, October 21, 1991, 25; *Traffic World*, November 26, 1990, 11.

38. *Trains*, November 1990, 47; Bill Fowler, "Chicago: SP's Last Frontier," *SP Trainline*, Spring 2016, 7–18; Don L. Hofsommer, "Katy Is Not a Museum," *Trains*, September 1982, 22–27; Kansas City Southern Industries, *10-K Report, 1988*, 1–2; Kansas City Southern Industries, *Annual Report, 1990*, 18; Kansas City Southern Industries, *Annual Report, 1995*, 2–3, 7–8; Kansas City Southern Industries, *Annual Report, 1996*, 2–3, 11–14; Kansas City Southern Industries, *Annual Report, 2000*, 2–9; *Traffic World*, October 1, 1990, 8–9; *Traffic World*, November 19, 1990, 14.

39. John F. Due, "Railroads: An Endangered Species and Possibilities of a Fatal Mistake," *Quarterly Review of Economics and Business* 21 (1981): 58–75; *Journal of Commerce*, January 3, 1986; *Des Moines Register*, December 17, 1986; *Waterloo Courier*, April 15, 1985.

40. Norfolk Southern Corporation, *Annual Report, 1989*, l; *Wall Street Journal*, September 25, 1986, November 23, 1987, June 5, 1988; Frank N. Wilner, "A Watershed for Rail Labor?," *Trains*, December 1987, 20–21; John G. Kneiling, "A System That Would Fly," *Trains*, June 1988, 36–39; Glenn Emery, "The Rail Surprise: Still Going Strong," *Insight*, May 1, 1989, 9–15; *Rail News Update*, June 8, 1988, 3.

41. *Wall Street Journal*, March 20, 1992, December 14, 1994, March 13, 1995; *Traffic World*, February 8, 1993, 10–15; *Traffic World*, March 20, 1995, 45–46; Chicago & North Western, *10-K Report, 1991*, 1–15, 28–39, 76–78; H. Roger Grant, *The North Western: A History of the Chicago & North Western System* (DeKalb: Northern Illinois University Press, 1996), 247–53.

42. *Traffic World*, November 13, 1995, 13–14; *Wall Street Journal*, November 30, 1995; *Des Moines Register*, January 30, February 8, 1996.

43. *Burlington Northern News*, April 1980, 3; Frank Malone, "BN Marketing Makes Its Mark," *Railway Age*, October 1984, 32–35; Burlington Northern, *Annual Report, 1985*, ii; *Business Week*, August 3, 1987, 66–67; Emery, "Rail Surprise," 9–19; Dan Piller, "BN Inc. Returns to Railroading," *Modern Railroads*, November 1989, 27–31; *Forbes*, March 30, 1992, 45–46; *Wall Street Journal*, April 6, 1993; Burlington Northern, *Annual Report, 1993*, 1, 20.

44. Santa Fe Southern Pacific, *Annual Report, 1983*, 3, 45; Santa Fe Southern Pacific, *Annual Report, 1986*, 3,9; Santa Fe Southern Pacific, *Annual Report, 1987*, 2; Santa Fe Southern Pacific, *Annual Report, 1991*, 2–3; *Los Angeles Times*, November 9, 1986.

45. *Forbes*, February 3, 1992, 86–87; *Wall Street Journal*, August 3, 1995; *Traffic World*, August 21, 1995, 27–28; Union Pacific, *Annual Report, 1996*, 1–12, 39–40; Saunders, *Main Lines*, 312–15; Maury Klein, *Union*

Pacific, the Reconfiguration: America's Greatest Railroad from 1969 to the Present (New York: Oxford University Press, 2011), 360–76.

46. Saunders, *Main Lines*, 308–12.

47. Ibid., 316–18.

48. Soo Line, *Annual Report, 1986*, 1–2; Soo Line, *Annual Report, 1987*, 1; Canadian Pacific, *Annual Report, 1989*, 1, 10, 12; Canadian Pacific, *Annual Report, 1990*, 2; Canadian Pacific, *Annual Report, 1997*, 4.

49. *Wall Street Journal*, February 11, 1998; Canadian National, *Annual Report, 1995*, 2; Canadian National, *Annual Report, 1997*, 5, 34; Canadian National, *Annual Report, 1998*, 2, 5–9, 32, 42–43, 56–57; Canadian National, *Annual Report, 1999*, 35; Tom Murray, "World's Best Railroad: Canadian National," *Trains*, November 2002, 32–45.

50. Lawrence H. Kaufman, *Leaders Count: The Story of BNSF Railway* (Austin: Texas Monthly, 2005), 204–70.

51. Burlington Northern Santa Fe, *Annual Report, 1995*, 3–4; *Railway*, September–October 1996, 1, 11; *Wall Street Journal*, May 15, 1998; Saunders, *Main Lines*, 300–306; Kaufman, *Leaders Count*, 271–325.

52. *BNSF Today*, December 20, 1999; Burlington Northern Santa Fe, *Annual Report, 1999*, 6–7; *Wall Street Journal*, July 21, 2000; Saunders, *Main Lines*, 349–51; Kaufman, *Leaders Count*, 327–41; Robert D. Krebs, *Riding the Rails: Inside the Business of America's Railroads* (Bloomington: Indiana University Press, 2018), 128–31.

53. Saunders, *Main Lines*, 322–28, 340–45.

54. *Traffic World*, October 7, 2002, 7–28

55. Kaufman, *Leaders Count*, 158–59, 292–93, 368–70; Krebs, *Riding the Rails*, 97; Jim McClellan, *Life with Trains: Memoir of a Railroader* (Bloomington: Indiana University Press, 2017), 91–95. On the general topic, see David J. DeBoer, *Piggyback and Containers: A History of Rail Intermodal on America's Steel Highways* (San Marino: Golden West Books, 1992).

56. *St. Louis Globe-Democrat*, May 21, October 31, 1968, February 6, August 30, November 16, 1969; Peter A. Hansen, "Give the People a Monument," *Trains*, April 1999, 62–72.

7. Rail Industry Survivors Face an Uncertain Future

1. *Wall Street Journal*, March 15, 2000; *Traffic World*, January 17, 2000, 8; Jim Giblin, "The Best of Times, the Worst of Times," *Rail News*, May 1999, 78–79; Brian Solomon, "Transformative Years: 1983–2001," *Trains*, October 2018, 18.

2. *Wall Street Journal*, March 15, 2000; Union Pacific, *Annual Report, 2000*, 1, 2, 20.

3. BNSF, *Annual Report, 2000*, 1, 2, 21, 26; *Wall Street Journal*, December 8, 2000.

4. Norfolk Southern, *Annual Report, 2000*, 5, 10, 26.

5. Kansas City Southern Industries, *Annual Report, 2000*, 2, 5, 6, 7, 10, 12.

6. Union Pacific, *Annual Report, 2001*, 1–2; Union Pacific, *Annual Report, 2002*, 10; Union Pacific, *Annual Report, 2009*, 2; Norfolk Southern, *Annual Report, 2001*, 3, 7; BNSF, *Annual Report, 2001*, 33; BNSF, *Annual Report, 2002*, 5–6; BNSF, *Annual Report, 2003*, 3.

7. Kansas City Southern, *Annual Report, 2005*, 3, 4, 7.

8. Union Pacific, *Annual Report, 2005*, 3–5, 10; BNSF, *Annual Report, 2005*, 1, 3, 7.

9. CPLtd, *Annual Report, 2000*, 1, 11; CP, *Annual Report, 2001*, 5; *Progressive Railroading*, June 2008, 42; Canadian Pacific, *Annual Report, 2007*, 2, 3, 40, 76.

10. TTX, *On Track* 22 (Summer 2006): 3; *Wall Street Journal*, January 24, 2007.

11. *St. Paul Pioneer Press*, June 10, 2005; *Wall Street Journal*, April 10, September 7, 2007.

12. *Traffic World*, June 9, 2008, 25; *Railway Age*, May 2008, 6; *Wall Street Journal*, July 25, 2008; Luther S. Miller, "They're at It Again," *Railway Age*, August 2008, 30–31; *Trains*, May 2008, 48–49; *Kansas City Star*, January 19, 2008.

13. *Wall Street Journal*, January 23, 2009; *Trains*, October 2006, 50–51; *Progressive Railroading*, September 2010, 55.

14. Lawrence H. Kaufman, "Why Buffet Is Betting on the Railroads," *Railway Age*, December 2009, 16–22; Jeff Stagl, "Buffet," *Progressive Railroading*, January 2010, 14–22; Berkshire Hathaway Inc., *Annual Report, 2011*, 10, 70.

15. *Trains*, January 2010, 50–51; Association of American Railroads, "Rail Facts for 2009," 1; Norfolk Southern, *Annual Report, 2010*, 1; Union Pacific, *Annual Report, 2010*, 22; *Railway Age*, September 2010, 4.

16. *Wall Street Journal*, April 26, 2011; Kansas City Southern, *Annual Report, 2011*, 3.

17. *Wall Street Journal*, January 22, March 27, 2013; Union Pacific, *Annual Report, 2012*, 3; *Economist*, April 13, 2013, 65.

18. Kansas City Southern, *Annual Report, 2013*, 2.

19. *Wall Street Journal*, April 20, May 18, December 5, 2012; *Economist*, March 9, 2013, 65; Canadian Pacific, *Annual Report, 2012*, 1; *Toronto Globe & Mail*, April 24, 2014; *Wall Street Journal*, October 13, 14, and 21, November 18 and 27, December 5, 9, 17, 22, and 24, 2015; *Wall Street Journal*, January 6, April 14, 2016; William C. Vantuono, "The Final Round of Mergers?," *Railway Age*, December 2015, 20–24, 48; *Economist*, February 13, 2016, 61–62.

20. *Wall Street Journal*, October 13, 14, and 21, November 18 and 27, December 5, 9, 17, 22, and 24, 2015; *Wall Street Journal*, January 6, April 14, 2016; William C. Vantuono, "The Final Round of Mergers?," *Railway Age*, December 2015, 20–24, 48; *Economist*, February 13, 2016, 61–62.

21. Tom Murray, "Black Diamonds: Lifeblood of American Railroads," *Trains Heavy Hauls* (2015), 6–13; Michael W. Blaszak, "The Future of Railroading Rides on Highways," *Trains Heavy Hauls* (2015), 31–39; Michael W. Blaszak, "Auto Racks in the Black," *Trains Heavy Hauls* (2015), 61–65; Michael W. Blaszak, "Your Next Meal Starts Here," *Trains Heavy Hauls* (2015), 16–23; Union Pacific, *Annual Report, 2015*, 6, 27, 28, 29; Kansas City Southern, *Annual Report, 2019*, 4, 5, 28–30; Bill Stephens, "Bigger in Texas," *Trains*, December 2019, 20–27; *Wall Street Journal*, January 20, February 10, April 19 and 21, July 20, August 23, October 12, December 18, 2017; *Wall Street Journal*, February 27, 2018; *Trains*, March 2018, 10–12.

22. *Wall Street Journal*, January 20, February 10, April 19 and 21, July 20, August 23, October 12, December 18, 2017; *Wall Street Journal*, February 27, 2018; *Trains*, March 2018, 10–12.

23. *Wall Street Journal*, September 20, October 26, 2018; *Wall Street Journal*, April 4, 2019; Union Pacific, *Annual Report, 2017*, 3; *Railway Age*, December 2018, 16.

24. *Railway Age*, April 2019, 9.

25. Historical production statistics and future projections are from "Future coal production depends on resources and technology, not just policy choices," US Energy Information Administration, accessed July 2019, https://www.eia.gov/todayinenergy/detail.php?id=31792; "Freight Rail in Your State," Association of American Railroads, accessed July 2019, https://www.aar.org/data-center/railroads-states/.

26. United States Census Bureau, accessed July 2019, https://www.census.gov/programs-surveys/geography/library/visualizations/center-of-population-1790-2010.html; Association of American Railroads, "Freight Rail"; AARoads, accessed July 2019, https://www.interstate-guide.com/state-index/; Association of American Railroads, "Freight Rail."

27. *Wall Street Journal*, March 22, April 7 and 21, May 9, 20, and 22, 2021.

28. *Trains*, June 2021, 4–5; *Trains*, July 2021, 4–6; Canadian Pacific, *Annual Report, 2021*, 14–15; Canadian Pacific, *Annual Report, 2022*, 13.

29. *Trains*, September 2022, 6.

30. *Wall Street Journal*, March 19, 2023; William C. Vantuono, "CPKC, a Historic Combination," *Railway Age*, April 2023, 11–12; "Canadian Pacific, Kansas City Southern Unite," *Trains*, June 2023, 4–5.

31. Don L. Hofsommer, *John H. Burdakin, Railroader* (East Lansing: Michigan State University Press, 2016), 72; Michael R. Haverty to Don L. Hofsommer, August 6, 2023.

The Missouri Pacific Railroad is a distinctively St. Louis institution. . . .
The prosperity of the railroad and that of the city are closely linked.

—*St. Louis Star and Times*, November 29, 1927

FIGURE B1B.1. A finely appointed observation car brought up the rear of a railroad's premier trains. Schwantes-Greever-Nolan Collection.

Selected Bibliography and Further Reading

Athearn, Robert G. *Union Pacific Country*. Chicago: Rand McNally, 1971.

Baldwin, W. W., prep. *Corporate History of the Chicago, Burlington & Quincy Railroad Company and Affiliates*. Chicago: CB&Q, 1921.

Barriger, John W. *Super Railroads for a Dynamic Economy*. New York: Simmons-Boardman, 1956.

Belasco, Warren James. *Americans on the Road: From Autocamp to Motel, 1910–1945*. Cambridge, MA: MIT Press, 1979.

Berger, Michael L. *The Devil Wagon in God's Country: The Automobile and Social Change in Rural America, 1893–1929*. Hamden, CT: Archon Books, 1979.

Blaszak, Michael W. "Chicago Railway History." In *Chicago, America's Railroad Capital: The Illustrated History, 1836 to Today*, by Brian Solomon, John Gruber, Michael Blaszak, and Chris Guss, 8–79. Minneapolis: Voyageur, 2014.

Botkin, Benjamin A., and Alvin F. Harlow. *A Treasury of Railroad Folklore*. New York: Crown, 1953.

Brown, John K. *The Baldwin Locomotive Works, 1831–1915*. Baltimore: Johns Hopkins University Press, 1995.

Bryant, Keith L. Jr. *Arthur E. Stilwell: Promoter with a Hunch*. Nashville: Vanderbilt University Press, 1971.

———. *History of the Atchison, Topeka and Santa Fe Railway*. New York: Macmillan, 1974.

Burton, W. J. "The Missouri Pacific History." Unpublished manuscript prepared for Missouri Pacific president P. J. Neff, July 1, 1956. A copy is preserved at the John Barriger III National Railroad Library within the Saint Louis Mercantile Library.

Carlson, Stephen P., and Fred W. Schneider III. *PCC: The Car That Fought Back*. Glendale, CA: Interurban, 1980.

Chandler, Alfred D. Jr., comp. and ed. *Giant Enterprise: Ford, General Motors and the Automobile Industry*. New York: Harcourt, Brace & World, 1964.

———. *The Railroads: The Nation's First Big Business*. New York: Harcourt, Brace & World, 1965.

———. *The Visible Hand: The Managerial Revolution in American Business*. Cambridge, MA: Harvard University Press, 1977.

Chandler, Lester V. *America's Greatest Depression, 1929–1941*. New York: Harper & Row, 1970.

Chapman, John Will. *Railroad Mergers*. New York: Simmons-Boardman, 1934.

Churrella, Albert J. *Steam to Diesel: Managerial Customs and Organizational Capabilities in the Twentieth-Century American Locomotive Industry*. Princeton, NJ: Princeton University Press, 1998.

Cordery, Simon. *The Iron Road in the Prairie State: The Story of Illinois Railroading*. Bloomington: Indiana University Press, 2016.

Corliss, Carleton J. *Main Line of Mid-America: The Story of the Illinois Central*. New York: Creative Age, 1950.

Currie, Earl J. *Burlington Northern: A Great Adventure, 1970–1979*. Pullman: Washington State University Press, 2020.

———. *Transformation of a Railroad Company: Burlington Northern, 1980–1995*. Pullman: Washington State University Press, 2020.

Davis, Colin J. *Power at Odds: The 1922 National Shopmen's Strike*. Urbana: University of Illinois Press, 1997.

Derleth, August. *The Milwaukee Road: Its First 100 Years*. New York: Creative Age, 1948.

DeRouin, Edward M. *Moving Mail and Express by Fall*. LaFox: Pixel, 2007.

Douglas, George H. *All Aboard: The Railroad in American Life*. New York: Marlowe, 1995. Reprint of 1992 edition.

Dubin, Arthur D. *Some Classic Trains*. Milwaukee: Kalmbach, 1964.

Flink, James I. *America Adopts the Automobile, 1895–1910*. Cambridge, MA: MIT Press, 1970.

———. *The Car Culture*. Cambridge: MIT Press, 1975.

Gallamore, Robert E., and John R. Meyer. *American Railroads: Decline and Renaissance in the Twentieth Century*. Cambridge, MA: Harvard University Press, 2014.

Galligan, William H. *Vision Accomplished: The History of the Kansas City Southern*. Bloomington: Indiana University Press, 2024.

Glabb, Charles N. *Kansas City and the Railroads: Community Policy in the Growth of a Regional Metropolis*.

Lawrence: University Press of Kansas, 1993. Reprint of 1962 edition.

Glendinnig, Gene. *The Chicago & Alton Railway: The Only Way*. DeKalb: Northern Illinois University Press, 2002.

Goddard, Stephen B. *Getting There: The Epic Struggle between Road and Rail in the American Century*. Chicago: University of Chicago Press, 1996. Reprint of 1994 edition.

Gordon, Sarah H. *Passage to Union: How Railroads Transformed American Life, 1829–1929*. Chicago: Ivan R. Dee, 1997.

Grant, H. Roger. *The Corn Belt Route: A History of the Chicago Great Western Railroad Company*. DeKalb: Northern Illinois University Press, 1984.

———. *Electric Interurbans and the American People*. Bloomington: Indiana University Press, 2016.

———. *"Follow the Flag": A History of the Wabash Railroad Company*. DeKalb: Northern Illinois University Press, 2004.

———. *Iowa Railroads: The Essays of Frank P. Donovan, Jr.* Iowa City: University of Iowa Press, 2000.

———. *Living in the Depot: The Two-Story Railroad Station*. Iowa City: University of Iowa Press, 1993.

———. *A Mighty Fine Road: A History of the Chicago, Rock Island & Pacific Railroad Company*. Bloomington: Indiana University Press, 2020.

———. *The North Western: A History of the Chicago & North Western Railway System*. DeKalb: Northern Illinois University Press, 1996.

Grant, H. Roger, and Charles W. Bohi. *The Country Railroad Station in America*. Boulder: Pruett, 1978.

Grant, H. Roger, Don L. Hofsommer, and Osmund Overby. *St. Louis Union Station: A Place for People, a Place for Trains*. St. Louis: St. Louis Mercantile Library, 1994.

Hampton, Taylor. *The Nickel Plate Road: The History of a Great Railroad*. Cleveland: World, 1947.

Hayes, William Edward. *Iron Road to Empire: The History of the Rock Island Lines*. New York: Simmons-Boardman, 1953.

Healy, Kent T. *Performance of the U.S. Railroads since World War II*. New York: Vantage, 1985.

Hilton, George W., and John F. Due. *The Electric Interurban Railways in America*. Stanford, CA: Stanford University Press, 1960.

Hines, Walker D. *War History of American Railroads*. New Haven, CT: Yale University Press, 1928.

Hofsommer, Don L. *The Hook & Eye: A History of the Iowa Central Railway*. Minneapolis: University of Minnesota Press, 2005.

———. *The Southern Pacific, 1901–1985*. College Station: Texas A&M University Press, 1986.

———. *Steel Trails of Hawkeyeland: Iowa's Railroad Experience*. Bloomington: Indiana University Press, 2005.

———. *The Tootin' Louie: A History of the Minneapolis & St. Louis Railway*. Minneapolis: University of Minnesota Press, 2005.

Hoogenboom, Ari, and Olive Hoogenboom. *A History of the ICC: From Panacea to Palliative*. New York: W. W. Norton, 1976.

Hubbard, Freeman. *Encyclopedia of North American Railroading: 150 Years of Railroading in the United States and Canada*. New York: McGraw-Hill, 1981.

Klein, Maury. *History of the Louisville & Nashville Railroad*. New York: Macmillan, 1972.

———. *Unfinished Business: The Railroad in American Life*. Hanover: University Press of New England, 1994.

———. *Union Pacific: The Rebirth, 1896–1969*. New York: Doubleday, 1989.

———. *Union Pacific: The Reconfiguration—America's Greatest Railroad from 1969 to the Present*. New York: Oxford University Press, 2011.

Lemly, James H. *The Gulf, Mobile & Ohio: A Railroad That Had to Expand or Expire*. Homewood: Richard D. Irwin, 1952.

Lind, Alan R. *From Horsecars to Streamliners: An Illustrated History of the St. Louis Car Company*. Park Forest: Transport History, 1978.

Long, Bryant Alder, and William Jefferson Dennis. *Mail by Rail: The Story of the Postal Transportation Service*. New York: Simmons-Boardman, 1951.

Maiken, Peter T. *Night Trains: The Pullman System in the Golden Years of Rail Travel*. Chicago: Lakme, 1989.

Martin, Albro. *Enterprise Denied: Origins of the Decline of American Railroads, 1897–1917*. New York: Columbia University Press, 1971.

———. *Railroad Triumphant: The Growth, Rejection, and Rebirth of a Vital American Force*. New York: Oxford University Press, 1992.

Masterson, V. V. *The Katy Railroad and the Last Frontier*. Norman: University of Oklahoma Press, 1952.

Meier, Albert E., and John P. Hoschek. *Over the Road: A History of Intercity Bus Transportation in the United States*. Upper Montclair, NJ: Motor Bus Society, 1975.

Miner, H. Craig. *The Rebirth of the Missouri Pacific*. College Station: Texas A&M University Press, 1983.

Moore, Truman E. *The Traveling Man: The Story of the American Traveling Salesman*. Garden City, NY: Random House, 1972.

O'Malley, Michael. *Keeping Watch: A History of American Time*. New York: Viking Penguin, 1990.

Overton, Richard C. *Burlington Route: A History of the Burlington Lines*. New York: Alfred A. Knopf, 1965.

Patton, Phil. *Open Road: A Celebration of the American Highway*. New York: Simon & Schuster, 1986.

Primm, James Neal. *Lion of the Valley: St. Louis, Missouri, 1764–1980*. 3rd ed. St. Louis: Missouri Historical Society Press, 1998.

Rae, John B. *The Automobile Industry*. Boston: Twayne, 1984.

Rehor, John A. *The Nickel Plate Story*. Milwaukee: Kalmbach, 1965.

Riegel, Robert Edgar. *The Story of the Western Railroads*. New York: Macmillan, 1926.

Rose, Joseph R. *American Wartime Transportation*. New York: Thomas Y. Crowell, 1953.

Roseman, V. S. *Railway Express: An Overview*. Denver: Rocky Mountain, 1992.

Rosen, William. *The Most Powerful Idea in the World: A Story of Steam, Industry, and Invention*. New York: Random House, 2010.

Saunders, Richard. *Merging Lines: American Railroads, 1900–1970*. DeKalb: Northern Illinois University Press, 2001.

———. *The Railroad Mergers and the Coming of Conrail*. Westport: Greenwood, 1978.

Schneider, Gregory L. *The Rock Island Requiem: The Collapse of a Mighty Fine Line*. Lawrence: University Press of Kansas, 2013.

Schramm, Jeff. *Out of Steam: Dieselization and American Railroads, 1920–1960*. Bethlehem, PA: Lehigh University Press, 2010.

Schwantes, Carlos A. *Going Places: Transportation Redefines the Twentieth Century West*. Bloomington: Indiana University Press, 2003.

Scott, Roy V. *Railroad Development in the Twentieth Century*. Ames: Iowa State University Press, 1985.

Stilgoe, John R. *Metropolitan Corridor: Railroads and the American Scene*. New Haven, CT: Yale University Press, 1983.

Storck, John, and Walter Darwin Teague. *Flour for Man's Bread: A History of Milling*. Minneapolis: University of Minnesota Press, 1952.

Stout, Greg. *Route of the Eagles: Missouri Pacific in the Streamlined Era*. Kansas City: White River Productions, 1995.

Stover, John F. *American Railroads*. Chicago: University of Chicago Press, 1961.

———. *History of the Baltimore and Ohio Railroad*. West Lafayette, IN: Purdue University Press, 1987.

———. *History of the Illinois Central Railroad*. New York: Macmillan, 1975.

Stringham, Paul H. *Illinois Terminal: The Electric Years*. Glendale, CA: Interurban, 1989.

Valle, James E. *The Iron Horse at War*. Berkeley: Howell-North, 1977.

Vance, James E. *The North American Railroad: Its Origin, Evolution, and Geography*. Baltimore: Johns Hopkins University Press, 1995.

Wilner, Frank N. *Railroad Mergers: History, Analysis, Insight*. Omaha: Simmons-Boardman, 1997.

Index

Railroads in Missouri and elsewhere had a lengthy and sometimes bewildering history of financial reorganization that resulted in a carrier's slight change of corporate title, such as from "railroad" to "railway" and even to "rail road." Thus, depending on the year, it was correct to speak of the St. Louis & San Francisco Railway or the St. Louis-San Francisco Railway. This index makes no attempt to differentiate between "railroad" or "railway" or even "system" as used at various times in corporate titles. Thus, all railroad corporate titles indexed below are italicized to avoid any confusion.

abandonment, railroad: *Chicago, Peoria & St. Louis*, 34, 67; *Colorado Midland*, 34; Missouri, 13, 79, 187, 194, 195, 216, 229, 230; mentioned, xiv, 33, 34, 54, 160, 177, 188, 192, 217, 221

accidents and safety, 21, 238, 254, 256

agriculture. *See* freight and express, agricultural commodities

Alton, Illinois, 112

Alton (*Chicago & Alton*): passenger traffic, 59, 60, 63, 70, 95, 102, 117; merger matters, 51, 112, 114, 239; freight traffic, 90, 113; mentioned, xviii, 8, 12, 130

Alton & Southern, 139, 143, 165–166

Amtrak: formation (1971), 176, 177, 178, 179; operations, 174, 196, 234; mentioned, xiv, 233

Anheuser-Busch, 75, 143, 202, 211

Arkansas & Missouri, 218

Arkansas railroad history, vii, 72, 75, 77, 79, 140, 142, 153, 185, 196, 208, 218

Atchison, Topeka & Santa Fe: Argentine yard, Kansas City, 90, 123, 163, 187, 243; freight traffic, 8, 49, 80, 90, 100, 101, 104, 113, 123, 140, 141, 142, 143, 162, 183, 184, 186; map, 9; merger matters, xvi, 114, 208, 210, 212, 213, 214, 221, 222, 226, 231, 232; passenger traffic, vi, 62, 68, 90, 91, 117, 118, 119, 120, 127, 128, 130, 132, 143, 151, 154, 156, 178, 179; proposed extension to St. Louis, 8, 9, 12, 13, 34, 114; Santa Fe Industries, 168, 190, 213, 221, 226; tracks across Missouri, 17, 54, 123, 134, 140, 151; mentioned, xvi, 34, 70, 71, 86, 134, 135, 161, 162, 168, 186, 201, 204, 221, 233, 249

automobile competition with railroads, 9, 13, 19, 28, 36, 57, 66, 67, 81, 11, 114, 153

automobiles, 12, 18, 20, 21, 25, 26, 27, 30, 31, 32, 38, 89, 93, 112, 148

automobiles hauled by rail, 90, 141, 142, 163, 183, 230, 238, 253

aviation, commercial: air travel, 68, 69; Ozark Airlines, 148; statistics, 68, 116, 119, 148; transcontinental air-rail coordination (1929), 67; Trans World Airlines (TWA), 68, 69; mentioned, 17, 21–23, 30, 81, 83, 158

Baltimore & Ohio: merger matters, 112, 164, 210; passenger traffic, 60, 66, 92, 115, 121, 127, 129, 131, 132, 146–148, 151, 152, 153, 154, 178; mentioned, xvii, 38, 52, 101, 155, 156

Barriger, John W., III, 188

beer. *See* freight and express, beer

Berkshire Hathaway, 246, 247

Bevier & Southern, 71, 79, 143

Biaggini, Benjamin, 213, 214

Big Four. See New York Central

BNSF Railway Company, xvi, 246, 247

Boonville, Missouri, 53, 79

boosterism, 66, 98, 256

bridges, history of, 3, 19, 67, 76, 79, 112, 124, 138, 139, 202, 210, 241

Burlington Northern: Burlington Resources, 226; merger matters, xvi, 164–165, 173, 176–177, 192, 209, 211, 212, 213, 215, 218, 219, 220, 223, 231–232, 224, 225, 226; mentioned, 178, 181, 182, 183, 186, 187, 201

Burlington Northern Santa Fe (BNSF), 246

buses, intercity: Missouri Pacific Transportation Company, 70–71; mentioned, 70, 148

California railroad history, xv, 3, 90, 118, 123, 128, 141, 149, 186, 208, 210, 225, 226, 230, 232

Canadian Pacific, xvii, xix, 55, 164, 231, 232, 245, 248, 249, 251, 252, 254

Canadian Pacific Kansas City (CPKC): merger matters, xvi; mentioned, xix, 236, 255

281

Canadian National: acquisition of *Illinois Central*, 231; mentioned, xvi, xvii, 55, 207, 232, 242, 243, 248, 250, 252, 252

Cape Girardeau, Missouri, 51, 141, 143

Carrollton, Missouri, 70, 144

Carter, Jimmy (president), 193, 195, 199, 207, 216

cattle shipment by rail. *See* freight and express, livestock

centralized traffic control (CTC), 100, 112, 113, 143, 187, 241

Charleston, Missouri, 70

Chicago, Burlington & Quincy (*Burlington*): freight traffic, 49, 72, 75, 78, 103, 143, 163; merger matters, 176; passenger traffic, x, 58, 61, 62, 63; mentioned, xiv, xv, xvi, 70, 178, 187, 200, 228

Chicago, Illinois: railroad connections, 8, 9, 18, 33, 34, 35, 36, 43, 59, 60, 62, 63, 64, 83, 90, 92; mentioned, xii, xiv, xvi, 29, 55, 66, 68, 75, 116, 119, 127

Chicago, Milwaukee, St. Paul & Pacific (*Milwaukee Road*): bankruptcy 1920s, 34, 35; Chicago Milwaukee Corporation, 180; decline and dismemberment, xvii, xix, 190–192, 193, 194, 195, 206, 207, 220, 224, 227, 233, 239, 245: financial woes, 112, 161, 191; freight traffic, 49, 79, 101, 103, 203; passenger traffic, 43, 119, 127, 129; mentioned, 8, 35, 38, 70, 88, 112, 162, 171, 180, 193, 210

Chicago, Peoria & St. Louis, 34, 67

Chicago, Rock Island & Pacific (*Rock Island*): connection St. Louis-Kansas City (1904), 7, 11–13, 18–19; decline and dismemberment, 171, 190, 205, 228–230, 60–161, 168, 172, 173, 193–195, 203, 205–210; financial woes, 112, 191, 203; freight traffic, 49, 73, 75, 77, 81, 123, 163, 173, 181, 183, 184; passenger traffic, 62–63, 77, 80, 81, 104, 119, 120, 127, 128, 148, 151, 156, 177; mentioned, xix, 33, 51, 52, 54, 55, 79, 88, 101, 103, 112, 117, 134, 166, 204

Chicago & Alton. See Alton (*Chicago & Alton*)

Chicago & Eastern Illinois, 51, 58, 92, 95, 117, 164, 203

Chicago & North Western: Northwest Industries, Union Pacific acquisition, 171, 225, 226, 232, 237; mentioned, xviii, 171, 172, 206, 220

Chicago Great Western: freight traffic, 81, 114, 141, 161, 164; merger matters, xviii, 164, 172, 206, 220, 225; passenger traffic, 81, 88, 114, 120, 153; mentioned, 8, 77, 78, 82, 83, 112, 113, 119, 127, 144, 161, 162, 163, 188

Chillicothe, Missouri, 130, 233

Cincinnati, Ohio, 60, 135, 148, 153, 156

circus by rail, 153

coal traffic. *See* freight and express, coal

Colorado railroad history, v, xviii, 75, 119, 185, 203, 230

commuter trains, St. Louis, 67, 68

competition: rail with highway and air, 32, 34–35, 46–59, 66, 67, 81, 82, 125, 148, 153, 158, 187; mentioned, xiii, 9, 13, 19, 22, 26, 27, 30, 44, 57, 59, 62, 119

Conrail: formation, 180, 220; split between *CSX* and *Norfolk Southern*, 221, 232; mentioned, xvii, 233

Cotton Belt. See *St. Louis Southwestern*

Council Bluffs, Iowa, 134, 135, 203

CSX Corporation, xvii, 221, 222, 232, 233, 243, 246, 248, 249, 250, 251

Dakota, Minnesota & Eastern, 245

Delta, Missouri, 49, 167

Denver & Rio Grande Western, xviii, 130, 210, 221, 223

Deramus, William Neal, III, 188, 206

deregulation, railroad, xv, 216, 217, 224, 233, 237, 247

diesel engines and locomotives. *See* locomotives, diesel

dinner in the diner. *See* railroad dining cars

Dockery, Andrew M. (governor), 28

dogs and railroads, 24

"doodlebug." *See* rail motor cars

Downing, Robert W., 180

Eads, James Buchanan, 3

Eads Bridge, St. Louis, 3, 138, 241

East St. Louis, Illinois, 75, 77, 79, 137, 142, 143, 153, 163, 202, 216, 223

Eisenhower, Dwight D. (president), 154, 160, 177

Eldon, Missouri, 53, 70, 230, 265

Excelsior Springs, Missouri, 33, 233

Ford, Gerald (president), 192, 199

freight and express: beer, 75, 141, 143, 185, 202; coal, xviii, 13, 29, 49, 77, 79, 82, 110, 113, 141, 143, 176, 181, 182, 183, 202, 206, 211, 219, 225; express, 39, 40, 41, 49, 69, 92, 94, 98, 100, 115, 132, 134–136, 138, 140 149–150; freight handling facilities, 79, 184, 185 fruit, 83, 13, 149; grain, 6, 47, 49, 79, 80, 110, 140, 141, 176, 181, 184, 186, 193, 202, 206, 211, 219, 220, 222, 223, 224; intermodal, 182, 186, 187, 232, 233, 238, 242, 243, 245, 247, 249, 251, 253; less-than-carload (LCL), 72, 73, 75; livestock, 73, 74, 80, 123, 141, 139, 183, 184; Railway Express Agency, 39, 92, 98, 100, 135, 136, 140 149; named freight trains, 51, 73, 75, 77, 141, 142, 186. 216, 223, 230, 233; perishables, 75, 116, 140, 208, 243; piggyback, trailer-on-flat car (TOFC), 141, 149, 163, 183, 211, 230, 233; statistics, 73, 81, 84; strawberries, 140, 185; trackside industries, 49; unit trains, 181, 182. 184, 250; mentioned, 51

"*Frisco*." See *St. Louis-San Francisco*

Gateway Western, 223, 227, 239

General Motors, Electro-Motive Division (EMD), 70, 89, 101, 113, 120, 126

"Golden State Route," 13, 113, 119, 205, 208, 209, 210, 213, 214, 230

Gould, Jay, 12, 34, 55, 185

grain shipment by rail. *See* freight and express, grain

Grand Trunk Western, 207, 210, 233, 255

Great Depression, 1930s, 47, 49–51, 52, 57, 80–81

Gulf, Mobile & Ohio: acquisition by Illinois Central, 181, 210, 239; formation, 51, 52; passenger traffic, 53, 117, 120, 127, 129, 130, 132, 146, 148, 151, 153, 178, 179; mentioned, xviii, 51, 90, 112, 114, 144, 156

Gulf Coast Lines, 185

Gulf of Mexico, 8, 206, 211

Hannibal, Missouri, 24, 49, 69, 239

Hannibal & St. Joseph, xiv, xv

Harrison, E. Hunter, 248, 249, 250, 251, 255

Harvey, Fred, xii, 136, 138, 196

Haverty, Michael, xx, 227, 243, 245, 249, 255

Hermann, Missouri, 53

highways and roads: Good Roads conference (St. Louis), 27, 28; Good Roads trains, 27, 28; highway trails, 31, 32; road trips, 30–31; mentioned, 27

Hoover, Herbert (president), 50

Illinois Central: freight traffic, 90, 94, 109, 161; passenger traffic, 59, 63, 64, 95, 115, 127, 130, 135, 146, 147, 148, 149, 153, 156; mentioned, xvi, xvii, 20, 27, 50, 103, 133, 134, 162, 163, 166, 168, 171, 181
Illinois Central Gulf, 181, 190, 210, 221, 222
Illinois railroad history: interurban electric railways, xviii, 7, 38, 75, 115, 129; mentioned, vii, 8, 34, 55, 70, 78, 92, 138, 143, 148, 153, 156
Illinois Terminal (formerly *Illinois Traction*): passenger traffic, 38, 129; mentioned, xviii, 75, 115, 218
Independence, Missouri, 122
India as a railroad destination, 3
Indianapolis, Indiana, xvii, 19–20, 142, 148, 175, 176
Interstate Commerce Commission, 56, 114, 158, 160, 166, 168, 173, 178, 190, 191
interurban (electric) and street railways: Missouri Interurban Companies by name, 36, 57; mentioned, 37, 38
Iowa, Chicago & Eastern, 233, 245
Iowa & Minnesota Rail Link (IMRL), 231, 233
Iowa railroad history, 245
Iron Mountain Route. *See* St. Louis, Iron Mountain & Southern

Jefferson City, Missouri (state capital), 70
Jenks, Downing, 203, 213
jitney fad (1914–1915), 25, 26
Johnson, Lyndon B. (president), 160, 164
Joplin, Missouri, 57, 118, 127, 128, 141, 153
Jones, Casey, 20

Kansas City, Missouri: freight traffic, 75, 79, 90, 112, 123, 140, 141, 163, 183, 184, 185, 186, 208, 210, 212, 214, 215, 216, 225; railroad history, xii, xiv, xvi, xix, 3, 7, 8, 9, 11, 12, 18, 19, 35, 36, 57, 173, 193, 195, 203, 228, 229, 230; passenger traffic, 33, 43, 58, 62, 70, 75, 83, 118, 119, 120, 127–131, 140, 147, 150, 151, 156, 178, 196; Union Station, 3, 66, 117, 120, 140, 148, 150, 195, 228, 233, 234; mentioned, xvii, xviii, 13, 31, 133, 134, 135, 153, 154, 162, 176, 182, 187, 194, 206, 207, 220, 222
Kansas City Southern: acquisition by *Canadian Pacific*, xvi, xviii, 248, 251, 254, 255; freight traffic, 6, 7–8, 140, 206, 222, 242, 243, 248, 249; Kansas City Southern Industries, 238; Mexico connections, 239, 243, 245, 247, 252; passenger traffic, 128, 130, 133; Stilwell Financial, 238; mentioned, 29, 52, 55, 56, 78, 81, 119, 224, 227, 231, 236, 246, 247
Kansas City Terminal, 79, 195, 203, 210, 228, 243
Kansas railroad history, 13, 31, 36, 57, 70, 90, 113, 118, 123, 140, 154, 163, 184, 208, 219
"Katy." *See Missouri-Kansas-Texas*
Kennedy, John F. (president), 160, 162, 164
Kirkwood, Missouri, 67
Korean War, 145, 146
Krebs, Robert D., 226, 231, 232, 238

Lambert, Albert Bond, 17, 23
Langdon, Jervis, 160, 161, 173
Lebanon, Missouri, 28
Little Rock, Arkansas, 116, 119, 128, 133
Lindbergh, Charles A., 17, 23
livestock. *See* freight and express, livestock

locomotives, diesel, 60, 61, 62, 63, 77, 101, 113, 114, 115, 116, 117, 120, 122, 123, 126, 128, 129, 130, 144, 157, 162, 163, 166, 167, 198
locomotives, electric, 38
locomotives, steam: manufacturers, 30, 113; replacement by diesel motive power, 60, 63, 77, 101, 113, 114, 117, 123, 128, 140, 145; statistics, 78, 144; wheel arrangement, 78; mentioned, vi, xiii, 7, 18, 35, 37, 48, 144, 153, 154, 162
Loree, Leonor, 52, 55–56
Los Angeles, California, xvi, 13, 62, 116, 122, 127, 130, 133, 134, 135, 142, 143, 151, 156, 175, 179, 186, 196, 213, 226, 245
Louisiana, Missouri, 49, 70
Louisiana Purchase Exposition (St. Louis, 1904). *See* World's Fairs, St. Louis (1904)
Louisville, Kentucky, 127, 147, 153, 207, 231
Louisville & Nashville, xvii, 66, 127, 129, 133, 147, 148, 152, 153, 156, 178, 210

MacArthur Bridge (St. Louis), 139, 241
Macon, Missouri, 27, 141
Malden, Missouri, 72
Manufacturers: Anheuser-Busch connection, 202; mentioned, 79
Marceline, Missouri, 53, 114, 162, 178
McKeen car ("doodlebug"), 68
Memphis, Tennessee, xvi, 66, 116, 120, 127, 133, 134, 135, 148, 153, 213, 226
Menk, Louis W., 211
Merchants Bridge (St. Louis), 241
Merchants' Refrigerator Dispatch, 140
Mexico and Mexico City: Missouri connections, 5, 38, 116, 247, 248, 249, 254; Mexico railroad history, 242, 243, 245, 252; mentioned, 252, 227, 231
Minneapolis, Minnesota, xii, xvii, xix, 33, 36, 75, 83, 119, 127, 134, 135, 151, 153, 156, 186, 193, 203, 206, 220, 239
Minneapolis & St. Louis, xii
Minnesota railroad history, xvii, 5, 36, 119, 194, 239
Mississippi River, 3, 8, 19, 34, 38, 67, 79, 112, 124, 138, 141, 143, 163, 176
Missouri & Arkansas, 79
Missouri & North Arkansas, 51
Missouri & Northern Arkansas, 218
Missouri history, xii, xiii, xiv, xv. *See* Missouri railroad companies listed by name
Missouri-Illinois, 51, 70
Missouri-Kansas-Texas (*Katy*): financial woes, 188; freight traffic, 51, 75, 81, 138, 140, 184, 198, 222; history, xviii, xix, 6, 52, 79, 168, 187; map, 74, 189; passenger traffic, 8, 58, 66, 81, 115, 116, 119–120, 121, 127, 129, 130, 131, 134, 148, 153, 163; Union Pacific acquisition, xviii, xix, 222, 259; mentioned, 14, 48, 50, 55, 74, 112, 203
Missouri Pacific: bankruptcy and reorganization, 93, 112, 201, 203; freight traffic, 49, 75, 77, 79, 81, 138, 140, 143, 166, 167, 182, 184, 185, 202, 211; history, xiv, xviii, 4, 5, 6, 12, 51, 54, 78, 91, 164, 212, 256; map, 4, 65; Missouri Pacific Transportation Company (intercity buses), 70–71; operations, 35, 101, 145, 196; passenger traffic, v, 43, 54, 60, 67, 68, 69, 81, 115, 116, 117, 120, 121, 127, 128, 130, 146, 147, 148, 151, 153, 156, 175, 178, 179; Union Pacific Acquisition, 213,

215, 216; mentioned, xvii, 21, 29, 35, 54, 69, 98, 114, 122, 132, 133, 134, 150, 154, 155, 210, 221, 228, 230, 249, 257

Missouri railroad accidents, 21

Missouri railroad construction projects, 3

Missouri railroad map, xi

Missouri railroad short lines, 51, 77, 79

Missouri railroad statistics, xii, 53, 84

Missouri River, xii, xiv, 35

Moberly, Missouri, 183, 187

Mobile & Ohio, 51, 53, 117

Monett, Missouri, 140

Municipal Bridge (St. Louis), 76, 79, 202

music, railroad, 204

"*MoPac.*" See *Missouri Pacific*

National Road, 32

Neosho, Missouri, 28, 79

New Orleans, Louisiana, xvi, 119, 128, 134, 145, 148, 149, 213, 226, 231

New York, Chicago & St. Louis (*Nickel Plate*), xviii, 117, 118, 123, 127, 130, 144, 146, 147, 153, 164

New York Central (*New York Central & Hudson River*), xiii, xvii, 20, 60, 93, 109, 15, 120, 127, 129, 132, 142, 146, 147, 150, 153, 164, 176

Nixon, Richard M. (president), 178, 191, 192

Norfolk & Western, xviii, 164, 178, 180, 181, 183, 186, 203, 210

Norfolk Southern, xviii, 221, 232, 233, 238, 239, 242, 243, 246, 247, 248

North American Free Trade Agreement (NAFTA), 223, 231, 238, 242, 245

Ohio River, 192

oil, 6–7, 25, 89, 90, 180, 229, 247, 248

Oklahoma railroad history, xvi, 6, 7, 13, 36, 66, 68, 75, 115, 121, 127, 134, 136, 148, 186, 222, 242

Omaha, Nebraska, xviii, 68, 70, 118, 127, 147, 173, 183

Overland Route, 210, 225

Ozark Plateau, 66, 140, 257

Pacific Coast, 3, 5, 207, 252

Pacific Railroad of Missouri, 3, 5

passenger train: air conditioning, 31, 38, 50, 59, 60, 62, 63, 66, 120; links between Missouri and Texas, vii, 58; curtailment/discontinuance, 34, 52, 53, 66, 69, 84, 94, 95, 152, 153, 156, 163, 173, 177; dining cars, 60, 62, 86, 104, 131, 132, 146, 174, 229; named trains, 17, 20, 34, 43, 58–59, 60–63, 80, 115, 129, 151. *See also* "passenger traffic" for individual railroads; parlor cars, 33, 115, 151; ridership trends (1921–1945), 5, 33, 102, 38, 44, 52, 53, 57, 58, 66, 69, 81, 92, 94, 102, 104, 108, 114; ridership trends (1946–2023), 115, 117, 145, 148, 152, 153, 156, 173, 174–175, 176, 178–179, 196; sleeping cars. *See* sleeping cars (Pullman); streamliners, v, xiii, 60, 61, 62, 63, 77, 91, 113; 115, 123, 126, 128, 129, 130, 134, 176, 251; travel, 33, 66

Penn Central, 164, 178, 179

Pennsylvania, xvii, 17, 23, 43, 52, 59, 60, 66, 67, 68, 71, 88, 92, 105, 109, 115, 116, 117, 120, 121, 127, 129, 132, 145, 146, 151, 164

Perry, Missouri, 35

Pittsburgh, Pennsylvania, 60, 133, 148, 156, 178

Poplar Bluff, Missouri, 70

Post Office Department. *See* Railway Post Office

precision scheduled railroading, 240, 248

Progressive Era railroad regulation, 9, 12–13, 28, 44

Prohibition, 79

Pullman cars. *See* sleeping cars (Pullman)

Pullman Company, 94, 96, 104, 116

Pullman porters, 148

Quanah, Acme & Pacific, 58, 75

rail motor cars ("doodlebugs"), 67, 68, 69, 70, 77

"Rail Renaissance," 245, 247

railroad abandonment. *See* abandonment, railroads

railroad brotherhoods. *See* railroad worklife

railroad passenger trains. *See* passenger trains

railroad politics, 50

railroad publishing, 42, 43, 54

railroad safety. *See* accidents and safety

railroad standardization during the 1880s, 135

railroad stations and depots: layout and function, 40–41, 62–63, 97–98; Kansas City Union Station. *See* Kansas City, Missouri, Union Station; St. Louis Union Station. *See* St. Louis, Missouri, Union Station; mentioned, 6, 24, 52, 70, 79, 100, 140, 150, 151, 163, 185, 187, 230, 246

railroad statistics: 1930s, 50, 66; 1940s, 158; 1950s, 160; mentioned, 47

railroad worklife: dispatchers, 29; employment statistics, 29, 162, 219–220, 250, 253; "featherbedders," 162; labor unions. *See* railway brotherhoods; strikes, 110, 113, 125, 180, 195; work rules, xiii, 125, 156, 162, 218, 224; mentioned, 53

railway brotherhoods, 123, 125, 194, 195, 203, 209, 218

Railway Express Agency. *See* freight and express, Railway Express Agency

Railway Post Office (RPO): elimination of mail by train, 154, 155, 156; mail by train, railway post office cars (RPO), 24, 69, 132, 134, 135, 136, 149, 150, 151, 153; mentioned, xv, 68, 94, 115, 158, 177

Reagan, Ronald (president), 199, 200, 220

Reed, John, 212, 214

regulation of railroads. *See* Progressive Era railroad regulation

Rolla, Missouri, 183, 211

Roosevelt, Franklin D. (president), 50

Roosevelt, Theodore (president), 27, 44

Rose, Matthew, K., 238, 246, 247, 250, 251

San Francisco, California, xvi, 52, 58, 66, 67, 68, 90, 116, 130, 132

Seaboard Air Line, 23

Sedalia, Missouri, 70

short lines. *See* Missouri railroad history, short lines

sleeping cars (Pullman): operations, 33, 38, 94, 95, 96, 104, 116, 178; routes across Missouri, 33; routes from Missouri to distant cities, 19, 38, 58–59, 66, 92, 115, 121, 129, 130, 131, 134, 146, 148, 151, 153, 156; mentioned, xii, 60, 66, 68, 115, 119, 148, 149, 174, 178, 229, 259

Soo Line (*Minneapolis, St. Paul & Sault Ste. Marie*), xvii, xix, 164, 207, 224, 227, 231, 233, 239, 255

Southern, xviii, 27, 117, 127, 164, 210

Southern Pacific: acquisition of *Chicago, Rock Island & Pacific* properties, 166, 171, 173, 190, 208, 216; relationship with *St. Louis Southwestern* (*Cotton Belt*), 164, 208, 209, 214, 215, 216; mentioned, xix, 52, 127, 156, 164, 166, 210, 213, 221, 222, 223, 226, 227

spatial relationships (railroad), 6, 8, 33, 58–59

speed, matters of, 19–21, 23, 33, 39, 62, 64, 66, 67, 71, 115, 123, 149, 174, 177, 186, 214, 220, 226, 231, 232, 250

sports and railroads, 59–60, 146

Springfield, Missouri, 28, 38, 66, 127, 141, 148, 156, 157, 183, 187, 212

Staggers Rail Act (1980), 216, 217, 218, 219, 220, 222, 224, 246, 251, 252

stations and depots. *See* railroad stations & depots

St. Charles, Missouri, 47, 67, 79, 177

Stilwell, Arthur, xii, 8, 12

St. Joseph, Missouri: local railroads, 79–80; mentioned, 36, 53, 70, 75, 91, 130, 141

St. Joseph & Grand Island, 68

St. Louis, Missouri: commercial outreach, vii, 6, 143, 182, 185, 240, 241; history, xii, xiv, xviii, 28, 243; industries, 7, 18, 30, 37, 75, 138, 139, 140, 143, 183, 184, 202; maps, xi, 4, 9, 65, 76; passenger trains, 58, 67, 68, 69, 92, 115, 117, 119, 120, 121, 127, 130, 131, 145, 150, 151, 152, 153, 156, 157, 176, 178, 179, 196; railroad connections to the East Coast, xiii, 17, 20, 59, 73, 129; railroad connections to Iowa and Minnesota, xii, 59; railroad connections to Texas, Arkansas, and Louisiana, 6, 7, 43, 55, 58, 59, 77, 134, 142, 163; railroad connections within Missouri, xix, 7, 11, 12, 13, 19, 227; relationship with Chicago, xv, 59, 60, 63, 64, 66, 95, 146; relationship with Kansas City, 33, 118, 126, 203, 216, 228, 230, 239; regulation. *See* Progressive Era railroad regulation; spatial relationships, v, xvi, xvii, 3, 5, 8, 18, 37, 53, 70, 75, 90, 114, 130, 132, 133, 134, 175, 208, 210, 212; Union Station. *See* St. Louis Union Station; World's Fair of 1904. *See* Louisiana Purchase Exposition (1904); mentioned, 25, 26, 27, 32, 34, 35, 52, 58, 79, 83, 109, 116, 137, 154, 222, 223, 229

St. Louis, Iron Mountain & Southern (formerly *St. Louis & Iron Mountain* until 1874), xviii, 6, 24

St. Louis, Kansas City & Colorado: abandonment, 12–13, 229–230; acquisition by Chicago, Rock Island & Pacific, 11–13; freight traffic, 127, 229; history, 7, 11–13, 18, 19, 210, 216, 228; passenger traffic, 19, 128

St Louis & Hannibal, 35, 69

St. Louis Car Company, 7, 37, 70

St. Louis Railway Club, 2

St. Louis-San Francisco (*Frisco*): acquisition by *Burlington Northern*, xvi, 211, 212, 213, 220, 231; freight traffic, 49, 75, 77, 79, 123, 138, 140, 141, 142, 143, 183, 184, 186, 187, 203; history, 6, 78, 114, 144, 187, 218; passenger traffic, 66, 67, 91, 92, 115, 120, 121, 127, 128, 129, 131, 134, 136, 145, 147, 148, 151, 156, 163; timetable art, 258, 263; mentioned, 5, 27, 28, 29, 54, 55, 153, 155, 156, 157, 164, 210, 228

St. Louis Southwestern (*Cotton Belt*): advertising, 260, 261; *Blue Streak Merchandise*, 73, 75, 77, 141, 216; freight traffic, 49, 71, 72, 78, 92, 137, 142, 207, 216; highway operations, 71; passenger traffic, 59, 66, 117, 148, 152–153; Southern Pacific connection, 52, 208, 209, 210, 214, 230; mentioned, vii, xviii, xix, 8, 6, 12, 51, 52, 55, 114, 117, 138, 144, 164, 165, 166, 167, 215

St. Louis Union Station: *Amtrak*. *See Amtrak*; history, 3, 67, 97, 99, 153, 173, 196, 233, 234; operations, 92, 145, 149, 151, 156; passenger traffic trends, post 1945, 116, 117, 173, 196; railroad owners and users, 118; World War II, 94, 96, 97; mentioned, xii, 24, 66, 120, 121, 135, 136, 138, 195, 228

St. Louis World Fair of 1904. *See* World's Fairs, St. Louis (1904)

St. Paul, Minnesota, xii, xiv, 33, 119, 134, 135, 48, 156, 186, 219, 231

street railways. *See* interurban (electric) and street railways

Surface Transportation Board (STB), 227, 239, 243, 246, 250, 254

telegraphy: Western Union, 40, 62, 196; mentioned, 29, 39, 40, 62, 63, 90, 100, 163, 187

Terminal Railroad Association of St. Louis, 8, 67, 78, 79, 116, 137, 138, 143, 153, 166, 202, 223, 240, 241

Texas & Pacific, 203

Texas railroad history: freight traffic, 7, 75, 123, 141, 142, 143, 149, 183, 184, 185, 186, 196, 243, 248, 260; passenger traffic, 5, 38, 43, 58, 66, 115, 116, 119, 121, 128, 130, 131, 132, 134, 146, 151, 153, 163, 178, 196; mentioned, v, xvi, 6, 7, 13, 36, 55, 90, 173, 208, 216, 219, 227, 230, 231, 239

timekeeping, 22

timetables and guides: *Official Guide of the Railways*, 33, 179; mentioned, 4, 20, 31, 48, 68, 74, 102, 105, 118, 128, 129, 133, 153, 172, 175, 179, 242, 256, 261, 262, 263

tourism, 25, 28, 58, 83, 154

Train of Tomorrow, 120

travel by train. *See* passenger train, travel

traveling salesmen ("commercial travelers" or "knights of the grip"), 40–41

Troy, Missouri, 79

trucking, intercity, 9, 13, 70–72, 73, 74, 82, 89, 90, 92, 111, 112, 116, 136, 141, 149, 151, 158, 175, 177, 181, 183, 208, 217, 218, 222

Truman, Harry (president), 122–123

Union Pacific: acquisition of *Chicago & North Western*, xix, 225, 226, 227, 237; acquisition of *Missouri-Kansas-Texas*, 188, 222; acquisition of *Missouri Pacific*, 12, 166, 212, 213; acquisition of Southern Pacific, xix, 226, 227, 230, 232, 239, 252; Champlin Petroleum Company, 180; freight traffic, 140, 183, 184, 203, 208, 243, 249, 250; history, xviii, 161, 166, 168, 172, 173, 190, 221, 226, 232, 238, 239, 245, 246, 247, 248, 252, 259; passenger traffic, 62, 119, 120, 128, 130, 178; mentioned, xviii, 30, 31, 104, 122, 134, 154, 162, 201, 214, 215, 216, 224, 227, 230, 251

United States Railroad Administration (USRA), 9, 10, 12–13, 34, 44

vacations, 38, 54, 58, 83, 92, 94, 95, 145, 256, 257

Wabash: freight traffic, 49, 74, 75, 81, 138, 140, 141, 141, 147, 149, 185; history, 78, 112, 164, 228, 233; passenger traffic, xix, 59, 62, 66, 67, 68, 81, 94, 115, 117, 119, 120, 126, 127, 130, 131, 146, 151, 153; mentioned, xiv, xviii, 8, 12, 51, 79, 95, 178, 238

Warrensburg, Missouri, 21
Ward, Michael, 246
Watkins, Hayes T., 221
Washington, DC, 17, 50, 66, 104, 121, 129, 132, 147, 154, 179, 181, 196
Western Pacific, 58, 213, 214, 215, 216, 221
women and railroads, 88, 97, 102, 107, 108
World War I and Missouri railroads: federal takeover of the railroads. *See* United States Railroad Administration; mentioned, 8, 9, 10, 34
World War II and Missouri railroads: advertising, 88, 102, 103, 105; Pearl Harbor attack, 90; national defense pre-Pearl Harbor (1941), 88; postwar adjustments, 110, 111, 112, 115; production for war, 89; Red Cross and United Service Organizations (USO), 97, 98; statistics, xii, 88, 89, 102, 103, 109; troop movements, 95, 96, 105, 106; troop trains, 96; wartime operations, 88, 90, 91, 92, 94, 100, 101, 104, 105, 108; women, 88; mentioned, 87, 109
World's Fairs: Buffalo (1901), 13; Chicago (1893), 11; New York (1939), 84, 87; officially sanctioned World's Fairs, 13; St. Louis (1904), xii, 7, 8, 11, 12, 18, 21, 265; mentioned, 20, 66

Don L. Hofsommer holds a doctorate from Oklahoma State University and is author of numerous books and articles on railroads. Among his many titles are several books on the railroads of Iowa. Hofsommer taught at several colleges and universities, most recently at St. Cloud State University, from which he retired.

Carlos A. Schwantes holds a doctorate in American history from the University of Michigan. He is author or editor of twenty books and numerous professional journal articles. During his fifty-year career in the classroom he taught history at four different colleges and universities, including most recently the University of Missouri–St. Louis (2001–2016). At UMSL he frequently taught classes both on Missouri as the Gateway to the West and on the railroads of the United States.

For Indiana University Press

Sabrina Black *Editorial Assistant*

Tony Brewer *Artist and Book Designer*

Anna Francis *Assistant Acquisitions Editor*

Anna Garnai *Production Coordinator*

Dave Hulsey *Associate Director and Director of Sales and Marketing*

Katie Huggins *Production Manager*

Alyssa Nicole Lucas *Marketing and Publicity Manager*

David Miller *Lead Project Manager/Editor*

Dan Pyle *Online Publishing Manager*

Jennifer Witzke *Senior Artist and Book Designer*